CHESTERTON AND TOLKIEN AS THEOLOGIANS

CHESTERTON AND TOLKIEN AS THEOLOGIANS

The Fantasy of the Real

ALISON MILBANK

t&t clark

Published by T&T Clark

The Tower Building, 11 York Road, London SE1 7NX

80 Maiden Lane, Suite 704, New York, NY 10038

A Continuum imprint

www.continuumbooks.com

All rights reserved. No part of this publication may be reproduced or transmitted in any form or by any means, electronic or mechanical, including photocopying, recording or any information storage or retrieval system, without permission in writing from the publishers.

Copyright © Alison Milbank, 2009

First edition published in hardback, 2007
This edition published, 2008

Alison Milbank has asserted her right under the Copyright, Designs and Patents Act, 1988, to be identified as the Author of this work.

Material from *Tree and Leaf Including the Poem Mythopoeia, The Homecoming of Beorhtnoth Beorhthelm's Son* by J. R. R. Tolkien reprinted by permission of HarperCollins Publishers Ltd. © J. R. R. Tolkien, 2001.

British Library Cataloguing-in-Publication Data
A catalogue record for this book is available from the British Library

Typeset by RefineCatch Limited, Bungay, Suffolk
Printed on acid-free paper in Great Britain by MPG Biddles Ltd, King's Lynn, Norfolk

ISBN-10: 0-567-39041-1 (paperback)
ISBN-13: 978-0-567-39041-7 (paperback)

CONTENTS

Acknowledgements
vii

Preface
viii

INTRODUCTION
Fairies, Fusiliers and Thomists
1

PART 1
Poiesis
29

CHAPTER 1
Making Strange: The Fantastic
29

CHAPTER 2
The Grotesque
56

CHAPTER 3
Paradox and Riddles
87

PART 2
Praxis
117

CHAPTER 4
Fairy Economics: Gift-Exchange
117

CHAPTER 5
Fairy Poetics: Make-Believe
142

Conclusion
162

Bibliography
170

Index
179

ACKNOWLEDGEMENTS

THIS BOOK had its origin in a series of public lectures I was invited to give at the Christian Studies Centre in Charlottesville in 2002, and I am grateful to Revd Dr Drew Trotter for the invitation, and to the audience for their enthusiastic and scholarly interest. I am also indebted to a number of the brilliant students who participated in my course on Religion and Fantasy at the University of Virginia, especially Dag Rowe and Hill Harman, and to Chiara Colombi and her splendid thesis on the hobbits. Versions of chapters in this book have appeared in *The Lord of the Rings and Philosophy*, edited by Gregory Bassham and Eric Bronson; and *Tolkien Influenced and Influencing: 17th Tolkien Society Seminar*, edited by Matthew Vernon. I thank the editors of those volumes for permission to reprint them. I also thank the copyright holders of the poetry of David Jones and J. R. R. Tolkien for permission to quote from their verse. Individuals to whom I owe ideas and criticism include Stratford Caldecott, Peter Candler, Patrick Curry, Curtis Gruenler, John Milbank, Peter Slade and Priscilla Tolkien. I am most grateful to Thomas Kraft, Dominic Mattos and Slav Todorov at Continuum, who have been unfailingly helpful, patient and efficient. John Sargant has been the most careful and learned of proofreaders, and has contributed greatly to the clarity of the book. I dedicate this volume to Arabella and Sebastian Milbank, who knew and loved Middle-earth long before I did.

PREFACE

IN THIS BOOK I aim to demonstrate that the essayist, poet, Christian apologist and writer of fantastic tales G. K. Chesterton was an important influence both on Tolkien's fiction and his literary criticism of the fairy tale. In Part 1, I shall offer a literary reading of Tolkien's writing through what I discern to be his specifically Chestertonian poetics. I shall then proceed to argue in Part 2 that it is through these same stylistic tropes that an implicitly Tolkienesque theology of art emerges: literature is shown to perform theology.

The book was prompted by the difficulties I encountered when I first taught Tolkien in the context of a university English department. While it was relatively easy to enjoy the texts themselves as literary artefacts, and to open them to the close reading techniques of the Practical Criticism tradition, searching for a contemporary intellectual or theoretical context in which to situate Tolkien's fiction proved to be quite problematic. Certainly there was much excellent work available by Tom Shippey and Jane Chance on Tolkien's Anglo-Saxon sources, while Verlyn Flieger's study of the influence of Owen Barfield on Tolkien gave his Inklings membership real theological weight.[1] John Garth's important study of Tolkien and his circle of school-friends in the context of World War I had not yet been published, but now provides important new considerations which I have taken into account.[2] There was, however, a dearth of straightforwardly *literary* analysis of Tolkien's manner of writing, which was quite surprising. I was teaching a graduate course on literary modernism at the time and this led me, in the face of this lacuna, to bring some insights from modernist aesthetics and its indebtedness to the symbolists to bear upon Tolkien's work.

PREFACE

Tolkien's project to create a mythological past for his own northern culture is a recognizably modernist endeavour, and parallels a poem such as T. S. Eliot's *The Waste Land* of 1922, which has recourse to James Frazer's comparative anthropology, in order to provide a 'primitive' frame of fertility cult for a critique of the present. Modernist writing reaches back to assert the influence of earlier culture on the present through the 'mythic method', while simultaneously stressing the gap between modernity and the past through ironic juxtaposition. Tolkien likewise dramatizes that temporal chasm through his portrayal of the crossed yet opposite trajectories of humans and elves, and by his complex interweaving of familiar and strange elements in the world of Middle-earth.[3]

Other features in Tolkien's fiction that resemble modernist art include the self-referentiality of the work, which creates its own little world of meaning. In this separation and elevation of the work of art, modernism inherited aspects of symbolist theory, as in so much else.[4] What modernism further developed was the element of quotation and allusiveness, so that new writing might be engendered from older material to make something fresh. Tom Shippey and other medieval scholars have shown to what an extent Tolkien created his trilogy out of *Beowulf* and other Anglo-Saxon and Nordic sources with a high degree of deliberate allusiveness. Another common feature is the deliberate mixing-up of low and high styles, of demotic and elevated language. Yet while Tolkien deploys this blend in the alternation between 'Roman' Gondor and hobbit speech, for example, he does not destabilise the elevated in the way that James Joyce does. Tolkien's approach is more akin to that of David Jones in his wartime epic *In Parenthesis*, which juxtaposes ordinary soldier talk of a range of periods with mythic tales in order to give heroism and significance to the common people.

What is fascinating about Tolkien's writing, in my view, is the way in which, like Jones, Eliot and Claudel, he employs certain key symbolist and modernist tropes for broadly religious ends, in the sense that his work seeks to accord transcendent significance to human life and activity. He was unlucky in publishing after World War II in a very different intellectual climate from that of the modernist heyday, in a populist era that privileged brevity, realism and naturalism over

PREFACE

epic ambition and modernist artifice. In this he again resembles David Jones, whose *In Parenthesis* did not appear until 1937, and his masterwork, the long poetic sequence *Anathémata*, a decade later. Although Jones achieved a certain *succès à clef*, he did not find a general receptive audience for his work. As will be seen below, I have traced a link between Tolkien and Jones through the philosopher Jacques Maritain. Nevertheless, they are of course very different writers, despite their shared Catholicism. The balanced and seamless beauty of Tolkien's created universe is of quite a different order from the fragmentary use of Jones's mythic material and his deliberate indecorum.

Beyond this noting of formal comparison with modernism however, the problem is far more pressingly one of trying to ascertain what contemporary writing Tolkien had read outside his professional work. For this I examined his published letters as well as his essays and was struck by the (relative) frequency with which he referred quite casually to the earlier writer of fantastic fiction, G. K. Chesterton. One remark, 'Chesterton once said that it is our duty to keep the flag of the world flying', shows that Tolkien had read *Orthodoxy*, Chesterton's intellectual journey to faith through his own version of natural religion.[5] On another occasion he cites Chesterton's remark that anything that is announced as 'here to stay' is bound shortly to be replaced.[6] And in 1944 his young daughter is, no doubt at parental suggestion, 'wading through *The Ballad of the White Horse*', by Chesterton, only for Tolkien to realize that Chesterton was actually no expert in things northern. G. K. Chesterton was admired by Tolkien's friend C. S. Lewis for his universal history, *The Everlasting Man*, to which Lewis attributed his conversion to theism, but Chesterton was also famous for his fantastic stories, plays and poetry, as well as for his advocacy of fairy-stories.[7] After his conversion to Roman Catholicism in 1922, Chesterton was also the leading Catholic public intellectual of pre-war Britain, who helped the Church's public recognition as indigenous and English through the little priest from Essex, Father Brown, who became the popular successor to Sherlock Holmes.

Reading Chesterton's 'The Ballad of the White Horse' after *The Lord of the Rings* is to recognize a great affinity and a common

PREFACE

project. Despite the anachronism of Chesterton's ballad form for an Anglo-Saxon voice, the whole spirit of King Alfred's position on the cusp between paganism and Christianity is true to Tolkien's understanding of *Beowulf* as a poem that is a careful preservation by a Christian of pagan tradition. Alfred has the ancient White Horse of the Oxfordshire vale recut, 'Because it is only Christian men/ Guard even heathen things', just as Tolkien argues that it is Christianity that preserves the pagan in his essay, 'Beowulf: the Monsters and the Critics'.[8] Moreover, the spirit of Alfred's coalition of Gael, Celt, Saxon and Roman to defeat the Danish invaders is not only reminiscent of the alliance of the Free Peoples of the West in Tolkien's novel, but their sign is a broken sword, like that of Aragorn. The courage with which they enter a battle against fearful odds is also Tolkienesque in the manner of the Anglo-Saxon poem, 'The Battle of Maldon', to which Tolkien wrote an epilogue, 'The Homecoming of Beorhtnoth Beorhthelm's Son', about two servants who retrieve their master's corpse from the battlefield. (According to Humphrey Carpenter, this poem was in existence in 1945, soon after the re-reading of 'The Ballad of the White Horse').[9] Tolkien quotes in his epilogue the celebrated battle cry from 'The Battle of Maldon': 'Heart shall be bolder, harder be purpose,/ More proud the spirit as our power lessens'.[10] The spirit of those lines is echoed in two stanzas from 'The Ballad of the White Horse', which became important rallying cries for the nation in times of crisis in both World War I and World War II:

> I tell you naught for your comfort,
> Yea, naught for your desire,
> Save that the sky grows darker yet
> And the sea rises higher.
>
> Night shall be thrice night over you,
> And heaven an iron cope.
> Do you have joy without a cause,
> Yea, faith without a hope?[11]

Maisie Ward notes that these lines appeared in *The Times* leader at the time of the evacuation of Crete in World War II, where Tolkien may have found the impetus to look again at the poem and commend it to his daughter.[12] The speaker of these lines is no Anglo-Saxon, however, but the Blessed Virgin Mary, who appears to Alfred in a vision on the small river islet of Athelney. Not only does Chesterton's poem anticipate the gaiety and courage in the face of seemingly undefeatable evil of *The Lord of the Rings*, but the Queen of Heaven's prophetic words and appearance on the islet may also have contributed to the portrayal of the elf queen Galadriel with her mirror of prophecy and her final appearance at the Tongue between the two rivers, where she says farewell to the Fellowship. In a response to Father Robert Murray, Tolkien confirmed that his conception of Galadriel had been influenced by his devotion to the Blessed Virgin.[13]

It is in Tolkien's great essay, 'On Fairy-Stories', however, that Chesterton is cited most carefully and specifically. In the discussion on the appropriateness of fairy-tales for children, Tolkien quotes a short piece, 'On Household Gods and Goddesses', published originally in 1922 but reprinted in *The Coloured Lands*, Maisie Ward's selection of early stories and poems by Chesterton, which was published in 1938. 'Chesterton once remarked that the children in whose company he saw Maeterlinck's *Blue Bird* were dissatisfied "because it did not end with a Day of Judgement, and it was not revealed to the hero and heroine that the Dog had been faithful and the Cat faithless." "For children," he says, "are innocent and love justice; while most of us are wicked and naturally prefer mercy"'.[14] Tolkien here cites Chesterton's awareness of children's sense of justice against Andrew Lang's tendency to soften some of the material he adapted for the child readers of his Fairy Books. Since Tolkien's approach to other writers is often quite negative (probably because he was so absolute a creative artist), any positive reference is particularly significant. Furthermore, Tolkien defines his own theory of what fantasy can achieve by building on and beyond what he calls 'Chestertonian fantasy', which is the sudden realization of the familiar seen as if for the first time. Tolkien calls this 'Mooreeffoc' – 'a fantastic word, but it could be seen written up in every town in this land. It is Coffee-room, viewed from the inside through a glass door, as it was seen by Dickens on a dark London day; and it was used by Chesterton to denote the queerness of things that have become trite, when they are seen suddenly from a new angle'.[15] Although Tolkien might have read Chesterton's 1906 study of Charles Dickens, from which this observation originally derives, it is much more likely that he knew it from Maisie Ward's introduction to *The Coloured Lands*, where she cites the same usage by Chesterton of Dickens and then goes on in similar language to Tolkien: 'Dickens read it in the gloom and despondency of a foggy London night during his slavery at Murdstone and Grinby. Gloomy fantasy is truth read backwards. Cheerful fantasy is the creation of a new form wherein man, become creator, co-operates with God'.[16] If Tolkien did indeed take his reference from Ward, then there also he found confirmation of his sub-creation thesis in the 'On Fairy-Stories' essay. The evidence that this was his source was greatly strengthened for me by some conversations with Miss Priscilla Tolkien, who kindly confirmed both her father's liking for Chesterton and his possession of *The Coloured Lands*, which was published the year before he gave the St Andrews lecture that became 'On Fairy-Stories'.[17]

Ward suggests that the Chestertonian fantasy, which is not so much an escape from the world as 'an extension of reality', developed after Chesterton became a Catholic.[18] Tolkien, a Catholic like Chesterton and Ward herself, shares their positive attitude to human making and art of all kinds, but his essay makes a sharp distinction between his own fantasy that opens the imaginative hoard and gives its contents freedom, and Chestertonian 'Mooreeffoc', which can only 'act as a time telescope on one spot'.[19] And yet his own position is not so very different from Chesterton's. 'Fantasy, he writes, 'is made out of the Primary World, but a good craftsman loves his material', and his creation will indeed make more luminous the simple realities of our own world: 'the wonder of the things, such as stone, and wood, and iron; tree and grass; house and fire; bread and wine'.[20] Moreover, the second of Tolkien's functions of the fairy-tale – recovery of a clear view – is exactly what Chesterton's art aims at. In particular, this is evident in the story that opens Ward's selection, 'The Coloured Lands', in which a bored and dissatisfied child is presented by a mysterious man with spectacles of various colours through which to see reality. This man tells of his own dissatisfaction even with these coloured perspectives, so that he is taken by a wizard to see the paintbox of creation, and is invited to make his own sort of world. As he splashes the air in front of him with the pigments, 'they remained where you had thrown them, as a bird hangs in the air'.[21] Adding reds and yellows, greens and white blobs, the man slowly discovers that the world he has painted – or actually constructed – is the very same house and garden with which he had earlier been so dissatisfied. 'That is how they came to be there. I thought you would be interested to know it', he announces to the bored child, who is now left to look at his own home and garden 'with a new look in his eyes'.[22] This is indeed a story of recovery of the real, of seeing the familiar anew, but it is also a story about co-creation. It makes 'Leaf by Niggle', written by Tolkien during World War II and published in 1945, read like a riposte. In Tolkien's tale, a painter of a particular tree manages to paint just one leaf of it during his lifetime, but is granted a vision of its completion in the afterlife. His artistic originality is thereby verified, but it is God himself who brings it to reality. The sense of creative fantasy is stronger in Tolkien's tale, since Niggle manages his own leaf, whereas the man in spectacles creates what is already there in a sense, but the stories are overwhelmingly similar in tone and topic. Although each story has an element of a fulfilment beyond this contingent world of phenomena, the human artefact in each case is real and participates in some sense in the divine creation.

In these few quotations from Chesterton, we have begun to see a common attitude to the relation of paganism and Christianity, and to English history. Common also is a religious tradition and its expression in fiction. Most centrally, the two writers share a view of art as revealing the createdness of the world, and the creative vocation of the artist in remaking it. Each writer sees art itself as mediatory: a theological tool for opening human eyes to see the reality of God and the reality, albeit contingent, of the world beyond the self. Because of Tolkien's membership of the Inklings group, we are accustomed to thinking of him as a writer of pure fantasy, like Charles Williams or C. S. Lewis. Interpreting his work through Chesterton, I hope to show that he is equally concerned with realism

PREFACE

and with writing fictions about real things, or at least in using fantasy and the fictive to restore our true relations with what Auden called 'those wordless creatures who are there as well'.[23]

I have given here the evidence for the influence of Chesterton on Tolkien, but what follows is by no means a study of reception. What I have tried to do rather is use each author to illuminate the other in terms of the development of a unique modern theological poetics. I shall treat Chesterton and Tolkien seriously as literary artists by taking stylistics as my mode of enquiry into the inner workings of their writing and, in particular, tropes that were in literary use in their own time, such as defamiliarization. In so doing, I wish to demonstrate that it is in this way that each writer engages theological and philosophical ideas. I am not so much seeking to find Christian doctrines in the *content* of their fiction as in the *manner* in which they write. It is precisely through this formal means that both authors contrived to adumbrate a Catholic and realist praxis and ethics, which will be the subject of the second part of this book. Although this approach necessarily offers new readings of Chesterton's technique, this is undertaken in order to illuminate Tolkien's ultimately more ambitious and far-reaching writing. The two writers are not identical, but they form crucial links in a developing tradition of British Christian poetics from George MacDonald to the present day. By using the earlier author as a golden key to unlock aspects of the later, one opens a way in which to reveal the power of Tolkien's imagined universe as openly fictive but equally real.

Notes

1. T. A. Shippey, *The Road to Middle-earth* (London: George Allen and Unwin, 1982), and *J. R. R. Tolkien: Author of the Century* (London: HarperCollins, 2000); Jane Chance, *Tolkien the Medievalist* (Routledge Studies in Medieval Culture and Religion, London: Routledge, 2002); Verlyn Flieger, *Splintered Light: Logos and Language in Tolkien's World* (Kent, OH: Kent State University Press, rev. edn, 2002).

2. John Garth, *Tolkien and the Great War: The Threshold of Middle-earth* (London: HarperCollins, 2003).

3. On Tolkien's art as modernist in its reinvention of the 'primitive', see Patchen Mortimer, 'Tolkien and Modernism', *Tolkien Studies* 2, (1) (2005)

PREFACE

pp. 113–29; and Patrick Curry, *Defending Middle-earth: Tolkien, Myth and Modernity* (London: HarperCollins, 1998). Joe Kraus takes an opposite perspective in 'Tolkien, Modernism, and the Importance of Tradition', in *The Lord of the Rings and Philosophy*, ed. Gregory Bassham and Eric Bronson (Chicago: Open Court, 2003), pp. 137–49.

4. Michael Levenson, *The Genealogy of Modernism: A Study of English Literary Doctrine, 1908–1922* (Cambridge: Cambridge University Press, 1984).
5. *The Letters of J. R. R. Tolkien*, ed. Humphrey Carpenter and Christopher Tolkien (London: George Allen and Unwin, 1981), p. 402.
6. *Letters of Tolkien*, p. 246.
7. C. S. Lewis, *Surprised by Joy: The Shape of My Early Life* (London: Geoffrey Bles, 1955), pp. 210–11.
8. J. R. R. Tolkien, 'Beowulf: the Monsters and the Critics,' *Proceedings of the British Academy*, 22 (London: Oxford University Press, 1937), pp. 245–95. 'The Ballad of the White Horse,' in *The Collected Poems of G. K. Chesterton* (London: Cecil Palmer, 1927), p. 233.
9. Humphrey Carpenter, *J. R. R. Tolkien: A Biography* (London: George Allen and Unwin, 1977), p. 214.
10. J. R. R. Tolkien, 'The Homecoming of Beorhtnoth Beorhthelm's Son', in *Tree and Leaf Including the Poem Mythopoeia, The Homecoming of Beorhtnoth Beorthelm's Son* (London: HarperCollins, 2001), p. 141.
11. Chesterton, *The Collected Poems*, p. 232.
12. Maisie Ward, *Gilbert Keith Chesterton* (London: Sheed and Ward, 1944), pp. 245–6.
13. *Letters of Tolkien*, pp. 171–2.
14. G. K. Chesterton, *The Coloured Lands*, illustrated by the author, ed. Maisie Ward (London: Sheed and Ward, 1938), p. 195, quoted in Tolkien, *Tree and Leaf*, p. 44.
15. Tolkien, *Tree and Leaf*, p. 52.
16. Chesterton, *The Coloured Lands*, p. 15.
17. *Tree and Leaf* gives the date of that lecture as 1938 in its introductory note, but Humphrey Carpenter's biography, *J. R. R. Tolkien*, p. 191, corrects this to 1939.
18. Chesterton, *The Coloured Lands*, pp. 9 & 16.
19. Tolkien, *Tree and Leaf*, p. 53.
20. Tolkien, *Tree and Leaf*, p. 53.
21. Chesterton, *The Coloured Lands*, p. 29.
22. Chesterton, *The Coloured Lands*, p. 30.
23. 'Objects,' in W. H. Auden, *Collected Poems*, ed. Edward Mendelson (New York: Vintage, 1991), p. 624.

INTRODUCTION: FAIRIES, FUSILIERS AND THOMISTS

'The Fairies' Farewell'

Farewell, rewards and fairies,
   Good housewives now may say,
For now foul sluts in dairies
   Do fare as well as they.
And though they sweep their hearths no less
   Than maids were wont to do,
Yet who of late for cleanness
   Finds sixpence in her shoe?

Lament, lament, old Abbeys,
   The Fairies' lost command!
They did but change Priests' babies,
   But some have changed your land.
And all your children, sprung from thence,
   Are now grown Puritans,
Who live as Changelings ever since
   For love of your demains.

At morning and at evening both
   You merry were and glad,
So little care of sleep or sloth
   These pretty ladies had;

INTRODUCTION

> When Tom came home from labour,
>   Or Cis to milking rose,
> Then merrily went their tabor,
>   And nimbly went their toes.
>
> Witness those rings and roundelays
>   Of theirs, which yet remain,
> Were footed in Queen Mary's days
>   On many a grassy plain;
> But since of late, Elizabeth,
>   And later, James came in,
> They never danced on any heath
>   As when the time hath been.
>
> By which we note the Fairies
>   Were of the old Profession.
> Their songs were 'Ave Mary's,
>   Their dances were Procession.
> But now, alas, they all are dead;
>   Or gone beyond the seas;
> Or farther for Religion fled;
>   Or else they take their ease.
>
> A tell-tale in their company
>   They never could endure!
> And whoso kept not secretly
>   Their mirth, was punished, sure;
> It was a just and Christian deed
>   To pinch such black and blue.
> Oh how the commonwealth doth want
>   Such Justices as you![1]

When Chesterton wrote his 'Ethics of Elfland' defence of fairy-tale logic in 1908, and Tolkien his early faërie poetry and stories such as 'Goblin Feet', fairies were still fashionable and even avant-garde. Most studies of the post-Romantic resurgence of fairies concentrate on the Victorian period, when Pre-Raphaelites painted elvish sirens in ultra-realist style, and Tennyson led the vogue for poems about curses and enchantment, and tales of mermen and sorceresses.² The Edwardian and Georgian periods, however, were equally enthralled by the fairy world, as the aesthetes' embrace of the supernatural became popular with the mainstream, leading to the publication of anthologies of fairy poetry, such as Alfred Noyes's *Magic Casements* of 1908 and R. S. Bates's collection of the following year, and various gift books in aid of the war effort with fairy illustrations.³ Walter de la Mare's fairy play, *Crossings*, which is by no means merely a children's production, was produced in 1923, and even the detective novelist Agatha Christie wrote a series of short stories that involved a fairy figure in the supernatural helper, Mr Harley Quin. Adults of Tolkien's generation – combatants of the Great War – grew up on Juliana Ewing's *The Brownies*, George MacDonald's *The Princess and the Goblin* and Andrew Lang's variously coloured *Fairy Books* of folk tales from around the world. They had clapped their hands at performances of *Peter Pan* in order to resurrect Tinkerbell by their belief in fairies. John Garth points out that Tolkien too saw this play at the age of eighteen, and considered it 'indescribable but shall never forget it as long as I live [sic]'.⁴ Rather than being rendered irrelevant by the war, *Peter Pan* took on a deeper meaning as thousands of young men died and never grew up: for them dying truly was 'an awfully great adventure'. One of the brothers for whom *Peter Pan* was written, George Llewelyn-Davies, died with its prototype *The Little White Bird* tucked into his kit-bag, while many soldiers received Estella Canziani's 'Piper of Dreams' postcard, which shows tiny elflike creatures around a child or Robin Goodfellow figure who plays a pipe at the foot of a great tree.⁵

While the popularity of fairy topics amid the horrors of trench warfare might be interpreted as nostalgic evocations of home, this does not explain the deliberate bringing together of magical and fighting realities in volumes such as Robert Graves's *Fairies and Fusiliers* of 1917. A poem called, in Georgian style, 'Faun' is followed immediately by 'A Dead Boche', with the theme of desecration linking the two. Similarly, in David Jones's World War I poem *In Parenthesis*, the enchanted wood of Mametz precipitates the soldiers into an encounter with the Queen of the Woods, who garlands them with crowns of flowers as they fall dead amid its brambles.⁶ Fairy

INTRODUCTION

encounter is equally serious in Kipling's short story, 'Fairy-kist', where it refers to the trauma of shell-shock.[7]

So writers who designate the Great War as the event that halted interest in fairies are only partially correct. It is true that the delicate arabesque style of the art fairy-tale of the 1890s, which continued in the gift books particularly, associated fairies with pure gratuity: art for art's sake. In an illustration by Edmund Dulac for his Red Cross fundraising volume, for example, the fairy godmother is drawn with the same clear line as the human Cinderella, but she is all white in the shade of the blue night, as if lit from within.[8] Mounted on separate sheets of paper, within a printed border and protected by tissue paper inserts, such tenebrous images detached themselves like Isis behind her veil from the world of the reader, just as the books themselves sought to distance themselves from the marketplace as presents – gift books – rather than commodities. Fairies are thus associated with art and with the unreal.

Chesterton's and Tolkien's fairies are not of this ethereal kind. They have more in common with Jones's perilous yet tutelary Queen of the Woods than the arabesques of Arthur Rackham and Dulac. What they do share with the Georgian poets and artists is a renewal of the association of fairies with nation and locality. The revival of the folk-tale and other traditional material in the Romantic period was associated with the rise of nationalism. In order to claim national status, it was necessary to establish one's native cultural imaginary, as in the case of the Grimm brothers' enterprise in Germany, or the adoption of Dante as national poet in the Italian *risorgimento*. Bishop Percy's promotion of the English ballad (including 'The Fairies' Farewell', which he reprinted in his *Reliques*) and the Arthurian vogue are two British examples of this attempt at an 'imagined community'.[9] Krishan Kumar has demonstrated that a specifically British late-Victorian and Edwardian need to maintain an imperial identity led to a mode of nationalism that was quite differently inflected from that of other imperial nations. It involved a kind of self-emptying and an ethic of service to the Empire as a whole, rather than to the British Isles.[10] Sympathetic and complementary to this is a kind of English localism, whereby the particular place takes on a specific value rather than the nation or land as a whole.

INTRODUCTION

For this reason there are as many classical fauns and nymphs as indigenous fairies in the poetic and artistic landscapes of the early twentieth century, as in the story 'The Curate's Friend' by E. M. Forster, where it is stated: 'There is nothing particularly classical about a faun: it is only that the Greeks and Italians have ever had the sharpest eyes. You will find him in "The Tempest" and the "Benedicite;" and any country which has beech clumps and sloping grass and very clear streams may reasonably produce him.'[11] Fauns here are international and yet locally specific. They mediate between classical paganism and Christianity, for the Benedicite is a canticle sung at Morning Prayer. And in the story, of course, it is the faun who is the curate's (somewhat dangerous) friend. The perilousness embodied by the faun renders the otherness of the landscape visible and at the same time sacred and valuable.

Edward Thomas wrote about a more 'national' and yet unideological fairy in his poem 'Lob', which was written during his service on the western front. It begins with a conversation between the narrator and an old Wiltshireman:

> At hawthorn-time in Wiltshire travelling
> In search of something chance would never bring,
> An old man's face, by life and weather cut
> And coloured, – rough, brown, sweet as any nut,
> A land face, sea-blue-eyed, – hung in my mind
> When I had left him many a mile behind.
> All he said was: 'Nobody can't stop 'ee. It's
> A footpath, right enough. You see those bits
> Of mounds – that's where they opened up the barrows
> Sixty years since, while I was scaring sparrows.
> They thought as there was something to find there,
> But couldn't find it, by digging, anywhere'.[12]

Although the old man is a figure of specific 'Englishness', his role is that of a liberator rather than a protector of identity. He establishes the freedom of access to the countryside, the 'right of way' that to this day marks out the English landscape as penetrable, unlike the private land of the USA, where access is denied outside the National

INTRODUCTION

Parks. The Wiltshireman is not, however, just a local inhabitant. Never found again, another voice informs the narrator that

> The man was wild
> And wandered. His home was where he was free.
> Everybody has met one such man as he.
> Does he keep clear old paths that no one uses
> But once a lifetime when he loves or muses?
> He is English as this gate, these flowers, this mire.
> And when at eight years old Lob-lie-by-the-fire
> Came in my books, this was the man I saw.
> He has been in England as long as dove and daw.[13]

A wanderer the length and breadth of England like Chesterton's 'rolling English drunkard', he is an embodiment of 'the right to roam', and the common law that establishes the public footpath by usage over time. It is he who names the flowers, the birds and the features of the landscape, such as the Hog's Back on the Surrey border. He is also the soldier who fought and died in a range of English battles:

> One of the lords of No Man's Land, good Lob, –
> Although he was seen dying at Waterloo,
> Hastings, Agincourt, and Sedgemoor too, –
> Lives yet.[14]

In that sense he recalls another poem by Chesterton of 1907, 'The Secret People', in which the common people fight for the nation in wars that they may not necessarily understand, and which enrich others. The poem concludes, 'But we are the people of England; and we have not spoken yet./ Smile at us, pay us, pass us. But do not quite forget'.[15] Chesterton's 'secret people' too are 'lords of No Man's Land', both in the sense of a freedom of access and also of those who fight for Britain at the western front.

There is more still to Lob, however: he is also a fairy-tale hero and an actual spirit: Herne the Hunter and Hob or Robin Goodfellow. The fairy here is revealed as the guarantor of the land and its integrity from possession by the powerful. This is also true of Rudyard Kipling's Puck in the story 'Puck of Pook's Hill' of 1906, and its sequel, 'Rewards and Fairies', who questions the child protagonists' assumption of the land as their own and asserts his own rights of ownership. Puck offers the children visions of characters who have made England what she is: Roman, Celtic, Norman and Jewish. None of them is native, yet all belong. The British, of any race or period, are only the trustees of the land, in the manner of the National Trust, which was established in 1895.[16] Fairies express both the independence of the landscape and its mediation in a period during which it was opening up to urban working-class people as the bicycle and the train were allowing them access to its delights in a way lost to them after enclosure.

The alert Tolkienian will already have detected in Thomas's Lob some familiar features. In his nut-brown appearance, his manner and occupation he is highly reminiscent of Tom Bombadil and may, I would suggest, have been an influence on Tolkien's character, especially in his association with barrows. Tom shares Lob's freedom: he is his own master. Although Tom is more bound to one locality than Lob, who wanders from Exeter to Leeds, in both figures their freedom comes from non-appropriation. Tom, like Lob and Puck/Robin Goodfellow is a guarantor of the integrity of the natural order. It is in this context that one should understand Tolkien's celebrated desire to 'restore to the English an epic tradition and present them with a mythology of their own'.[17] Although it is for the English people, its Englishness is that of 'its tongue and soil', and needs to be 'somewhat cool and clear, be redolent of our "air" (the clime and soil of the North West . . .)'.[18] England here is both a cultural construct – a language – and the land itself. It is not to be equated with the people who inhabit both the land and the English language. *The Silmarillion*, which was Tolkien's attempt in this direction, has no story that justifies possession of Middle-earth for any particular group and no foundation myth. The elves themselves, Eru's first-born, are only exiles and asylum-seekers upon the earth, and even their love and protection of its natural beauty is somewhat ambiguous, since it seeks to arrest the effects of time. What, paradoxically, *The Silmarillion* offers the English are stories of great

INTRODUCTION

beauty and clarity, but of increasing fall and loss. It is a quality that the poet and painter David Jones described as Celtic: 'a certain affection for the intimate creatureliness of things – a care for, and appreciation of the particular genius of places, men, trees, animals, and yet withal a pervading sense of metamorphosis and mutability. That trees are men walking. That words "bind and loose" material things'.[19] And as in English fairy-tradition since Chaucer's Wife of Bath, Tolkien's fairies – with the exception of Tom Bombadil – are leaving 'England' to sail into the west. Tolkien's myth is another 'Fairies' Farewell'.

Neither Chesterton nor Tolkien was an imperialist, and their adherence to the local and even the national was far from uncritical. In 'The Flag of the World' chapter in *Orthodoxy*, Chesterton indeed claimed that to love a country or a town was essentially to love it despite its faults, and to be aware of them so as to improve and reform the place. This is in contrast to jingoists who have to find some reason, some 'theory of England', in order to love it and to justify it. Chesterton goes on, however, to point out that morality, looked at historically, did not proceed from some rational Rousseauian social contract but from an awareness of the sacredness of a place. Even the Ten Commandments, according to Chesterton, were 'a code of regimental orders, issued to protect a certain ark across a certain desert'.[20] To assert that there are fairies somewhere, therefore, is to witness to that site's intrinsic sacrality. So, 'old nurses did not tell children about the grass, but about the fairies that dance on the grass; and the old Greeks could not see the trees for the dryads'.[21]

Something of this was going on generally in Edwardian and Georgian employment of fairy themes: it became a way to import meaning to the natural world in a post-Darwinian age. It was also a way to introduce a sense of the holy in an increasingly disenchanted and secularized society. 'Disenchantment', a word coined by Max Weber, referred to the way in which the modern world could be mastered through calculation. There were, he believed, 'no mysterious incalculable powers at work' in the world, and thus no need for recourse to magic.[22] It is this 'disenchantment' thesis that Christian writers of the fantastic, such as Chesterton and Tolkien, are quite rightly refuting. They realize, however, that it is not enough to

INTRODUCTION

present their readers with the world described in tones of wonder, which is sometimes how the admirers of the Oxford Inklings present them as proceeding. The challenge to a religious fullness of experience must be intellectually engaged and in some sense entered into before re-enchantment can be effected. This book will seek to lay bare the way in which this is achieved, and to explore the theology of these two writers by means of their employment of literary tropes. For Chesterton, however, re-enchantment came by logic and reason: it was equally intellectual if not 'intellectualist'. Although he restores the dryads to the woods and the fairies to the grass as a necessary mediation, it is by turning nineteenth-century positivism on its head using its own field of discourse.

'The Ethics of Elfland' chapter in Chesterton's intellectual autobiography *Orthodoxy* still has power to shock in an era which sees Victorian attitudes to science re-emerging in the rhetoric of popularizers such as Richard Dawkins. Here Chesterton argues against the determinism of his own day that sees in science a foolproof method of explication of phenomena, without the causal sequence that would justify such a claim.

> I observed that learned men in spectacles were talking of the actual things that happened – dawn and death and so on – as if *they* were rational and inevitable. They talked as if the fact that trees bear fruit were just as *necessary* as the fact that two and one trees make three. But it is not. There is an enormous difference by the test of fairyland; which is the test of the imagination. You cannot *imagine* two and one not making three. But you can easily imagine trees not growing fruit; you can imagine them growing golden candlesticks or tigers hanging by the tail. These men in spectacles spoke much of a man named Newton, who was hit by an apple, and who discovered a law. But they could not be got to see the distinction between a true law, a law of reason, and the mere fact of apples falling.[23]

Chesterton surprisingly follows David Hume here in making a sharp distinction between the laws of mental relations and the observations of scientific method, to which he refuses to give the word 'law', and instead speaks of 'weird repetitions'. Indeed, he goes on to argue that fairy-tales are more logical – and sceptical – than science, for they do not too easily assume a cause/effect sequence. Facts of nature have an arbitrary quality which, Chesterton argues, is best expressed by the words 'enchantment' or 'spell'.[24] Logic is better learnt from the witch in the fairy-tale who says, ' "Blow the horn, and the ogre's castle will fall"; but she does not say it as if it were something in which the effect obviously grew out of the cause'.[25] For it is not a law, even though the witch may have seen the castle fall on numerous occasions, since 'a law implies we know the nature of the generalisation and enactment; not merely that we have noticed some of its effects'.[26]

What Chesterton is pointing out here is that the materialist science of his day with its necessarianism is actually implying a purpose and causality that does not belong to such a discourse, but is inherently religious. Even the phrase 'natural selection' is unfortunate in implying a mechanism and even a telos: a sort of natural theology. And a natural religion is what Chesterton himself draws out of his study of the fairy-tale. First, he derives a narrative ontology, whereby life itself has the character of a fairy-tale, in the sense that it has an entelechy: he feels himself to be part of a story. This comes through a sense of self-consciousness, or rather a sense of consciousness of being part of a world. It sounds obvious but logically to have this awareness is already to impart meaning to experience. To *see* the world is to wonder at it: the wonder is therefore not some sentimental patronage but a kind of shock. Secondly, such an awareness of the thisness of the world calls out gratitude; for admiration, as Chesterton points out, has included within it an element of praise. So from existence as a surprise Chesterton derives its creator, as the one whom he desires to thank. Even the repetitions in nature speak to him not of tiredness and clockwork but 'a theatrical encore': 'There was something personal in the world, as in a work of art; whatever it meant it meant violently'.[27] Thirdly, he goes on to argue that the proper form of thanks is some form of humility or restraint. He cites the fairy-tale prohibition against Cinderella staying at the ball after midnight as evidence that the happiness of existence rests on an incomprehensible condition, from which he derives a sense of the fallenness of the world, and that what exists has something of the quality of goods saved from a wreck.

INTRODUCTION

Chesterton's 'natural religion' is pretty complete but quite unlike the natural theology of the eighteenth-century deists, in which God was in a sort of continuum with the created order, but at the same time oddly absent. God is not here a *deus absconditus* at the end of a chain of being, but revealed and active in every phenomenon and experience. Moreover, it is the cultural production, the fairy-tale, mediated by 'the solemn and star-appointed priestess at once of democracy and tradition' – his nurse – that shows him how to interpret the natural world.[28] Indeed, the chapter tends to privilege mediatory figures in the fairy-tale itself, such as the fairy-godmother or the witch aiding the hero to destroy the ogre's castle. In Chesterton's view, everything is waving madly at us to indicate its divine origin and its storied character. Mediation is therefore not a distantiation from God but an enabling of this realization of divine purpose.

And it is from this recognition that the theology of the art of invention of stories, fantastic or otherwise, is derived. To tell a story, whether one's own or a traditional tale, is to mediate the world in its intentionality and narrative character. It is therefore no surprise that our own age has such trouble with plotmaking in novels, resorting either to historical pastiche, novels based on real events, or postmodern bricolage. For to tell a story is to affirm that there is meaning to life, and that experience is shaped and has an entelechy.

This also has implications for all sorts of mediations. In our amoral market economy, economic transactions have taken on the fatalism of nineteenth-century science, with a similarly unacknowledged 'magic' quality to the distribution and sale of commodities. Similarly, our political system has trouble in relating central and local powers and has downplayed the roles of trades union and local education authority alike. The Church of England is itself denigrating the role of the local parish in favour of 'fresh expressions' of Church, which seek to address people in their specific age-group, consumer choices or networks, rather than as members together of a local (and international) society.

Chesterton's 'Ethics of Elfland' by contrast embraces the localism of the Edwardian and Georgian fairy in its specificity, but renders it universal: that is, we are all storied beings but our narratives are refracted and specific. Fairyland is everywhere about us, but we can never possess it. The 'incomprehensible condition' limits us to one woman, one place and one nation, but our allegiance is to the world. Without that specific and local sense of sacrality, however, the universal cannot be understood, just as we need a concept of a tree in order to appreciate the sycamore in our back-garden.

Similarly, Chesterton's elfland is not a *hortus conclusus* like the fairyland of the aesthetes but a way of looking at the world as storied and gifted. Another feature that allies it with Thomas's 'Lob' is its stress on the independence of the world from our perception and ownership. It truly is 'no man's land', but we have rights of access and use, just as in common law one may legally pick blackberries on a public footpath.

This has philosophical consequences for both Chesterton and Tolkien. The independence of the created order from our appropriation is underpinned in both writers by a strong philosophical realism, whereby the world of objects is not the product of our own mental perceptions but has its own reality. Faërie, as Tolkien understands it in his extended essay on fairy-stories, is the site where we encounter other beings and the world itself not just as 'enchanted' but as 'other.' As with 'The Ethics of Elfland', enchantment is a mode of relationality as well: neither Tolkien nor Chesterton has the nominalist individualism that would see each thing as totally separately named from every other. Instead, the created nature of the world renders it both related to God as its origin yet separated from its Creator by its contingency.

With my remarks above about realism, contingency and narrative ethics I have begun to move from literature to theology and to employ the discourse of medieval scholasticism. This, like the fairies, experienced a revival in the period under discussion, from the encyclical *Aeterni Patris* of 1879, in which Leo XIII commended the teaching of Aquinas and which led to the use of the *Summa* in the training of seminarians.[29] It was part of a move to find a philosophical basis for a whole programme of cultural life that could answer the intellectual challenges of modernism. Its Aristotelianism was, moreover, a way of mediation between 'pure' revelation and natural theology. A similar programme of Catholic social thought of the same period sought to find a middle way between the excesses

INTRODUCTION

of capitalism on the one hand, which denied the rights of workers, and socialism on the other, which was seen as denying the rights of the individual. Popes Leo XIII and Pius XI promoted in particular the role of voluntary associations, such as trades unions and craft guilds on the medieval model, as necessary mediations between the self and the state.

Chesterton's eventual adherence to the distributist movement, which sought the widest extension of relatively small private ownership of property, was in accord both with the 'third way' of Catholic social teaching and with Aquinas's views on property. Aquinas argues that property belongs primarily to God, but through Him to human needs. There is therefore a relative right to the use and enjoyment of the goods of the earth. Private property for Aquinas is important for social order and individual responsibility, but owes also a responsibility to the common good and to love between people. He commends attempts to limit the size of estates in ancient Greece.[30] In *An Essay on the Restoration of Property*, Chesterton's friend Hilaire Belloc argued that the common people had lost property they formerly enjoyed through enclosure and the onslaughts of capitalist modes of production.[31] It is easy to criticize distributism as nostalgic, although its wisdom is again becoming apparent as the effects of global warming lead to the need for more local production of food and self-sufficiency. What is important for the argument of this book is its promotion of property as both one's own – to use and enjoy – and yet as a common resource. It becomes mediatory of the self and a good that can be used for just exchanges, in contrast to the imaginary paper economy of a financial world and the interest payments of the banking system. Stratford Caldecott has pointed out the distributist elements in Tolkien's Shire, both in small-scale land ownership and devolved local governement.[32] There is also a somewhat 'anarchic' absence of law and policing, with the king a very long way off. The Shire communities are therefore mainly self-regulating and self-policing.

In distributism, property and money can be seen: they are rendered visible and real, and their mediatory character is acknowledged. It is a mediation that binds people together and allows the 'thingness' of property a sacred nature. It thus ties in with a

INTRODUCTION

theological realism as well as with an incarnational theology. Chesterton was a great friend of the Revd Conrad Noel of Thaxted, who was a leader among the Christian Socialists, and with whom he spoke at the Christian Social Union.[33] It is worth remembering that there was a great closeness between Guild Socialism, communism and distributism in the first half of the twentieth century, with a figure such as Eric Gill being associated with all three movements. The socialism represented by Noel, Stewart Headlam and Percy Dearmer was not only located in the theology of the incarnation but in Anglo-Catholic sacramentalism. As William Oddie has pointed out, Chesterton's views on patriotism, for example, owe a great deal to Noel's theology:

> Chesterton's essay appeared in a book called *England: a Nation* (1904), edited by his friend Lucian Oldershaw. This volume also included an essay by Fr Conrad Noel, one of the Catholic minded Anglican clergy who was at this time, I believe, having a considerable influence over the early development of Chesterton's religious beliefs. Noel . . . takes Chesterton's argument – that we can only have a true and universal love for all mankind if we first love those who are close to us – he takes this argument, which is essentially the Aristotelian argument, that we can only know the universal if we first know the particular – one stage further by pointing out that a Christian understands God's universal presence because he first receives God himself in sacramental form.
>
> 'The Divine Presence in the Mass', he wrote, 'adored as a presence distinct, exclusive, cut off from and incompatible with God's Universal presence in the world, becomes an insupportable heresy. So, too, with the love of country. A worship of the nation that is narrow, and excludes admiration for the traditions and heroisms of other countries, that is in effect a denial of the universal workings of God's Spirit, is the turning of a great and legitimate sacrament into a blasphemous fable and dangerous deceit. That God is contained within wafer or country is as necessary a proposition as it is orthodox.' A sacrament, in other words, is that which contains the universal within the particular.[34]

The socialism represented by Noel was guild socialism and had distinctly anarcho-syndicalist features, which stressed the importance

INTRODUCTION

of mediating structures and local organization. Chesterton's hymn, 'O God of earth and altar,' with its implicitly medieval vision of an integrated society, was published in the (significantly titled) *English Hymnal* of 1906, which was the production of Dearmer, Noel and friends.[35] Noel moved to Thaxted in Essex as incumbent in 1910, where he set about restoring all the colour and ceremony of medieval Catholicism with processions, music by Holst, dancing and maypoles, all of which coexisted with the red flag and revolutionary socialism. It was thus a most embodied politics, which, like that of Stuart Headlam who defended the music-hall, had a positive attitude to human life and culture of all sorts. Although Chesterton moved away from Anglicanism to become a Roman Catholic in 1922, this Anglo-Catholic association is important in giving a certain specific colouring to his Catholic theology. In his *The Catholic Church and Conversion*, Chesterton cites as one reason for his movement away from the Anglo-Catholicism of his friends its too national character: 'But I did not start out with the idea of saving the English Church, but of finding the Catholic Church. If the two were one, so much the better; but I had never conceived of Catholicism as a sort of showy attribute or attraction to be tacked on to my own national body, but as the inmost soul of the true body, wherever it might be'.[36]

The theology of the later Anglo-Catholics was influenced by Coleridge and F. D. Maurice as much as by the Oxford Movement; it looked to the early Church fathers for its socialist precedents. Chesterton's own theology, by contrast, has more in common with medieval scholasticism, although the bizarre truth is that he seems to have invented it for himself. Even when commissioned to write a study of Thomas Aquinas, he sent for a list of titles from his old friend and prototype of Father Brown, Father John O'Connor, and then, according to his secretary, flipped through them rapidly and never referred to them again.[37] Much of what one can describe as Thomistic in Chesterton dates from before any contact with O'Connor or Aquinas, as we shall see below. In contrast, Tolkien was not only brought up as a Catholic and thus sat through sermons by those trained in Aquinas, but owned a copy of the *Summa* which has some marginal notes.[38]

INTRODUCTION

Monsignor John O'Connor, however, first translated Jacques Maritain's *Art and Scholasticism* into English in 1923 with the help of the artist and writer Eric Gill, whose confessor he had become. Along with *St Thomas Aquinas* in 1922 and *Theonas* the following year, Maritain's writing preached the centrality of Aquinas and the scholastic tradition not only to Christian theology but to art and culture as a whole. The influence on Catholic intellectuals was immense, especially in the Ditchling community around Eric Gill and David Jones, where Maritain's works seem to have been used as a kind of textbook.[39] Already, as was mentioned earlier, there had been a return to Aquinas in the training given to Catholic seminarians, but it was Maritain and Etienne Gilson who drew lay Catholics like Chesterton and Gill to see his value in formulating a unified theory of civil and cultural life. According to Ward, Gill was a good friend of Chesterton, and the two shared a political attachment to distributism, with Gill contributing articles to *G. K's Weekly*.[40]

The first and most radical of Thomas's ideas, according to Chesterton, is that 'there *is* an Is'.[41] When a child looks out of the window he knows that there is something there. Chesterton differs here from Humean scepticism, because he points out that it is impossible to do anything or trust the reality of the eye itself if what one sees – the grass – is 'a mere green impression on the mind'.[42] From this one established point Chesterton shows how Thomas's great and complex system all proceeds. As Thomas puts it: 'Our intellect, therefore, knows being [*ens*] naturally, and whatever essentially belongs to a being as such; and upon this knowledge is founded the knowledge of first principles'.[43]

There are two immediate corollaries to this central point: first, if the child sees the grass, he knows it is not true to say that he does not see it. A thing cannot be and not be and from this, Chesterton argues, comes 'the everlasting duel between Yes and No'.[44] Secondly, that which we see is not complete, because it is always in a process of change. 'Ice is melted into cold water and cold water is heated into hot water; it cannot be all three at once'.[45] There is a mutability in the things we see but this does not lead to a Heraclitean flux. Rather, its incompletion, its 'becomingness' presupposes the existence of completion:

INTRODUCTION

> Looking at Being as it is now, as the baby looks at the grass, we see a second thing about it; in quite popular language, it *looks* secondary and dependent. Existence exists; but it is not sufficiently self-existent; and it would never become so merely by going on existing. The same primary sense which tells us it is Being, tells us that it is not perfect Being; not merely imperfect in the popular controversial sense of containing sin or sorrow; but imperfect as Being; less actual than the actuality it implies.[46]

The potentialities in the mutable phenomena that we see have their fulfilment in God, in whom they already exist. Without this potentiality there can be no concept of change at all, and Chesterton points out the inconsistency of using the language of change in evolutionary theory, since unless one accords an intentionality to the process there can only be flux. The mutability of things can deceive us if we try to hold onto them as ends in themselves; but

> as things tending to a greater end, they are even more real than we think them. If they seem to have a relative unreality (so to speak) it is because they are potential and not actual; they are unfulfilled, like packets of seeds or boxes of fireworks. They have it in them to be more real than they are. And there is an upper world of what the Schoolman called Fruition or Fulfillment, in which all this relative relativity becomes actuality; in which the trees burst into flower or the rockets into flame.[47]

There is one further element in this metaphysics that we need in order to understand Tolkien's philosophy, which is that the child does not just see one thing but many. He sees things – grass and grain – and he sees qualities that they hold in common, as well as ones by which they differ. It is this difference of things that Chesterton points to as especially the worldview of Christianity; its Creator of variety is like an artist, in contrast to an Asian philosophy of change as a misleading veil of illusion, and individuation with it. In Thomas this leads to a rejection of nominalism, and promotion of a moderate and participatory realism. For Tolkien the element I would stress is the otherness or objectivity of things. Only through the reality of the world can the mind, according to Thomas, reach out to otherness and become the object. As Maritain writes, 'it is in

INTRODUCTION

its totality reaching out towards the object, towards the other *as other*; it needs the dominating contact of the object, but only that it may be enriched by it . . . fertilised by being, rightly subjected to the real'.[48]

To sum up, Aquinas, according to Chesterton, teaches 'the reality of things, the mutability of things, the diversity of things'.[49] And, as this book will argue, this is a philosophy that can be found at every level of Tolkien's fictional project, from his invention of languages, to the workings of his fictional world and its ethics, to the meta-level of his theory of art.

The world Tolkien invents is, of course, fictional, but it is famously realistic in its density and completeness of realization. To invent a world at all, as fantasy writers continue to do, is to commit to metaphysics. As Kath Filmer-Roberts has argued, it is well-nigh impossible to write non-theistic fantasy because an intentionality in the act of creation of Being and beings is inherent in the whole enterprise.[50] It is significant that the archmodernist James Joyce, despite his rejection of Catholicism, sought the authority of Thomist aesthetics for his Stephen Dedalus in *Portrait of the Artist as a Young Man*, and Stephen continues his scholastic reflections in chapter 2 of *Ulysses*. For the fantasy writer not only mimics the divine act of creation but he or she, by creating a self-consistent, independent world also witnesses to the existence of an Is: to *Ens*.

Tolkien shows himself to be fully aware of this metaphysical dimension to fantasy writing in his essay 'On Fairy-Stories'. In the section discussing how fantasy can help us towards recovery, he states that: 'recovery (which includes return and renewal of health) is a re-gaining – regaining of a clear view. I do not say "seeing things as they are" and involve myself with the philosophers, though I might venture to say "seeing things as we are (or were) meant to see them" – as things apart from ourselves'.[51]

He goes on to move beyond what he calls 'Chestertonian fantasy' by which things are presented strangely so that we might see them afresh, because this does not free things enough. Paradoxically, it is the invention of creative fantasy which allows the gems to turn into 'flowers or flames'[52] rather like the 'trees burst[ing] into flower or the rockets into flame' of the upper world described in Chesterton's

INTRODUCTION

study of Aquinas quoted earlier. The 'things in themselves' to which Tolkien alludes are those elements of phenomena to which Kant, a critical idealist, believes we have no access, and to which he gives the term, 'noumena'. Despite his apologetic tone, Tolkien is actually saying something quite radical: that fiction in the form of fantastic recreation of the world can give us access to the real by freeing the world of objects from our appropriation of them. Maritain states that Kant's mistake was in believing 'that the act of knowing consists in *creating* the other, not in *becoming* the other, he foolishly reversed the order of dependence between the object of knowledge and the human intellect and made the human intellect the measure and law of the object'.[53] In reaching out to understand the grass as grass in Thomistic fashion, rather than being trapped by the subjectivity of Kantian perception, Tolkien's story-maker becomes the lover of nature and not her slave.

This Thomistic stress on the freedom of the created order is already emphasized by Chesterton in *Orthodoxy*, where he compares God to an artist: 'A poet is so separate from his poem that he himself speaks of it as a little thing he has "thrown off".'[54] Similarly God, in making the world, set it free in the manner of a dramatist, leaving its performance to human actors and stage managers. In Tolkien's own creation myth in *The Silmarillion*, Eru, 'the One' makes the great gods or spirits called the Ainur, to whom he proposes themes of music, out of which each finds his own particular melody, by which polyphony or harmony with the world is conceived. It is Eru or Ilúvatar's 'secret fire' of Being, Eä, which gives existence to the world, but he allows his themes to be freely developed by the Ainur, even incorporating the discord of the fallen Melkor into a yet more wonderful music. This story adds a further level of freedom, so that the creation derives wholly from Ilúvatar but has the contribution of the Ainur. However, once it has been actualized by Ilúvatar, he shows it to the Ainur as the fruition of their own vision: he shows them themselves.

The Ainur then come to look at the creation and are amazed, especially by the children of Ilúvatar, the elves and men, who had not been part of their own thought. 'Therefore when they beheld them, the more did they love them, being things other than themselves, strange and free, wherein they saw the mind of Ilúvatar reflected anew'.[55] So in each part of the creative act there is a consequent setting free of a variety of things and peoples to be themselves. Yet to have variety and diversity is not to have a dead materialism, since every work of the Ainur's hands reveals the wisdom of the Creator.[56]

So Tolkien's myth is faithful to Thomistic philosophy in its stress on God as Creator, the freedom of creation and its diversity. Its mutability is also a strong theme throughout Tolkien's work. It is already present in his account of the creation of the two main orders of the Children of Ilúvatar: the elves are immortal except by slaughter, or at least they shall live as long as the world endures; men are mortal but have a destiny beyond the world. Human beings are therefore mutable in that their body changes and dies, but their end is a supernatural one, which accords with Thomas Aquinas's anthropology in which the natural end for Man is a supernatural one, namely participation in the divine life, achievable through the Fall only by grace. The elves in contrast seem immutable in that they do not age and endure, but they witness to mutability, which they suffer, and which gives them a certain pathos. This is all the stronger in that, while not subject to death in the manner of human beings, the elves do begin to fade and lose their strength and power. To a degree greater than humanity they are wedded to the material cosmos, and yet they are always nostalgic for return to the Blessed Realm beyond the sea, from which they are exiled. So they are in a way mutable in that they are faded and have lost complete actuality, but their mutability is to do with the loss of past things, whereas the mutability of men and hobbits is focused on an unachieved future.

This contrast in perspective also has something to do with the diverse vocations of humans and elves. The latter are presented primarily as artists in Tolkien's world, while the former are concerned with action. This follows precisely the Thomistic (and Aristotelian) distinction between *poiesis* and *praxis*, which Maritain discusses at length in *Art and Scholasticism*, Eric Gill in his essay *Art and Prudence*, and David Jones in *Epoch and Artist*.[57] Action – *praxis* – in this context consists 'of the *free* use (*free* being here emphatic) of our faculties or in the exercise of our free will considered not in relation to things themselves or the works of our hands, but simply in relation to the use to which we put our freedom.'[58] The sphere of morality and the human good is that of action, and Maritain sets up prudence as its central virtue, by which our acts are measured against their ultimate end, which is God himself. In contrast, making (*poiesis*) is productive action, which is judged in relation to the thing produced and its perfecting. It is governed by the virtue of art. Hence the humans in Tolkien's world are primarily men of action, involved in public projects, government and defence; it is the elves who are the makers, following the example of the Ainur such as Aulë whose 'delight and pride' were 'in the deed of making, and in the thing made'.[59] The ethics of this distinction are explored in the story 'Leaf by Niggle'; which I discussed in the Preface in relation to co-creation. Niggle the artist is wholly consumed with the desire to paint a great tree, his real picture, before he has to make what is clearly the journey of death. In the story Niggle is unable to complete his work because of constant interruptions by his neighbour Parish and his practical needs. After a spell in a purgatorial hospital in which he learns the value of practical work, Niggle is released partly because 'he took a great deal of pains with leaves, just for their own sake'.[60] In Thomistic terms, he sought the perfecting of the work. At the end of a train journey he discovers the tree he had tried to paint, now an actual tree in a landscape and completely finished. ' "It's a gift!" he said. He was referring to his art, and also to the result; but he was using the word quite literally.'[61] He plans more work, and with the assistance of Parish, who helps rather than interrupting him, Niggle completes a whole landscape, house and garden. This story is partly about the value of artistic production, but also seeks to bring together Parish's *praxis* and Niggle's *poiesis*, which find their integration and fulfilment in heaven's 'mystical comradeship' as Chesterton put it in *Thomas Aquinas*.[62] It is typical of Tolkien that he should write about a piece of art coming true, since that was the triumphant theological conclusion to 'On Fairy-Stories' in which he looked to a time when all tales would come true in the *eschaton* (the end of time and inauguration of God's kingdom). The art that is created in 'Leaf by Niggle', however, is not just a piece of fine art, but also of practical use: people can come and live in it and be refreshed by it. Here prudence has not been sacrificed to Art as

Maritain (and Chesterton) claimed happened at the Renaissance, but there has been a return to an earlier medieval conception of art as serving society, which was being revived in communities like that of Eric Gill at the time that Tolkien was writing. In its conception of art as related to society, the arts and craft movement departs from high modernism's conception of the role of the avant-garde.

The art of the elves is similarly functional in the sense that they make objects rather than paint canvases: in modern terms they make applied rather than pure art. They are designers rather than painters. The nearest to 'pure art' are the Silmarils made by Fëanor, either through a 'new thought' or because he dreaded the possible destruction of the two Trees that lit the Blessed Realm, so that they 'might be preserved imperishable'.[63] Although the Silmarils are wonderful as objects, Fëanor hoards them, refuses them as aid to the Valar in undoing the destruction of the Two Trees, and later they are the cause of war and all sorts of disasters. Maritain helps to make sense of the fault here. Not only should the artist aim always and solely at the good of the work itself but he makes always a new thing; he does not merely imitate an old idea. The makers of the Silmarils were not concentrating wholly on the jewels as an end in themselves but as holders of something else, nor were they thinking primarily of the jewels as new things. There is consequently an ambiguity in the original project, which was aimed at preservation, and this is later confirmed by Fëanor's failure to use the jewels for a good purpose. They have become evidence of an art for art's sake aesethetic, and spend much of the time locked up. Maritain does allow a look backward to artistic production, because he claims that it restores the relation of people and things lost after the Fall: for beauty 'has the savour of the terrestrial paradise, because it restores, for a moment, the peace and simultaneous delight of the intellect and the senses'.[64] But generally art must have a purpose that is servile, because it is oriented to usefulness, or liberal in providing intellectual joy. Both purposes are located in present experience or future use.

In *The Lord of the Rings* Galadriel, Celeborn and the Lothlórien Elves are presented very much as correct artists in scholastic terms. As Maritain urges, they put themselves in all that they make: 'Leaf and branch, water and stone. They have the hue and beauty of all

INTRODUCTION

these things under the twilight of Lórien that we love; for we put the thought of all that we love into all that we make'.[65] Not only are all the things they make beautiful and pleasing to sight, but they are useful and serve the common good.[66] Like Niggle's Parish they unite art and prudence. Their cloaks are light and allow the wearer to blend into the landscape; their rope magically undoes itself, and their boats do not sink. Although the phial of light Galadriel gives to Frodo contains the light of Elendil's star, it orients that ancient source of illumination to future needs. And because all these objects are given to the Fellowship, Galadriel accepts her own fading and mutability (as she does also in resisting the temptation to take the Ring when Frodo offers it to her), offering her work to an unknown world to come. Her great lament, sung as the Fellowship floats away from Lórien down the River, does mourn the loss of Eldamar, but it contains a hope that other races may indeed reach it: 'maybe thou shalt find Valimar'.[67]

Maritain also describes the qualities that the beautiful must possess for scholastic philosophy: integrity, proportion and radiance or clarity. The first refers to fullness of being, so that elvish art's enchanted quality, whereby the rope has all the qualities one might hope for – silken smoothness, toughness, easy coiling and even visibility in the dark – to such an extent that it seems to have a life of its own, witnesses to its fullness of ropey being, or form. Elvish art clearly has proportion and unity; but most of all it has clarity or radiance, or what Aquinas terms, *splendor formae*, a splendour in its form. This means more than integrity. As Maritain puts it, '*splendor formae* . . . that is to say, the principle which constitutes and achieves things in their essence and qualities, which is, finally . . . the ontological secret that they bear within them, their spiritual being, their operating mystery – the form, indeed, is above all the proper *clarity* of every thing. Besides, every form is a vestige or a ray of the creative Intelligence imprinted at the heart of created being'.[68] Such a philosophy depends upon a neo-Platonic theory of light as intellectual energy, which is given off by a beautiful object or person from its source in God. The poet Dante constructs his whole Paradise out of such 'light intellectual full of love'.[69] Tolkien too seems to hold to such a celestial physics in his use of objects whose radiance similarly has a heavenly origin. The Silmarils, the three rings of the elves, Narya, Nenya and Vilya, and the little phial given to Frodo, all have the radiance and clarity of divine connection, and even the rope has a silvery sheen. Their actual illumination has an intelligibility, which reveals their nature and its 'operating mystery'. For the elves all remember the realm of the gods: the ontological origins of Middle-earth itself.

Aquinas also has something to contribute to the problem of the Ring of Power. Sauron, its maker, erred as an artist, in stealing knowledge to forge it from others, so that he did not put his own *habitus* within it. He erred in not seeking the good of the work but his own power. He erred also morally in separating art from prudence completely, with no thought of the common good, or of according his making to the divine order. Despite this, the Ring appears beautiful to Frodo when he first acquires it: 'the gold looked very fair and pure, and Frodo thought how rich and beautiful was its colour, how perfect was its roundness. It was an admirable thing and altogether precious'.[70] In Thomistic terms it certainly has integrity, in that it appears complete in itself. Its proportion, its inner qualities that render it round and golden also seem unified. What it lacks is clarity or radiance, because it actually hides words visible only in the fire. Moreover it lacks any vestige of its createdness: the integrity seems to subsume it, so that it becomes an isolated 'precious' object that subsumes divinity to itself. No one can free themselves from it once they own it and therefore, as Tolkien indicated in his essay 'On Fairy-Stories', it reveals nothing of the primary world. 'By the forging of Gram cold iron was revealed', but the Ring's power tells us little of the virtues of gold in themselves.

Paradoxically, Sauron too becomes the slave rather than the lover of his own work, and its destruction immediately leads to his own downfall. By denying clarity and relation to origin to the Ring, it became magical rather than enchanted. And in trying to be god, with his perversions of creation in his genetically modified orcs, Sauron is reduced to a great fiery Eye, which is fixed on the Ring. For Tolkien shows us that to be most like God is to be creative, and to allow one's creation true freedom. Tolkien as a creator, or sub-creator, has indeed given birth to a whole world, of different races and landscapes, beliefs and cultures. Its success too is due to the entire devotion to *poiesis*, to the perfecting of the work itself by its author. But its satisfying depth is not simply due to its complexity and detail, as in the Harry Potter series. It is due to its integrity and proportion, but also to its clarity, so that it provides a philosophical clue to the primary world we know: like Middle-earth, this world means more than it seems. In a real sense *The Lord of the Rings* does not need gods or a Christian subtext to be a religious work: because there is a mediatory radiance in every detail of its world, rendering it both wholly real and yet witnessing to a reality beyond itself and providing, as Tolkien wrote in 'Mythopoeia', 'from mirrored truth the likeness of the True'.[71]

We have come a long way from Edwardian fairies to reach Thomistic metaphysics, but I hope it is evident that they have in common an interest in mediation. In the three chapters of the next part, we shall see how Chesterton's and Tolkien's ideas similarly rely on mediation: that is, they are literary constructs in which, I shall demonstrate, the theology emerges within and through the stylistic modes and tropes that they employ to tell their stories. From what I have said, I hope it is clear that such mediation is not supposed to be transparent but rather radiant, and itself having the *integritas* and proportion of the work of art as Aquinas saw it. In the final part, I shall examine the poetics that builds upon these tropes to form not just an aesthetics but an ethics based on trust in the fairy or enchanted nature of mediation: the poetic justice of Richard Corbett's 'sixpence in her shoe'. To conclude, I shall return to making and action, to argue for a theology that like the fairies restores the world to us in all the fullness of its reality.

Notes

1. Richard Corbett, 'The Fairies' Farewell', in *Reliques of Ancient English Poetry*, ed. Thomas Percy, 3 vols (London: L. J. Dodsley, 1765), 3, pp. 209–12.

2. See, for example, Jeremy Maas, Pamela White Trimpe, Charlotte Gere and others, *Victorian Fairy Painting*, ed. Jane Martineau (London: Royal Academy of Arts, 1998); Jack Zipes, *Victorian Fairy Tales: The Revolt of the Fairies and the Elves* (London: Methuen, 1987); Alison Packer, Stella Beddoie and Liane Jarrett, *Fairies*

INTRODUCTION

in *Legend and the Arts* (London: Cameron and Tayleur, 1980); Diana Purkiss, *Troublesome Things: A History of Fairies and Fairy-Stories* (Harmondsworth: Penguin, 2001); Nicola Bown, *Fairies in Nineteenth-Century Art and Literature* (Cambridge: Cambridge University Press, 2001).

3. Cicely Barker's Flower Fairy series developed out of postcards she designed during the war. The first book in the series, on British flowers, was published in 1923. Edmund Gosse edited *The Allies' Fairy Book* in 1916 and there are fairy illustrations in Edmund Dulac's *Picture Book For the French Red Cross* (London: Hodder and Stoughton, 1915).

4. Quoted by John Garth, *Tolkien and the Great War*, p. 73.

5. Maas *et al.*, *Victorian Fairy Painting*, pp. 151–2.

6. David Jones, *In Parenthesis* (London: Faber, 1937), p. 185.

7. Rudyard Kipling, 'Fairy-kist,' in *Limits and Renewals* (London: Macmillan, 1932).

8. Dulac, *Picture Book*, p. 73.

9. The phrase comes from an influential study of the rise of nationalism by Benedict Anderson, *Imagined Communities: Reflections on the Origin and Spread of Nationalism* (London: Verso, 1983).

10. Krishan Kumar, *The Making of English National Identity* (Cambridge: Cambridge University Press, 2003).

11. E. M. Forster, *Collected Short Stories* (Harmondsworth: Penguin, 1972), p. 86.

12. Edward Thomas, 'Lob', *Poems of Edward Thomas*, introduced by Walter de la Mare (Oxford: Oxford University Press, 1975), p. 36.

13. *Poems of Edward Thomas*, p. 37.

14. *Poems of Edward Thomas*, p. 39.

15. Chesterton, *The Collected Poems*, p. 160.

16. It is significant that the National Trust's impetus came from writers of fairy-stories such as Ruskin and Morris, while Collingwood became a scholar on the subject.

17. *Letters of Tolkien*, p. 231.

18. *Letters of Tolkien*, p. 144.

19. Quoted in Rowan Willams, *Grace and Necessity: Reflections on Art and Love* (London and Harrisburg PA: Continuum/Morehouse, 2005), p. 63.

20. G. K. Chesterton, *Orthodoxy* (London: Bodley Head, 1908), p. 108.

21. Chesterton, *Orthodoxy*, p. 73.

22. 'Science as a Vocation', in Peter Lansman and Irving Velody (eds), *Max Weber* (London: Unwin, Hyman, 1989), p. 13.

23. Chesterton, *Orthodoxy*, p. 75.

24. Chesterton, *Orthodoxy*, p. 79.

25. Chesterton, *Orthodoxy*, p. 76.

INTRODUCTION

26. Chesterton, *Orthodoxy*, p. 77.
27. Chesterton, *Orthodoxy*, p. 101.
28. Chesterton, *Orthodoxy*, p. 72.
29. *Actes de Leo XIII*, 2 vols (Paris: Maison de la Bonne Presse, 1903). See also Romanus Cessario, *A Short History of Thomism* (Washington DC: Catholic University of America, 2005); and James A. Weisheipl, OP, 'The Revival of Thomism: An Historical Survey', *http://www.op.org/Domcentral/study/revival.htm* (accessed 17 July 2006).
30. Thomas Aquinas, *Summa Theologica*, literally translated by Fathers of the English Dominican Province (London: Burns Oates and Washbourne, 1920), Part 2, Q. 66, p. 66–70.
31. Hilaire Belloc, *An Essay on the Restoration of Property* (Norfolk VA: HIS Press, 2002).
32. Stratford Caldecott, *Secret Fire: The Spiritual Vision of J. R. R. Tolkien* (London: Darton, Longman and Todd, 2003), pp. 124–7.
33. See Ward, *Chesterton*, pp. 143–4.
34. William Oddie, 'Mass Communication and the Culture of Death', http://www.chesterton.lt/index.php?id=316 (accessed 5 January 2007).
35. *The English Hymnal*, ed. Percy Dearmer, Ralph Vaughan Williams *et al.* (Oxford: Oxford University Press, 1906), no. 562. It is in the national section, just one hymn away from the national anthem, but that last has a Part 2 with a corrective stress on peace, justice and international brotherhood! Scott Holland's 'Judge Eternal, throned in splendour' was also included at no. 423. His talk to The Christian Social Union was the subject of Chesterton's poem of the same title, which is quoted in Ward, *Chesterton*, pp. 143–4.
36. G. K. Chesterton, *The Catholic Church and Conversion* (London: Burns and Oates, 1960), p. 23.
37. Ward, *Chesterton*, p. 525.
38. I base this information upon a copy of the *Summa* offered for sale in an Oxford bookseller's in 2007, which has signatures verified as that of Tolkien. Paper slips inserted in various sections are taken from bibliographies of Anglo-Saxon studies, showing, I believe, that Tolkien used these volumes. The youth of the signatures and the topics of obedience, and the relation of love and passion, may even mark out the period of Tolkien's courtship and unofficial engagement. His mentor, Father Francis Morgan, opposed the engagement because of Tolkien's youth. See Carpenter, pp. 43–5.
39. Jacques Maritain, *Art and Scholasticism*, trans. J. Scanlon (London: Sheed and Ward, 1930). David Jones, *Epoch and Artist: Selected Writings*, ed. Harman Grisewood (London: Faber, 1959), p. 30.
40. Ward, *Chesterton*, pp. 422–3.

INTRODUCTION

41. G. K. Chesterton, *Thomas Aquinas and Saint Francis of Assisi*, p. 153.
42. Chesterton, *Aquinas*, p. 152.
43. Thomas Aquinas, *Summa Contra Gentiles*, trans. Vernon Bourke and Anton Pegis, 5 vols (Notre Dame IN: University of Notre Dame Press, 1975), II, ch. 83, 31, pp. 281–2.
44. Chesterton, *Aquinas*, p. 15
45. Chesterton, *Aquinas*, p. 154.
46. Chesterton, *Aquinas*, p. 158.
47. Chesterton, *Aquinas*, p. 164–5.
48. Jacques Maritain, *Theonas: Conversations of a Sage* (London: Sheed and Ward, 1923), p. 9.
49. Chesterton, *Aquinas*, p. 168.
50. Kath Filmer-Roberts, 'Presence and Absence: God in Fantasy Literature', *Christianity and Literature* 47(1) (1997), pp. 59–76.
51. J. R. R. Tolkien, 'On Fairy-Stories', in *Tree and Leaf*, p. 58.
52. Tolkien, *Tree and Leaf*, p. 59.
53. Maritain, *Theonas*, p. 9.
54. Chesterton, *Orthodoxy*, p. 125–6.
55. J. R. R. Tolkien, *The Silmarillion*, ed. Christopher Tolkien (London: Harper-Collins, 1999), p. 18.
56. On Tolkien's creation myth and the Thomist presentation of creation, see Jonathan McIntosh's unpublished paper, ' "I have Kindled You with the Flame Imperishable": Tolkien, Aquinas, and the Metaphysics of Faërie'.
57. Jones, 'Art and Sacrament', in *Epoch and Artist*, pp. 143–7; Eric Gill, *Art and Prudence* (Ditchling: Golden Cockerel Press, 1928).
58. Maritain, *Art and Scholasticism*, p. 5.
59. Tolkien, *The Silmarillion*, p. 19.
60. J. R. R. Tolkien, 'Leaf by Niggle', in *Tree and Leaf*, p. 106.
61. Tolkien, *Tree and Leaf*, p. 110.
62. Chesterton, *Aquinas*, p. 107.
63. Tolkien, *The Silmarillion*, p. 67.
64. Maritain, *Art and Scholasticism*, p. 19.
65. Tolkien, *The Lord of the Rings*, p. 361.
66. Maritain, *Art and Scholasticism*, p. 19.
67. Tolkien, *The Lord of the Rings*, p. 369.
68. Maritain, *Art and Scholasticism*, p. 20.
69. Dante Alighieri, *Paradiso*, Bollingen edition (New Haven: Yale University Press, 1973), p. 290.
70. Tolkien, *The Lord of the Rings*, p. 59.
71. Tolkien, *Tree and Leaf*, p. 90.

PART 1: POIESIS

CHAPTER

1

MAKING STRANGE: THE FANTASTIC

> 'I knew that Art had won, and snapt
> The Covenant of Things.'[1]

As A YOUNG MAN in the 1890s, Chesterton's wit was often expended on the fashions and orthodoxies of the day, of which aestheticism was one of the easiest to hold to ridicule, having received Gilbert and Sullivan's comic treatment in *Patience* as long ago as 1881. Yet despite the critical attitude to decadence in poems like the one quoted above, Chesterton was not only personally affected by the scepticism and melancholia of the *fin de siècle* to such a degree that Borges compares him to Oscar Wilde, but was also himself affected by the intellectual crisis of which aestheticism was one response.[2] In this chapter we shall see how it was precisely as a child of his time, responding to the crisis of language as representation and communication, that Chesterton came to use what literary critics would now see as proto-modernist techniques in order to invert the inversions of Wildean decadence, and find new ways to restore language as a signifying medium of the real world: namely, by the fantastic.

In her important study, *Language and Decadence in the Victorian Fin de Siècle*, Linda Dowling has shown that the late Victorian period suffered a loss of confidence in the Romantics' conception of the religious basis of language.[3] After revelation by Max Müller and other neo-grammarians of the arbitrariness of the relation between words and the ideas or things to which they refer, there ensued a general sense of linguistic demoralization and decadence, akin to that of the 'silver' age of Latin poetry as a falling away in the later Empire from the health and muscularity of the Ciceronian – and republican – style. Dowling proceeds to interpret nineteenth-century decadence less as a positive programme than 'a perception about the materiality and autonomy of its own linguistic medium'.[4] Art-for-art's-sake is all one is left with if what Chesterton would call 'the covenant of things' breaks down, and the symbol can no longer be said to participate, in Coleridgean fashion, in that which it symbolizes. In literature, the result of this breakdown is twofold. First, literary language as a medium or a material becomes an end in itself, as in the jewel-like excrescence of the prose-poem; secondly, it becomes a dead end, and art or poetry becomes a memorial for a lost presence. Max Beerbohm, a barometer as well as satirist of his times (and one who managed to be friends with both Wilde and Chesterton), draws attention to this turn to the funereal in his critique of the style of Walter Pater, whose epilogue to *Studies in the Renaissance* had been taken as an aestheticist *credo*: 'Even then I was angry that he should treat English as a dead language, bored by that sedulous ritual wherewith he laid out every sentence as if in a shroud.'[5]

Much later, the Catholic poet and artist, David Jones, in his preface to the long modernist poem *Anathémata* looked back to the early twentieth century as the time when he and others became aware of what he called 'the Break':

> Most now see that in the nineteenth century, Western Man moved across a Rubicon which, if as unseen as the 38th Parallel, seems to have been as definitive as the Styx ... But it was not the memory-effacing Lethe that was crossed; and consequently, although man has found much to his liking, advantage, and considerable wonderment, he has still retained ineradicable longings for, as it were, the farther shore. ... Our Break had reference to something which was affecting the entire world of sacrament and sign.[6]

Interestingly, he too uses the language of the underworld with the reference to the River Styx, and it is typical of modernist epics such as T. S. Eliot's *The Waste Land* and Ezra Pound's *Cantos* that they should be written as if from the perspective of a dead world, or take their protagonists on an initiation into the underworld as a rite granting prophetic authority, like that of Aeneas in book 6 of Virgil's *Aeneid*.

In Russia this same sense of the deadness of language led to a new concentration on the phenomenology of literary works and would lead to the development of linguistics and semiotics as academic disciplines. As for Wilde's supreme decadent Dorian Gray, so for critics such as Victor Shklovsky, 'it is simply expression that gives reality to things'.[7] Shklovsky, in particular, called for attention to the mortality of language: 'now words are dead, and language is like a graveyard'.[8] Unlike Jones, however, for Shklovsky the words are not moribund because of the loss of connection to communal meaning, but because of too much communality: we use words so often that we are habituated to them and cease to notice them at all: 'We are like the violinist who has ceased to feel the bow and strings, we have ceased to be artists in everyday life, we do not love our houses and clothes, and easily part from a life of which we are not aware. Only the creation of new forms of art can restore to man sensation of the world, can resurrect things and kill pessimism'.[9]

Here is a paragraph that might have come from Chesterton himself who, in the first decade of the new century, sought to find new fictional modes to reconnect his readers with the world of ordinary life, and in which he presented protagonists, such as Innocent Smith in *Manalive* (1912), who are true 'performance artists', aiming (quite literally with a shiny pistol in the case of Smith) to 'kill pessimism' by offering a Shopenhauerian philosopher the quick death his creed seems to sanction. *The Club of Queer Trades* (1905) shows organized attempts to release the bored bourgeois from the tedium of daily routine by means of the 'Adventure and Romance Agency', while *The Man Who Was Thursday* (1908) restores sensation through dowsing the startled reader in the genres of comedy, thriller, mystery, farce and fairy-tale in exhilarating succession.

In seeking to challenge lazy and lackadaisical usages of language – by locating a Surrey villa with the conventionally genteel address

'The Elms' in a truly arboreal position, for example, in 'The Singular Speculation of the House Agent' – Chesterton seems to be carrying out Shklovsky's programme, but his popular inclusive wit was the complete opposite of the style favoured by the Russian Futurist poets and artists, which was lauded by Shklovsky for its avant-garde obscurity. As only semi-comprehensible, such works remained poetic precisely because the reader could not move easily beyond the figurative language to understand what was meant. Indeed, the mode by which these works 'resurrected' language was achieved by the dismemberment of objects and their grotesque rearticulation. Thus art could be 'suspend[ed] in its own self-referential immunity' uncontaminated by the world beyond.[10]

Despite this, Shklovsky is most helpful in offering an analogue to Chesterton's project in his early work in another highly influential article, 'Art as Technique'. There he again states that our perception, even of art, becomes first habitual and then automatic, so that we do not really 'see' the objects described. Hence the purpose of art 'is to impart the sensation of things as they are perceived and not as they are known. The technique of art is to make objects "unfamiliar", to make forms difficult, to increase the difficulty and length of perception because the process of perception is an aesthetic end in itself and must be prolonged. Art is a way of experiencing the artfulness of an object'.[11]

The labour of making a poem or a picture is now something that can be experienced by the reader or viewer, and it is perhaps this remnant of the Carlylean work ethic (Carlyle being the subject of an appreciative essay by Chesterton) that links Russian formalism and English realism. Shklovsky takes his examples of this technique of 'defamiliarization' or making strange from Tolstoy, but every one is equally true of Chesterton's own writing. First there is the avoidance of direct naming, so that an event or familiar object is described as if for the first time. As 'eerie realism', this is a technique that Chesterton attributed to the London created by his beloved Dickens. He describes Dickens walking dreamily through the streets, so that objects are renewed in 'a trance of abstraction'. The most celebrated example of this defamiliarization, as was mentioned in the Preface, was the glass inscription over a street doorway read backwards on

MAKING STRANGE

the wrong side as MOOREEFFOC, which sends a Proustian shock through Dickens as it restores an early memory of coffee shops visited near St Martin's Lane in his unhappy youth. Chesterton imitates this effect to comic and satiric effect in the opening scene of his fantastic novel *The Ball and the Cross* (1905), in which the Satanic overreacher Professor Lucifer, steering his flying ship 'like a silver arrow' through the expanse of space, descries a new planet:

> 'It's a new world', he cried, with a dreadful mirth. 'It's a new planet and it shall bear my name. This star and not another vulgar one shall be "Lucifer, son of the morning". Here we will have no chartered lunacies, here we will have no gods. Here man shall be as innocent as the daisies, as innocent and as cruel – here the intellect –'
> 'There seems', said Michael, timidly, 'to be something sticking up in the middle of it'.
> 'So there is', said the Professor, leaning over the side of the ship, his spectacles shining with intellectual excitement. 'What can it be? It might of course be merely a –'[12]

The Professor breaks off to throw up his hands in astonished despair, and it is only by the quick attention of his captive, the monk Michael, that the flying ship avoids smashing straight into St Paul's Cathedral. Here the title of the novel, *The Ball and the Cross*, connects with its signified or indeed its referent (the actual ball and cross on top of the dome), and the very act by which the readers make the reconnection in their mind reorders and renews their understanding of that familiar London landmark. As in every Chestertonian example of this trope of 'making strange' a mini-drama of creation, fall and restoration is performed, here quite literally, as Lucifer's will-to-power is brought into abrupt collision with the resistance of the material. Indeed, the nature of 'fall' is itself defamiliarized here, where it is expressed by mastery of height, while a 'fall' brings the characters in contact with the holy in physical form as the iron cross topping the cathedral that literally saves them from death.

Shklovsky's second mode of defamiliarization is effected by an unusual point of view, which, in his example from a Tolstoyan short story, is that of a horse, and is used to criticize the practice of private property. Chesterton too uses the same principle of the unregarded perspective as a critique of human values in his short poem 'The Donkey':

> 'The tattered outlaw of the earth
> Of ancient crooked will;
> Starve, scourge, deride me: I am dumb,
> I keep my secret still.
>
> 'Fools! For I also had my hour,
> One far fierce hour and sweet:
> There was a shout about my ears,
> And palms before my feet.'[13]

Not only does the donkey, like Balaam's ass, answer back against human mistreatment, but he himself uses the avoidance of direct naming for his own defamiliarizing technique. He de-centres the gospel perspective of Jesus's entry into Jerusalem, 'riding upon an ass', with a more donkeyish integrity of vision than Tolstoy's horse, who delivers a long political sermon. Defamiliarization also works ethically in this poem, dividing the readership between metaphorical 'donkeys' who miss the point and think the speaking donkey voice in the poem mistakes adulation of Christ for praise of himself (which is also a temptation for Jesus since the praise turns to hatred later in the week!), and the believer who can now experience the story in a new way, in the manner of Ignatian kinaesthetic meditation on gospel events.

Shklovsky's third example of defamiliarization is the almost childlike description of something familiar as if it were seen for the first time. He uses the scene from *War and Peace* of Natasha's first visit to the opera, in which she misses the glamour and illusion but draws attention to the flat boards of painted scenery, the glue and the fat pants of the leading singer. The mechanisms of the artistic effect are relentlessly privileged over the opera as a whole, so that the performance appears ridiculous, demystified by the fresh gaze of the young visitor. All Chesterton's Father Brown detective stories are predicated on this trope, so that an illusion produced by the criminal is seen through by the innocent gaze of the childlike priest, such as the artistically irregular writing paper used for a suicide note, which Father Brown immediately sees is 'the wrong shape' – because it has had incriminating words cut off.[14] It requires the pastoral eye of the priest to recognize the likeness between the waiter and the gentleman diner in 'The Queer Feet', and thus unmask the thief who had played upon the snobbery that would not believe a waiter could imitate a guest, despite their identical evening clothes. To the social gaze a postman is 'no-one', whereas Father Brown sees the someone behind the uniform and thus the body of the victim in the sack in 'The Invisible Man'.

Yet whereas Tolstoy uses demystification of the opera to decry its artifice, Chesterton's attitude to the insubstantiality of theatrical effect is far less reductive. What follows is the opening of chapter 2 of Chesterton's *Autobiography*:

> The very first thing I can ever remember seeing with my own eyes was a young man walking across a bridge. He had a curly moustache and an attitude of confidence verging on swagger. He carried in his hand a disproportionately large key of shining yellow metal and wore a large golden or gilded crown. The bridge he was crossing sprang on one side from the edge of a highly perilous mountain chasm, the peaks of the range rising fantastically in the distance; and at the other end it joined the upper part of a tower of an almost excessively castellated castle. In the castle tower there was one window, out of which a young lady was looking. I cannot remember in the least what she looked like; but I will do battle with anyone who denies her superlative good looks.
>
> To those who may object that such a scene is rare in the home life of house-agents living immediately to the north of Kensington High Street, in the later seventies of the last century, I shall be compelled to admit, not that the scene was unreal, but that I saw it through a window more wonderful than the window in the tower; through the proscenium of a toy theatre constructed by my father; and that ... the young man in the crown was about six inches high and proved on investigation to be made of cardboard.[15]

There is indeed defamiliarization at work in this passage, as the reader moves from the apprehension of an actual young man, through a comic viewpoint to an uncomprehending problematization of perspective as he or she tries to imagine how the child Londoner came to see mountain chasms, which is finally resolved by an understanding of the scene as theatrical and thus cardboard and tinsel. Whereas Tolstoy's young Natasha, fresh from the country, is appalled by the unnaturalness of a cultural form whose conventions she does not understand, the artificiality of Chesterton's toy theatre is the creative work of his own father. Hence the Chestertonian reader moves from incomprehension to delight in artifice, just as the young man Chesterton moved from scepticism and agnosticism to embrace Christian belief and the goodness of creation whereas, as Shklovsky notes, 'Tolstoy found that his perceptions had unsettled his faith'.[16] For Tolstoyan defamiliarization sees society as a Platonic theatre of shadows in a cave from which he longs to escape, whereas Chesterton revises the Platonic myth and the Lockean model of the mind as passive audience of the play of images in a realist direction. The mind does indeed construct its idea of the real, but in joyful response to the otherness of the world beyond – an ideal-realism if you like. As we shall see in a later chapter of this study, Chesterton also revises the Romantic association of childhood with imagination to claim, inversely, that it is children who are the true realists. So the child Gilbert was not deceived by the man with the golden key's artifice, but liked it 'and indeed the things that now shine most in my memory were many of them technical accessories'.[17]

This emphasis on the reality of the mechanism of the process of making has implications for Chesterton's use of 'making strange', which is crucially different from that of the Russian formalists. For Shklovsky, defamiliarization privileges the viewer or reader over the object described or pictured: 'A work is created "artistically" so that its perception is impeded and the greatest possible effect is produced through the slowness of the perception. As a result of this lingering, the object is perceived not in its extension in space, but, so to speak, in its continuity'.[18] To use the technical terms that are themselves the creation of this same Russian literary school, this 'lingering' opens as large a gap as possible between the signifier (the word on the page) and its signified (what it means), thus separating it from any referent (the object described as a phenomenon in the world – in space). Instead the object is recreated in the mind of the perceiver as a new thing.

Such an idealist turn would lead to the combination of deliberately simple and repetitive diction with the complex and difficult meaning of Modernist poetry such as that of Gertrude Stein, whose volume *Tender Buttons* describes fruit, vegetables and household objects in such a bizarrely defamiliarized manner as to render them unrecognizable. Celery, for example, 'tastes tastes where in curled lashes and little bits and mostly in remains. A green acre is so selfish and pure and so enlivened'.[19] It would lead equally to the literary critical school of the so-called 'New Criticism', in which the work of art was separated from author and context to be viewed as a thing in itself. Philosophically, defamiliarization overcomes the Kantian problem of access to things-in-themselves by dramatizing the problem of moving from phenomena (which we can describe) to noumena (to which we have no access) through the perception of difficulty.

No Kantian, Chesterton's individual usage of defamiliarization thus becomes clear in its very difference: whereas Shklovsky problematizes understanding in order to empower its reach by the subject's mind, Chesterton does so to empower the object. His sense of the given reality of the world was with him intuitively as a child, but was later sharpened by his reading of Thomas Aquinas, or about him by writers such as Jacques Maritain, the neo-Thomist, whose work I have already shown he undoubtedly knew.

As we saw in the Introduction, central to Thomas's system is the belief that there *is something*: Being exists, and therefore 'there is a real bridge between the mind and reality'. Hence, according to Maritain, 'our art does not derive from itself alone what it imports to things; it spreads over them a secret which it first discovered in them, in their invisible substance or in their endless exchanges and correspondences'.[20] With this assumption, Chesterton can use his 'making strange' technique quite literally, as a device to sunder our lazy ownership of perception, so that we lose our apprehension of the phenomenal world in order to find it again: as itself, as something coming to us which is a mystery in its quiddity, its individuality and its difference from ourselves. The work that the imagination performs in uniting the 'before' and 'after' of the defamiliarization effect has a creative dimension, akin to that of the artist himself: 'It is by the way in which he changes the shape of the universe passing through his mind, in order to make a form apprehended in things shine upon a matter, that the artist impresses his signature upon his work. He recomposes for each, *according as the poetry changes him*, a world more real than the reality offered to the senses'.[21]

Chesterton the writer 'changes the shape of the universe' in order to give his readers the 'world more real' than our perceptions, while the reader then collaborates to make the effect work, and endeavours to apprehend the form: 'the real decisive quality that makes a thing itself'. This form is both within the object (as recognized or divined by the artist/reader) and within the mind of the perceiver, forming the bridge between them. To detect this form is both to see the object as itself but also as *more* than itself: objects are both revelatory and hidden; they mean more than they seem or, as Maritain has it, there is a secret. The suspension of understanding in the defamiliarization effect stages and precipitates this sense of a hidden secret, of what Maritain calls an 'ontological secret'. So the protagonist of Chesterton's *The Man Who Was Thursday* walks down a country lane at the end of the fantastic sequence of events feeling that 'he was in possession of some impossible good news, which made every other thing a triviliality, but an adorable triviality'.[22] The complex machinery of the spy thriller plot that finally burst like a nightmare becomes one great defamiliarization technique, performed so that ordinary life can now be seen as formed – given shape and meaning – by something both within and without it: namely, the transcendent.

Another way of thinking about this 'making strange' is in terms of rebirth. For Shklovsky 'words are dead, and language is like a graveyard' because they are too easy and familiar, and defamiliarization will not so much restore the meaning as arrest the perception in the materiality of the language as linguistic stuff. But for Chesterton the visual phenomenal field 'dies' as inert object (like Donne's 'Death thou shalt die'), in order to be reborn as a miracle, 'as if saved from a wreck', as Chesterton describes it in *Orthodoxy*. The reader moves from a 'fallen' perception of the world as dull or in his control to a 'redeemed' apprehension of it as God's creation and thus beautiful in the Aquinan sense of 'what gives pleasure on sight' and 'delights the soul by the bare fact of its being given to the intuition of the soul'.[23] Therefore both the things we make and the things we apprehend in this way have that 'savour of the terrestrial paradise', that I quoted earlier, because they truly do 'restore[s] for a brief moment the simultaneous peace and delight of the mind and the senses'.[24]

It is here that Tolkien's literary project opens out naturally from Chesterton's, as it is outlined in his lecture 'On Fairy-Stories', which was published in expanded form in 1947. As we have already seen, Chesterton is referred to more than once in 'On Fairy-Stories', and on one occasion from Chesterton's own essay on fairy-stories. Tolkien outlines the earlier writer's defamiliarizing techniques and shows that they are used 'to denote the queerness of things that have become trite, when they are seen suddenly from a new angle'.[25] Tolkien also realizes the theological basis of these tropes as indicating an attitude of humility towards the world beyond the self.

Interestingly, however, Tolkien grants this kind of fantasy only a limited power, not because it is wrong but because it does not go far enough. Whereas for Chesterton, as I have just shown, establishing the marvellous or transcendent *realism* of objects is the central aim, for Tolkien it is their *independence*. His first category for analysing the function of fantasy is at one with Chesterton: 'recovery', or 'regaining a clear view'. But he goes on: 'I do not say "seeing things as they are" and involve myself with the philosophers, though I might venture to say "seeing things as we are (or were) meant to see them" – as things apart from ourselves'.[26] For Tolkien, Chesterton does not take them far enough away from our appropriation. Tolkien uses the image of the dragon's hoard to explain our possessive attitude to things, as well as our weary boredom in relation to them. 'They have become like the things which once attracted us by their glitter, or their colour, or their shape, and we laid hands on them, and locked them in our hoard, acquired them, and acquiring ceased to look at them'.[27] Fantasy, in Tolkien's understanding, is an opening up of the hoard and letting the locked things fly away, to be transformed and reformed.

For this reason 'escape' is the second of Tolkien's characteristics of

Fantasy writing. It is not, he claims, escapism, or a flight from the real but towards it: 'we should meet the centaur and the dragon, and then perhaps suddenly behold, like the ancient shepherds, sheep, and dogs, and horses – and wolves'.[28] Similarly, Tolkien points out how, in a fairy-story, normal daily objects and materials, such as stone, wood and iron 'are made all the more luminous by their setting'.[29] All this approximates to Shklovsky's defamiliarization by change of point of view, whereby objects are seen as if for the first time. The word 'luminous' as used here evokes also the medieval scholastic tradition, in which it is by their 'lumen' or 'splendour' – their radiance – that objects reveal their divinely created origin: 'Every form, indeed, that is to say every light, is "a certain radiation proceeding from the first brightness"'.[30]

This all sounds Chestertonian but it is used, of course, for a very different purpose. Chesterton never takes the reader completely out of his own world as Tolkien does. For the aim of escape combined with a recovery of vision is to undergird Tolkien's imaginary or sub-created fictional universe, and allows him to employ defamilarization effects throughout his stories and novels for a slightly different function. Yet Middle-earth is not the self-enclosed alternative reality of much fantasy writing that claims to follow in Tolkien's footsteps, but bears a complicated relation to our own world. It is actually our own planet before Great Britain split off from the European landmass, and the terrain of the Shire is not dissimiliar to that of the Midlands in which Tolkien grew up. It is, however, deliberately 'made strange' not only by the foreign physical geography but by the hobbits themselves, who share so many mid-twentieth century English characteristics: their love of gardening, fish and chips and pipeweed; their bourgeois respectability: Bag End is an anglicization of the suburban 'cul de sac', and there is a recognizable small-town stolidity about Hobbiton. Tolkien acknowledged readily that the domestic imperturbability and courage of Sam Gamgee was based on his experience of the ordinary Tommies he fought alongside in the Great War, while the pubs, named The Ivy Bush and The Green Dragon, are very British local hostelries.[31]

The fusion of horizons between the Shire and Tolkien's modern British readers is, of course, problematized by the fact that hobbits are actually only half our size and, moreover, have overlarge feet covered in hair that they keep unshod. Furthermore, the Shire itself is supremely unimportant in the world of its own day in comparison to the imperial reach of early twentieth-century Great Britain. Treebeard the Ent has no entry for hobbits in his encyclopaedic list of living creatures, and to Éomer and the Rohirrim they are as fairies are to us: 'a little people in old songs and children's tales out of the North'. The preface to the first volume of *The Lord of the Rings* has the tone of an anthropology textbook in which hobbit life and customs are described with the careful accuracy and attention to minutiae of life of a study of Polynesian islanders, which gives the reader knowledge while at the same time distancing him or her from the characters as objects of scientific investigation.

The rendering of hobbits as strange, and their defamiliarization within their own fictional world, has a double effect: first, their distantiation renders them fictional, as a legend in their own narrative context; secondly – and conversely – this very lack of fit for a group with whom the reader has become quite comfortable as his or her primary perspective on events in the novel, renders the hobbits believable, rather in the manner in which historical criticism of the Bible privileges elements in the gospels as more credible if they do not fit easily with what the critic perceives to be an early church worldview. Hence the very legendary status of the hobbit world engenders what narrative theorists term a 'reality effect'. We believe in the ents, dwarves, etc., because we experience them through hobbit eyes; we believe in the hobbits partly because they are our focalizers – our point of view on events – and partly because after this relationship has been established, questions of their existence are introduced by those same groups or species to which hobbit eyes have made us accustomed. And this reality effect works both ways: first, to give integrity and context to the hobbits, and second, to give a sense of historicity to the world of Ents, Rohirrim and Middle-earth as a whole.

For although Tolkien's world is, in his own understanding, a 'sub-creation', it is achieved so thoroughly that it takes on a realism of its own. And every mode of fictional apparatus – maps, indices, appendices, supplementary versions of the novel and *The Silmarillion* itself – paradoxically render that world all the more credible. This is true of any successful fantasy to some extent: J. K. Rowling's fictional magical Britain of the Harry Potter stories has a similar density of lovingly imagined detail if not of metaphysics, while Philip Pullman's *Dark Materials* trilogy is spawning supplements in *Lyra's Oxford* and *The Book of Dust*. In both these recent projects, however, there is an equal reliance on defamiliarization at work, quite unlike the hermetic seal around the Earthsea world of Ursula Le Guin, despite the latter's psychological credibility. Rowling adds the celebrated Platform Nine and Three-Quarters to King's Cross Station as part of a parallel and intertwined co-reality, while Lyra's Oxford is, like Joan Aiken's London, an alternative version of a real place, undergirded by theories of infinite parallel universes in modern physics. Pullman's effective employment of animal daemons for each human in one world is his defamiliarizing equivalent of the hobbits' hairy feet.

But where Middle-earth differs from Rowling's and Pullman's visions is in its conception of magic. Rowling's children learn spells as the equivalents to Chemistry and Biology at school, in the manner of the positivist theory of magic in primitive culture as an early form of science rather than religion. Pullman's 'magic', that works through I Ching, alethiometer and subtle knife, has a similar instrumental and quasi-scientific character, appropriate to his materialist project. The success of Pullman and Rowling as writers primarily for children is due first to their ability to defamiliarize ordinary adolescent experience, to render it significant and narratable and, second, to their granting of real theurgic power to their young protagonists: they write myths of liberation.

In contrast, Tolkien's world has a complete taxonomy of magic in which subtle knife/wand magic is demythologized as the will-to-power and even as fetishistic: the Ring and its effects are viewed as much more dangerous and corrupting than any of the magic skills in Rowling and Pullman. There is, however, a more potent and universal magic in Tolkien's world by which the whole material cosmos is infused with a kind of enchantment, as if it had a radiance: a 'lumen'. This is the particular character of the elves, so that Sam sees them for the first time with 'the starlight glimmering on their hair and in their eyes'; but it is a property of everything in the novel: wood, stone and iron as in the traditional fairy-tale (which of course need have no actual fairy to guarantee its 'fairy' status) and the chasteness of its colour scheme of green, brown, yellow, blue and silver.[32] The distinction between universal enchantedness and instrumental magic is made in the very first chapter of *The Lord of the Rings*, in which the Ring's power allows Bilbo to disappear at the end of his birthday speech – '*This is the END. I am going. I am leaving NOW. GOOD-BYE!*' (p. 37) – leaving everyone feeling cheated and rather flat, whereas Gandalf's own fireworks (made by himself) are the stuff of legend and excitement. The fireworks are no less magic and mysterious:

> There were rockets like a flight of scintillating birds singing with sweet voices. There were green trees with trunks of dark smoke: their leaves opened like a whole spring unfolding in a moment, and their shining branches dropped glowing flowers down upon the astonished hobbits, disappearing with a sweet scent just before they touched their upturned faces. There were fountains of butterflies that flew glittering into the trees; there were pillars of coloured fires that rose and turned into eagles, or sailing ships, or a phalanx of flying swans; there was a red thunderstorm and a shower of yellow rain; there was a forest of silver spears that sprang suddenly into the air with a yell like an embattled army, and came down upon the water with a hiss like a hundred hot snakes. And there was also one last surprise, in honour of Bilbo, and it startled the hobbits exceedingly, as Gandalf intended. The lights went out. A great smoke went up. It shaped itself like a mountain seen in the distance, and began to glow at the summit. It spouted green and scarlet flames. Out flew a red-golden dragon – not life-size, but terribly life-like: fire came from his jaws, his eyes glared down; there was a roar, and he whizzed three times over the heads of the crowd. They all ducked, and many fell flat on their faces. The dragon passed like an express train, turned a somersault, and burst over Bywater with a deafening explosion. (p. 27)

I have given this description in its entirety because only cumulatively does the mysterious nature of the fireworks emerge. The passage begins with a simile, 'like . . . a flight of birds' and we recognize our own musings at an ordinary bonfire night display, but the language moves to direct statement: 'there *were* green trees', although the similitude is still maintained in the phrase about the leaves opening 'like' a whole spring. Next, however, the trees grow blossoms, which actually smell, and soon an entire woodland habitat has emerged, to be followed by items that are either eagles, ships or swans, to be followed by a scene realized out of Bilbo's past in *The Hobbit*. After this miraculous effect the dragon moves as if to attack the audience and the tone lurches anachronistically into the reader's present with the comic analogy of the express train, and the dragon too becomes oddly material by turning a somersault.

Not only does the passage in this way orchestrate a whole sequence of defamiliarization effects, but it leaves the reader hesitating as to the manner in which he or she should understand the experience. The anachronism of the express train is reminiscent of the intrusive authorial voice of *The Hobbit* that preserves the fusion of horizons of the parental bedtime story by referring back to the child auditor's own experience. Here it marks the distance between the earlier novel and *The Lord of the Rings* by leaving the interpretive quandary unresolved. The reader is left in the *aporia* of the making strange and for some readers of the novel, this is the point at which they give up, unable to take the story seriously.

Again, recourse to literary theory helps to make sense of what Tolkien's text is staging here in the work of a more recent narrative theorist, Tzvetan Todorov, from whom I take my usage of 'fantastic' in the title of this chapter. In his influential *The Fantastic: A Structural Approach to a Literary Genre*, first published in 1970, Todorov takes the difficulty that Shklovsky sees as central to the defamiliarizing effect in a metaphysical direction, so that he argues that the fantastic occurs when a text opens by assuming a world that accords with our own understanding of how the laws of space, time and so on operate.

> In a world which is indeed our world, the one we know, a world without devils, sylphides, or vampires, there occurs an event which cannot be explained by the laws of this same familiar world. The person who experiences the event must opt for one of two possible solutions: either he is the victim of an illusion of the senses, of a product of the imagination – and laws of the world then remain what

they are; or else the event has indeed taken place, it is an integral part of reality – but then this reality is controlled by laws unknown to us. Either the devil is an illusion, an imaginary being; or else he really exists, precisely like other living beings – with this reservation, that we encounter him infrequently.

The fantastic occupies the duration of this uncertainty. Once we choose one answer or the other, we leave the fantastic for a neighbouring genre, the uncanny or the marvellous. The fantastic is that hesitation experienced by a person who knows only the laws of nature, confronting an apparently supernatural event.[33]

Like the hobbits, Todorov's protagonist has to resolve an *impasse*: either the fantastic event is truly marvellous, like a fairy-tale, and one leaves realism and the world of the diurnal behind; or it is uncanny, and like Freud's interpretation of eerie, seemingly supernatural phenomena, one seeks an explanation in the psychology of the perceiver. The hobbits who, once the dragon threat has passed, seem quite unbothered by the miraculous elements of the fireworks, evidently resolve their hesitation by deciding the whole thing is a conjurer's illusion. The reader, however, is left rather more like the young Chesterton in front of the toy theatre, both acknowledging the fictive status of the fireworks as art – designed and made by Gandalf – but also their magical ability actually to be the things they represent, rather like the art of God in Dante's *Purgatorio* (10: 34–81), in which the proud are taught humility by living pictures that move and speak. The effect of these magical fireworks, however, is more complex than Todorov's dualities of miracle or secularity, for what they do is present the world of Middle-earth as perceived in *The Hobbit*, including its battle, forest, dragon and mountain, as all enchanted. The scenes of Bilbo's life are returned to him in all the richness of their own life, so that the plants and creatures are all in motion, having the fullness of being, and even the dragon is allowed to fly away. It is the world of things which are non-appropriated, allowed to be 'made strange' and Gandalf, like Tolkien's ideal fantasy writer in 'On Fairy-Stories', opens the hoard of images 'which once attracted' Bilbo 'by their glitter, or their colour, or their shape' and lets them escape, so as perhaps to prepare Bilbo psychologically for the renunciation of the Ring of Power. If he gives up the bad magic of the Ring, he can enjoy all the more a world of enchantment and art, and the 'radiance' of admitting a divine and thus non-possessive origin.

Tolkien's preference for independence over Chestertonian fantasy means that examples of the true fantastic in Todorov's definition are few. He does, however, have moments of actual hesitation in the plot of the novel that are equally revelatory of the distinction between true and false magic. So in book 2, chapter 4 the Fellowship reach the great Doors of Durin that lead into the mines of Moria, but are unable to enter. For hours Gandalf hesitates as he tries in vain to use spells or find the secret password that will grant them access. Only when he realizes that the words over the arch, 'Speak, Friend and Enter' (p. 300), are themselves the key, does he open the portal: the word 'friend' was all that was required. Legolas and Gimli had been bickering, and the door gave an example in its union of dwarf, elven and human iconography of the friendship that the Fellowship themselves need if they are to complete their task. The magic of command failed; the magic of enchantment creates community. Here Gandalf actually enacts a Shklovskian defamiliarization quite precisely because he has to stop seeing language as automatic, a route to something beyond itself; instead he must dwell upon the materiality of the word 'friend'. The performative nature of language here is close to modernist practice. Unlike Shklovsky, however, the defamiliarized word 'friend' is not divorced from context but restores it, so that the community is reformed by the renewal of their journey.

Chesterton's stories are much closer to Todorov than Tolkien's hesitations, because they belong primarily in the modern post-Enlightenment world that Todorov describes, in which the supernatural is a problem for thought. In particular his Father Brown detective stories are object-lessons in the fantastic, because each begins in a credible world of service flats, tea-shops or seaside resorts out of season, but then proceeds to destabilize that comfortable sense of normality by a mysterious fact that seems inexplicable in rational terms: a dead body vanishes from a room and appears in a tree; an arrow from heaven shoots someone; a dagger flies; an automatom commits a murder; the sun kills its worshipper. The reader is faced with a seemingly supernatural incursion into the real and tries to find an explanation in which both normal context and supernatural fact can be accommodated. Chesterton delights in setting up atheists as particularly prone to this conceptual confusion. So, for example, in 'The Resurrection of Father Brown', set in Latin America, Father Brown is assassinated but appears to have been miraculously brought back to life to be greeted by religious sceptics and populace alike as a miracle. He is alone in protesting that no miracle has occurred, and in 'The Oracle of the Dog' he presents the fantastic as a trope appropriate to modern agnosticism: 'It's the first effect of not believing in God that you lose your common sense and can't see things as they are. Anything that anybody talks about, and says there's a good deal in it, extends itself indefinitely like a vista in a nightmare'.[34]

Without a divine grounding for the real, it is oddly spectral, especially if one accepts the Kantian unknowability of the noumena. Every phenomenon, therefore, comes shadowed with mystery but with no categories with which to understand it – hence the infinite vista. Chesterton may have in mind the scene in George MacDonald's fantasy novel *Phantastes* (which may also in a different way have been the inspiration for the wardrobe scene in C. S. Lewis's *The Lion, the Witch and the Wardrobe*) in which the hero visits the eerie house of Darkness, where he opens a cupboard only to find it backless. It leads into an infinite void down which his shadow rushes towards him. The Shadow haunts the hero, preventing human contact and mediation.[35] Similarly, Chesterton sees agnosticism as opening onto this same negative transcendence.

Each Father Brown story stages the fantastic as a blockage to thought, an interpretive void, in order to allow Father Brown to exercise his priestly ministry by restoring the real, not as supernatural in a vague, ethereal sense, nor as something that is part of our mind alone but as truly real: Tolkien's 'things as we were meant to see them, apart from ourselves'. Hence the Father Brown stories often hinge on an object – cursed goblet, silver fish-knives, a jewel, a mutilated Bible – that appears uncanny but is later shorn of its superstitious aura and restored to communality with the phenomenal world. In the story 'The Head of Caesar', for example, Christabel Carstairs is blackmailed when she takes a coin from her brother's historic collection to give her lover, because the face reminds her of his profile. She does not mean to steal – and has no pecuniary motive to do so – but wishes to escape from the 'dead, dull gold and bronze and brass' of family life lived in thrall to this inheritance, in order to escape to the 'living and growing gold' of the gorse in the natural world outside.[36] Her action is approved by the narrator, who compares her brother's attitude to money to idolatry, which leads him to don a false nose and blackmail his own sister, whereas she had sought to return the fetishized object to use and to value as a token of her affection for her beloved.

The Todorovian fantastic is most interestingly at work in Chesterton's play *Magic*, which ran very successfully in 1913.[37] The plot hinges upon the actions of a professional musician who turns the red light outside a doctor's surgery to blue under the gaze of the doctor himself, a duke, a priest and a sneering American visitor, causing a nervous collapse in this last witness. The play lurches between belief and disbelief in the supernatural basis of the magician's spells. The first scene introduces a ghostly figure who claims to be a fairy but who is later revealed to be the professional conjuror; he then proceeds to perform a 'trick' that is completely inexplicable, and which he later claims to have been achieved with the aid of demonic forces. All the characters who witness the 'miracle' of the light change and other eerie effects are put into the hesitation of the fantastic – mainly atheists or agnostics, they cannot credit the supernatural yet have the evidence of their own eyes with which to contend. The effect is further complicated by the fact that it happens within a play and is, in that sense, a purely theatrical effect, so that *Magic* can be interpreted as a reflection upon the power of theatre to make us believe. The audience is, however, left still within the hesitation of the fantastic because the magician, while claiming the reality of his magic, agrees to furnish a possible explanation so that the prostrated young American may keep his materialist opinions and get well.

Indeed, in every mention of fairies in Chesterton – and there are a great number – it is impossible to work out if he literally believes in them or not. It is as if the existence of fairies represents possibility itself, and the mysterious nature of the material, so that all that can be managed is an entertaining of their existence not so much as a blockage to thought as a reverent agnosticism about the potentialities within the divine creation. Tolkien on the other hand, if the anecdote of Canon Norman Power is to be believed, really did believe in both dragons and fairies. After a talk at Worcester College, Oxford, Tolkien is reported as having emptied his pockets to retrieve a long soft piece of lizard skin, which he claimed was the shoe of a leprechaun.[38] This has to be balanced by the line in his poem 'Mythopoeia' in which he seems to imply that we look back into history and imagine the elves: what is indisputable, however, is that Tolkien does use fantastic effects in his fiction as Chesterton does, but for rather different ends.

One of the most interesting moments of fantastic hesitation is the scene in Fangorn Forest in chapter 5 of *The Two Towers*, in which the Fellowship remnant encounters the 'risen' Gandalf. At first all they see is an old beggar-man moving wearily among the trees, whom Gimli thinks they should kill, believing him to be Saruman. When the old man approaches, he is clearly more than a beggar: he moves 'with surprising speed' like the seemingly aged Professor de Worms in *The Man Who Was Thursday* who, despite his age and decrepitude, is able to chase the protagonist all over London. Moreover, a 'quick glint of white' (p. 482) appears for a moment from within the seeming Saruman's grey garments.

It takes two pages of text for Gandalf to be revealed to his friends, during which he converses with them in deliberately riddling fashion. Tolkien has quite deliberately modelled this encounter on the conflation of two stories of Jesus's resurrection appearances in the gospels. In John 20.11–18 Mary Magdalene encounters someone who she takes to be the gardener in Gethsemane, but realizes it is Christ when he speaks her name; in Luke 24.13–35 two disciples are joined by a third man on the road to Emmaus, who expounds to them the scriptures about the death of the messiah, and who is revealed as Christ in the breaking of bread together in the evening. Both stories have a period of misapprehension, followed by an epiphany. Tolkien imitates this structure and includes comforting words about the fate of the two lost hobbits, just as Luke's Jesus does about the death of Christ. He makes Gimli demand of the old man where he has hidden the hobbits, just as Mary asks of the 'gardener' where Jesus has been taken. The period of mystery and puzzlement in the gospel accounts is important in enabling a certain detachment from the Jesus his friends knew hitherto, so that they may receive him as risen. In the book of Acts, which is the sequel to Luke's gospel, the apostles move swiftly into acting *as* Christ: baptizing and healing in his name. Similarly, in John's gospel, Mary has to learn not to cling to the Jesus she knew, so that she may be his witness to others. A truly Todorovian period of hesitation is opened up in all the gospel accounts of the resurrection, particularly that of Mark, which ends appropriately with the problem of the empty tomb, provoking a real dilemma: is this a tomb robbery or something supernatural? Each gospel moves to situate belief in Christ on the other side of real doubt and despair; a movement of faith has to be made by protagonists and readers alike. Indeed, the stories make it really fantastic by having Christ eat, move through doors and have wounds that can be touched. Christ is neither ghost nor someone who did not really die: he crosses all known boundaries of existence.

Tolkien brings all this to bear upon his Gandalf resurrection scene, in which Gandalf too has gone beyond all forms of life known to Middle-earth, even to the extent of forgetting some things he once knew in the experience of his walk 'in dark thought' (p. 484). The hesitation suffered by the reader and characters alike is not one between natural and supernatural explanations, except at first. Rather it is about whether the figure is benign or dangerous, good or evil. Again, we can see how Tolkien takes the Chestertonian fantastic – which restores the real as uncanny in Todorovian terms – in a more marvellous direction. No naturalistic explanation is offered here akin to that of Father Brown's 'resurrection'. Instead, and in imitation of the Christian gospels, the Gandalf appearance takes the reader into a deeper supernatural dimension of Middle-earth, hitherto unknown. The hesitation element is still, however, preserved by the fact that Tolkien's narrative includes analogies not only with Christ's resurrection but also with his transfiguration. For when Legolas, like Mary, has recognized Gandalf he sees him alter before his eyes: 'They all gazed at him. His hair was white as snow in the sunshine, and gleaming white was his robe; the eyes under his deep brows were bright, piercing as the rays of the sun; power was in his hand. Between wonder, fear and joy they found no words to say' (pp. 483–4).

The dazzling brightness of Gandalf's robe echoes that of Jesus in Luke 9.29 and Mark 9.3, when he appears in glory to three chosen disciples on a mountain. Appropriately there are also three witnesses to Gandalf's transfiguration. But the event falls between the two gospel events of earthly transfiguring and postmortem resurrection. There is an element of death in Gandalf's falling into shadow, but he is not a human being. He is an angelic figure, one of the Maia, who are lesser Ainur. His return reveals more of who he actually is, as does Jesus's transfiguration, but Gandalf has actually been changed into something greater than he was by the experience: he is now Saruman in some sense. So the biblical echoes are not included in order to render the meaning of the event more authoritative, but to open out and extend its meaning – and even to destabilize it. Falling between two already mysterious categories, the event is difficult for the reader to comprehend, and in that sense Gandalf's return is rendered fantastical. The fantastic, however, has shifted from psychological versus marvellous to two sorts of marvellous that also bear with them elements of the real: the fantastic squared if you like.

Despite the realism of Tolkien's fictional world, he does not spell out its laws from the beginning but allows them to emerge gradually, as the reader encounters new races and cultures and deeper magic in the course of the narrative. When magic does occur, it tends to emerge in such a way as to render the world of the novel stranger than before, but not in such a way as to negate the earlier readerly assumptions. In part, this is the result of Tolkien's long immersion in his imaginary world and the depth of his engagement, but it also has to do with his theology. I have already drawn attention to his belief that fantasy aims towards the liberation of things to be themselves. By being freed into new life, however, they also become *more* than themselves. Maritain expresses this surpassing in a footnote to his essay 'The Frontiers of Poetry':

> A similar antimony is implicit in all things which (like the mind and art) touch the transcendental order and are realised either in a pure

state in God or 'by participation' in created subjects. As they tend (with an ineffective tendency which is none the less real) to the fullness of their essence *considered in itself* (transcendentally) *and in its pure formal line*, so they tend to surpass themselves, to cross the boundaries of their essence *considered in a created subject* (with the specific determinants there appropriate to it) and in so doing to escape from their *conditions of existence*.[39]

So in Tolkien's Middle-earth the more a tree realizes itself as a tree, it becomes a Huorn, which is something more than a tree; or like the Mallorns it participates in some way in the gold and silver of the original trees of the Valar: Telperion and Laurelin. Elves, who are in harmony with the natural world, thereby exceed their nature as created beings in order to share in the divine creativity. Elvish magic has this same effect on the objects that they make: they become themselves, only more so. Lembas, the elven waybread, sustains the hungry much more concentratedly than ordinary food and has a eucharistic quality; elven rope has a silken beauty, pliancy and ability to return itself that others would call magical; the leaders of the elves, who originate in the Blessed Realm, 'live at once in both worlds, and against both the Seen and Unseen they have great power' (p. 216). Not only do elves participate in a world beyond the natural, but they convey something of the spirit of the original divine creation in their art. So the cloaks that they give the Fellowship are an effective camouflage, because not only do they imitate the natural forms among which their wearers seek to hide, but actually participate in the leafiness and woodiness of Lórien. As Maritain says, 'as God makes created participations of His being exist outside Himself, so the artist puts himself – not what he sees but what he is – into what he makes'.[40] For Tolkien's elves, however, what they see has become part of them, so that their art is more truly magical than even Maritain's high Catholic vision of art can conceive. They do indeed, as Maritain puts it, 'create, as it were, in the second degree, continuing God's creation'.[41] But the letting-go of the form to be itself – its making strange – both indicates the divine origin of their art and renders the object magical or enchanted.

In that sense Tolkien does use the elves' and Gandalf's magic to defamiliarize the world in a Chestertonian manner, making it strange in order to take it away from our appropriation and restore it as enchanted. But Tolkien does seem to have a stronger sense of the role of imagination in completing the world, both within the story in the art of the elves and the magic of Gandalf and outside the story in the role of the writer of fantasy. 'The Man in Spectacles' in Chesterton's story discussed in the Preface found himself painting his own house that was already in existence. But Niggle imagines a tree that does not exist in the material world but only in his mind. He then encounters the eternal tree in which he recognizes his vision when he comes to the afterlife. There is thus a more Platonic tinge to Tolkien's view of the imagination, in which imagination exceeds the real and helps to complete the world: to add to the 'effoliation of creation' as Tolkien puts it.[42] Verlyn Flieger has pointed out the Neo-Platonic elements of the mode of creation by the Ainur, and the importance of the Blessed Realm and the elves points to a reality that contains *both* the material world and the real *mundus imaginalis*.[43] What is important is that in the ending of *The Lord of the Rings*, which leaves Frodo already smelling the Blessed Realm while Sam comes safe to his fireside in the Shire, Tolkien presents each realm as equally real, and equally part of Chesterton's 'covenant of things'.

Notes

1. G. K. Chesterton, 'On the Disastrous Spread of Aestheticism in All Classes', in *Greybeards at Play: Literature and Art for Old Gentlemen* (London: Brimley Johnson, 1900), p. 96.

2. Jorge Louis Borges, 'On Oscar Wilde', in *Selected Non-Fictions*, ed. Eliot Weinberger, trans. Esther Allen, Jill Levine and Eliot Weinberger (New York: Viking, 1999), pp. 314–16.

3. Linda Dowling, *Language and Decadence in the Victorian Fin de Siècle* (Princeton: Princeton University Press, 1986).

4. Dowling, *Language and Decadence*, p. 173.

5. Max Beerbohm, 'Diminuendo', in *Victorian Literature 1830–1900*, ed. Dorothy Mermin and Herbert F. Tucker (Fort Worth: Harcourt Brace, 2002), pp. 1097–1100 (1098).

6. David Jones, *The Anathémata: Fragments of an Attempted Writing* (London: Faber, 1952), pp. 15–16.

7. Oscar Wilde, *The Picture of Dorian Gray*, ed. Robert Mighall (Harmondsworth: Penguin, 2000), p. 104.

8. Victor Shklovsky, 'The Resurrection of the Word (1914)', in *Russian Formalism: A Collection of Articles and Texts in Translation*, ed. Stephen Bann and John E. Boult (Edinburgh: Scottish Academic Press, 1973), pp. 41–7 (41).

9. Shklovsky, 'Resurrection of the Word', p. 46.

10. Shklovsky, 'Resurrection of the Word' p. 46.

11. Victor Shklovsky, 'Art as Technique', in *Russian Formalist Criticism: Four Essays*, trans. Lee T. Lemon and Marion J. Reis (Lincoln: University of Nebraska Press, 1965), pp. 3–24 (12).

12. G. K. Chesterton, *The Ball and the Cross*, ed. Martin Gardner (New York: Dover, 1995), p. 1.

13. Chesterton, *The Collected Poems*, p. 297.

14. G. K. Chesterton, 'The Wrong Shape,' in *The Innocence of Father Brown* (London: Penguin, 1950), pp. 129–50.

15. G. K. Chesterton, *Autobiography* (Thirsk: House of Stratus, 2001), p. 15.

16. Shklovsky, 'Art as Technique', p. 18.

17. Chesterton, *Autobiography*, p. 27.

18. Shklovsky, 'Art as Technique', p. 22.

19. Gertrude Stein, *Writings and Lectures 1911–1945*, ed. Patricia Meyerowitz, intro. Elizabeth Sprigge (London: Peter Owen, 1967), *Tender Buttons: Objects, Food, Rooms*, p. 184.

20. Maritain, 'The Frontiers of Poetry', in *Art and Scholasticism*, pp. 68–94 (74).

21. Maritain, *Art and Scholasticism*, pp. 74–5.

22. G. K. Chesterton, *The Man Who Was Thursday: A Nightmare*, intro. Kingsley Amis (Harmondsworth: Penguin, 1986), p. 184.

23. Maritain, *Art and Scholasticism*, p. 19.

24. Maritain, *Art and Scholasticism*, p. 19.

25. Tolkien, *Tree and Leaf*, p. 58.

26. Tolkien, *Tree and Leaf*, p. 58.

27. Tolkien, *Tree and Leaf*, p. 58.

28. Tolkien, *Tree and Leaf*, p. 57.

29. Tolkien, *Tree and Leaf*, p. 59.

30. Maritain, *Art and Scholasticism*, p. 25.

31. On Sam's relation to the British soldier of the Great War, see Carpenter, *Tolkien*, p. 81; and Garth, *Tolkien and the Great War*, p. 310.

32. J. R. R. Tolkien, *The Lord of the Rings* (3 vols; London: HarperCollins, 1997), p. 106. All further references are to this edition and are given in the text. J. R. R. Tolkien, *The Hobbit: Or There and Back Again* (London: HarperCollins, 2001).

33. Tzvetan Todorov, *The Fantastic: A Structural Approach to a Literary Genre*,

foreword Robert Scholes, trans. Richard Howard (Ithaca NY: Cornell University Press, 1975), p. 14.

34. G. K. Chesterton, *The Incredulity of Father Brown* (Harmondsworth: Penguin, 1974), pp. 70–1.

35. George MacDonald, *Phantastes: A Fairy Romance*, intro. C. S. Lewis (Grand Rapids MI: Eerdmans, 2000), pp. 55–8.

36. G. K. Chesterton, 'The Head of Caesar', in *The Wisdom of Father Brown* (Harmondsworth: Penguin, 1970), p. 98.

37. G. K. Chesterton, *Magic: A Fantastic Comedy* (London: Martin Secker, 1926).

38. *J. R. R. Tolkien Centenary Conference*, ed. Wayne G. Hammond (Milton Keynes: Tolkien Society, 1992), pp. 15–16.

39. Maritain, *Art and Scholasticism*, p. 173.

40. Maritain, *Art and Scholasticism*, p. 74.

41. Maritain, *Art and Scholasticism*, p. 49.

42. Tolkien, *Tree and Leaf*, p. 73: 'So great is the bounty with which he has been treated that he may now, perhaps, fairly dare to guess that in Fantasy he may actually assist in the effoliation and multiple enrichment of creation'.

43. Verlyn Flieger, *Interrupted Music: The Making of Tolkien's Mythology* (Kent OH and London: Kent State University Press, 2005), p. 121–37.

CHAPTER 2

THE GROTESQUE

> But think of the Cosmos – conceive
> The universe – system and sphere,
> I must say with my heart on my sleeve,
> The shape is decidedly queer.[1]

ESPECIALLY IN ADJECTIVAL FORM, 'grotesque' is one of Chesterton's favourite words, even being used in the title of the poem quoted above, 'A Ballade on the Grotesque'. In his predilection for this aesthetic term, Chesterton is both entirely himself (he has a modest reputation as a contributor to its definition) and equally entirely of his age. From the Romantic period onwards, the grotesque – the deliberate employment of monstrous, excessive and hybrid figures and style – emerged as the quintessentially modern artistic mode, embracing both the creative excess of the artist or writer and also the democratic nature of nineteenth-century political aspiration. It was viewed as a populist mode, because it mixed together high and low forms and lacked generic decorum. Victor Hugo gave effective voice to this double function in the influential preface to his 1827 drama *Cromwell*. Building upon Chateaubriand and Schlegel's classification of modern Christian poetry as Romantic, Hugo locates this Romantic freedom in its dramatic quality. Dante, Milton and Shakespeare are all primarily dramatic and modern according to Hugo, because they allow the heights of sublimity to coexist with the depths of the vulgar, monstrous and grotesque.[2] It is in the drama of this clash of modes that realism emerges, and the energy of modern democracy.

The British Pre-Raphaelite painters – especially Dante Gabriel Rossetti – put this aesthetic to artistic use by including twisted figures, monstrously long necks or full lips and awkward gestures in their work, thus energizing what might otherwise be mere historical pastiche with the sense of the modern. Indeed, contemporary criticism as grotesque of the face and attitude of the young Christ and his mother in Millais's *Christ in the House of his Parents* (1849) misunderstood what was a deliberate move to signal the historical distance between the Palestine of the New Testament and the nineteenth century.[3] In France, writers such as Charles Baudelaire were attracted to Edgar Allan Poe for his *Tales of the Grotesque and the Arabesque* which refreshed old ideas of beauty as residing in nature, order and harmony with a new aesthetic that valued artifice, disorder and disharmony; he himself could write a poem about a dead carcase, 'Une Charogne'.[4]

The British poets and artists of the 1890s were hugely influenced by this French tradition and its privileging of the grotesque. 'If I am not grotesque, I am nothing', Aubrey Beardsley is reported to have said, and his art is a strange mixture of arabesque and fluid decoration, combined with monstrously exaggerated and ugly forms.[5] Appropriately he illustrated Oscar Wilde's play *Salome* (1894 in English translation), which climaxes in the heroine's embrace of the severed head of Jokanaan (John the Baptist), which she proceeds to kiss as truly beautiful. Like the exhibition *Sensation* at the Royal Academy in London in 1997, which included child mannequins with sexual parts for noses and mouths, the decadent usage of the grotesque is aimed to shock, to jolt the viewer or reader out of his or her habitual way of understanding reality.

Although it might seem strange that Chesterton, who was so anxious to find a way out of the velvet folds of late-Victorian aestheticism, should embrace the very mode that was so central to their philosophy, he shared the aesthetes' desire to disturb perception. As we have seen in the previous chapter, Chesterton uses estranging literary techniques for this very purpose but for opposite ends; rather than separate the work of art in its own material identity, Chesterton makes the object strange to us so that it may be reconnected by participation in a divine world. Similarly, he employs the grotesque for this purpose, but in this case he has an already-existing theological understanding of the grotesque to draw upon.

Victor Hugo assumes a religious conception of human nature in his *Cromwell* preface, which is based on Pascal's description of humanity as part beast and part angel: 'One day Christianity said to man "You are double, you are composed of two beings, the one perishable, the other immortal, the one carnal, the other ethereal, the one chained by appetites, needs and passions, the other carried on the wings of enthusiasm and reverie, the one always finally bending towards the earth, its mother, the other ceaselessly launching itself towards the heavens, its father"' (my translation).[6]

Every person in this Christian psychomachia is thus the hero of a drama, and hence the grotesque hybrid nature of humanity lends itself to a human comedy and tragedy that are democratic, common to all. In the early years of the twentieth century, Chesterton wrote monographs on two great exemplars of the democratic grotesque, Charles Dickens and Robert Browning.[7] Dickens's art is grotesque in its exaggeratedly monstrous characters (in which he imitates Hugo's own novels, such as *Notre Dame de Paris* with its hunchback Quasimodo), and in the way in which his narration galvanizes the inanimate world of objects, as if they had subjectivity and movement. Browning is an even closer adherent to Hugo in his poetic monologues, which display a character lurching between his diabolic and ethereal natures and trying to free himself from the constraints of 'appetites, needs and passions'. Browning's verse was Pre-Raphaelite in its deliberate awkwardnesses, being knotted and convoluted. He famously began his 'Soliloquy of the Spanish Cloister' with the word 'GR-R-R- . . .', which not only illustrates his ruggedness but the energy of his grotesque style.[8] And it was this aspect of the Hugoesque democratic grotesque that Chesterton emphasized in Browning: 'The element of the grotesque in art, like the element of the grotesque in nature, means, in the main, energy, the energy which takes its own forms and goes its own way. Browning's verse, in so far as it is grotesque, is not complex or artificial; it is natural and in the legitimate tradition of nature. The verse sprawls like the trees, dances like the dust; it is ragged like the thundercloud, it is top-heavy like the toadstool'.[9]

Chesterton perceives in Browning 'a sense of the uproarious force in things', so that not only are human characters revealed in their struggles but also the world of fungus and jellyfish. Similarly, as the subject of Browning's monologue uses his first-person narrative to assert himself as a human being with freedom and intentionality, so the bizarre presentation of Browning's grotesque style serves to render even the inanimate or abstract as equally full of potentiality: 'To present in a grotesque manner does certainly tend to touch the nerve of surprise, and thus to draw attention to the intrinsically miraculous character of the object itself'.[10] The way this works is that the monstrous oddity of the jellyfish or the eccentric character of a man provoke a sense of their incompleteness: there is something beyond to which they aspire.

In his *Criticisms and Appreciations of Charles Dickens*, Chesterton goes further by stating that 'in beauty, perhaps, there is something allied to sadness, certainly there is something akin to joy in the grotesque'.[11] The joy comes from the very lack of harmony and completion or boundedness, which allows for the possibility of more life, growth and development, whereas the perfection of beauty implies some sort of limit. As Hugh Kenner puts it, 'a grotesque is an energy which aborts, as if to express its dissatisfaction with available boundaries, as a dwarf may be nature's critique of a tailor's dummy'.[12] Hugo, notably, yoked the sublime and not the beautiful to the grotesque, since the sublime is caused by the baulking and then the overcoming of a blockage to thought: it takes the mind beyond itself. Chesterton may be remembering Ruskin's essay on the nature of Gothic in *The Stones of Venice* (1851–53), where he privileges the imperfection of Gothic building over later technical perfection as a source of its liveliness, 'here starting up into a monster, there germinating into a blossom, anon knitting itself to a branch ... or writhed into every form of nervous entanglement; but, even when most grateful, never for a moment languid, always quickset'.[13]

Chesterton explores the grotesque in relation to Gothic in his allegorical story 'On Gargoyles' (1910), which provides a potted history of art. It begins by sketching a society that worships the sun by using materials that imitate its light and are wholly clear and pure: lilies, crystal and water. After invasion and destruction of this shrine they build a second, which now encompasses all forms of life, since the sun shines on them all: 'The columns of the temple were carved like necks of giraffes; the dome was like an ugly tortoise, and the highest pinnacle was a monkey standing on his head with his tail pointing at the sun. And yet the whole was beautiful, because it was lifted up in one living and religious gesture as a man lifts his hands in prayer'.[14]

Chesterton describes this work in Hugoesque terms as Gothic, Romantic and Christian, 'for man is the ape upside down'. The rich people, however, object to this democratic art and in the riotous confusion that ensues, in which the temple is ruined, a stone hits the priest and he loses his memory. He sees the piles of oddities, forgets what they are there for and piles them in a heap while the rich applaud: 'This is real art! This is Realism! This is things as they really are!' The following paragraph provokes Chesterton's famous epigram: 'Realism is simply Romanticism that has lost its reason'.[15] Chesterton views the grotesque as a true form of realism, which is quite unlike this meaningless naturalism 'that has lost its reason'. It is faithful to the dual nature of humanity as bestial and divine, and to the Christian belief in the goodness of creation. He views Christianity, indeed, as a guardian of all monstrosities – 'a beauty created by controlling a million monsters of ugliness' in the same way as the Christian monks of Iceland and Britain preserved the pagan stories of dragons and dwarves in the *Edda* and poems like *Beowulf*.[16] In that sense, the grotesque is a mode of idealism as well as realism, since it offers a vision as well as describing what already is.

Although the tone and tenor of Tolkien's writing style is less colourful and bizarre than that of Chesterton who, as a final flourish to 'On Gargoyles', described his own essays as 'ungainly monsters', he is equally attracted to the monstrous and grotesque. From childhood he coveted dragons, and in adulthood wrote about them both in fantasy and *Beowulf* criticism, drew them and gave an illustrated lecture for children on the subject at the University Museum in Oxford.[17] Chesterton's vision of Christianity as controlling a million

THE GROTESQUE

monsters finds a parallel in Tolkien's attitude to the 'wilderness of dragons' of the Northern pagan past, which resembles that of the Christian author of *Beowulf* himself who looked 'back on the heroism and the sorrow' and felt in them 'something permanent and something symbolical'.[18] The dragons represent the dark forces that no one can fully withstand but they are not allegories, for then they would be mere puppet bodies for ideas and not really grotesque. Tolkien states that the writer of the poem was poised between a dark antiquity in which monsters like Grendel were an actual threat, and a Christian universe in which the dragon becomes an avatar for the forces over evil whom Christ has defeated: 'Done is a battell on the dragon blak;/Our campion Chryst confoundit hes his force', in the words of the Scottish poet William Dunbar in the late fifteenth century.[19] The distance between the writer of *Beowulf* and the events of the poem renders them both darker and more poetical, and similarly the distance between Tolkien the writer and the monsters he described rendered them more fascinating and powerful, while his own Christian background allowed them to be enjoyed as aesthetic objects. He wrote in 'On Fairy-Stories': 'I desired dragons with a profound desire. Of course, I in my timid body did not wish to have them in the neighbourhood ... But the world that contained even the imagination of Fáfnir [the dragon killed by Sigurd in the Volsung Saga] was richer and more beautiful, at whatever cost or peril'.[20] So the dragon Tolkien drew to illustrate the one who kills Beowulf was delicately drawn in pencil and watercolour wash, although his representation of the wily dragon Glórund (later Glaurung) who instigates one of the most tragic tales of *The Silmarillion*, that of Túrin and Níniel, is more obviously grotesque, with an ugly horned green head with yellow eyes on a huge yellow body, and taloned limbs that plant their claws right outside the limit of the picture to invade the text.[21]

Tolkien's illustrations of dragons, as well as the delight he takes in describing the winged Chrysophylax in *Farmer Giles of Ham* and even the more dangerous Smaug in *The Hobbit*, are examples of what Ruskin defines as the playful grotesque: 'art arising from healthful but irrational play of the imagination in times of rest', in which the mind jests 'sometimes with under-current of sternest pathos' with death and sin, and he gives as examples Holbein's *Dance of Death* and Dürer's *Knight and Death*.[22] It was this playful aspect of the grotesque that was developed in German criticism in the Romantic period, when the graceful undulations of arabesque decoration were not always seen as separate from the hybrid forms and often monstrous permutations of the grotesque.[23] From the time of Vasari's comments on Leonardo's grotesque heads, the use of the grotesque had been taken as evidence of the freedom of the artist to invent, and a measure of his creativity. Raphael's decorations of the Vatican loggia seemed to present decoration, both arabesque and grotesque, as an end in itself. Tolkien's little watercolour dragon, despite the words from *Beowulf* that accompany him – 'Now was the heart of the coiling beast stirred to come out to fight' – in modern English, is hardly ready for battle, with his tail well and truly knotted. He more resembles a manuscript decoration from the Gothic period, and in that sense is more arabesque (aimlessly decorative) than monstrous. When brought out for the museum lecture, Tolkien described him as a 'newly hatched dragonet' rather than Beowulf's destroyer.[24] In the context of Tolkien's extensive dragon lore, however, and the existence of the terrifying Glaurung, not to mention the hordes of firedrakes under Morgoth's command, the dragonet and tamed Chrysophylax are rather the playful grotesque of a Christian art that really can create beauty out of ugliness, and act as guardian to monsters, just as Farmer Giles does by taming Chrysophylax at his 'Worminghall' in Tolkien's children's story *Farmer Giles of Ham* (1949).

Like the German Romantic writers Jean Paul and the Schlegel brothers, Tolkien too believes in creative freedom: the 'world-dominion by creative act' of humanity, the status of man as 'sub-creator' and the right to fill the crannies of the world with goblins 'and sow the seed of dragons'.[25] This freedom is most obviously present in the grotesque, which recombines the forms of nature and art to make something new and surprising. There has to be some awkwardness in the combination to render it grotesque, so that the surprise becomes all the more evident, and is more prominent than the sense of a harmonious whole. In making something new, all fantasy writing is a mode of the grotesque, as Mary Shelley was aware when she made her Frankenstein create his monster out of body parts of a variety of people – an avatar of the Romantic artist as creator: fantasy foregrounds the sense of novelty and createdness. And Tolkien's most inventive fictional races and monsters have this grotesque quality, of which the ents are the clearest example. They could have been rendered beautiful by stressing the copper beechiness of their hair colour, or the bending grace of their walk. Tolkien, however, makes them a far more awkward hybrid form, and far more difficult to understand. First the ent is introduced by body-parts, as 'a large knob-knuckled hand' is laid on Merry and Pippin's shoulders and two great arms lift them up, after which a full picture is given:

> They found that they were looking at a most extraordinary face. It belonged to a large Man-like, almost Troll-like, figure, at least fourteen foot high, very sturdy, with a tall head, and hardly any neck. Whether it was clad in stuff like green and grey bark, or whether that was its hide, was difficult to say. At any rate the arms, at a short distance from the trunk, were not wrinkled, but covered with a brown smooth skin. The large feet had seven toes each. The lower part of the long face was covered with a sweeping grey beard, bushy, almost twiggy at the roots, thin and mossy at the ends. But at the moment the hobbits noted little but the eyes. These deep eyes were now surveying them, slow and solemn, but very penetrating. They were brown, shot with a green light. Often afterwards Pippin tried to describe his first impression of them. (p. 452)

The initial impression is of a person, especially since it is the voice that the hobbits hear first before the touch of the unknown hand. Geoffrey Harpham has pointed out that the grotesque orchestrates 'phenomena that both require and defeat definition: they are neither so regular that they settle easily into our categories, nor so unprecedented that we do not recognise them at all; they stand at the margin of consciousness between the known and the unknown, calling into question the adequacy of our ways of organizing the world'.[26]

Here Treebeard evokes both human and arboreal characteristics, but makes the classification of himself as one or the other really problematic. Words like 'arms' and 'trunk' are used of both trees and humans, the first primarily for people but applied metaphorically to trees, the second literally for trees and metaphorically applied to humans. As a human, Treebeard has certain monstrous features such as seven toes, enormous height and very little neck. As a tree he is equally grotesque in having a voice, no roots and ease of movement. The ambiguity about whether 'it' has hide or clothes makes it impossible to 'see' him, as was made evident in Peter Jackson's filmic representation of him as merely a walking tree. Jackson had to choose one option or the other for his realist aesthetic, so that Treebeard seemed somewhat comic and ridiculous, cosily picturesque in the manner of a Walt Disney animated character. By contrast, what renders Treebeard so impressive in the novel is his eyes, which are his most grotesque feature viewed as arboreal – since they imply agency and personality – and as human they have a whole cornucopia of natural, inanimate imagery applied to them: wells, the sun, ripples on a lake, something growing in the ground.

As in the 'making strange' of my previous chapter, so here the effect of the grotesque is first to destabilize perception; second to render unstable the human belief in itself as the centre of the universe; third to make the reader experience the wonder and ecstasy of pure otherness. This third element is again an otherness that is not an estrangement but a participation, for it has been structured through complex rearticulations of likeness and difference, so that the reader experiences himself or herself anew in the eyes of Treebeard, just as the hobbits do. And there is a fourth quality to the readerly experience, which is particularly the effect of the grotesque presentation of the ent: namely, an appreciation of the created nature of Treebeard. For the same difficulty in classifying the grotesque leads also to an understanding of the grotesque as an aesthetic mode: it is as if the scaffolding of artistic creation has been laid open to the reader for his or her admiration. We can believe in Treebeard at the same time as we are aware of him as a fictional creation. And it is in the ability to create – fiction is linked to the Latin verb *facere*, to make – that the artist comes closest to God. For us to recognize the world as God's creation, we have to see it as a work of art; for us to recognize the creative power of the artist, we similarly have both to

THE GROTESQUE

experience his or her fiction as a world but also be aware of its constructed nature.

Tolkien explores this created aspect of the grotesque in his myth of the origin of the dwarf race in *The Silmarillion*. It is Aulë, the smith of the Ainur, who out of pure desire to give life creates the dwarves. He can give them a certain measure of life and action, but he is unable to give them full freedom. Despite his good intentions they remain the creatures of his hand and mind, as Ilúvatar points out. Ilúvatar takes pity on these creatures and on Aulë's disobedience, and grants the seven dwarf lords the secret fire of existence, although they must sleep until after the awakening of his firstborn.[27] The dwarves, who are short, stone-hard and fierce, bear the marks of this somewhat botched creation, reflected also in their greed for gold and antipathy to trees. *The Lord of the Rings*, however, provides a means for the dwarf race to transcend its origins in the person of Gimli, who asks audaciously but non-materialistically for a golden hair of Galadriel rather than for anything more precious in worldly terms. Moreover, in Khazad-dûm, dwarf art and architecture is as fine as anything elvish, with a sublimity of size and ambition that is truly grotesque in the sense used by Ruskin to describe medieval art. The friendship that is forged between Gimli and Legolas the elf represents in artistic terms the union of the grotesque with the arabesque. This latter term was sometimes used in German aesthetic theory along with the grotesque, but in Schlegel it was differentiated as the convoluted and flowing line of decoration.[28] It too like the grotesque had an excessive element because it was often purely decorative, and without any obvious function beyond delight in line itself. The elves similarly have a tendency to preservation for its own sake and an immortal nature, which one might see as representing the eternal line of the arabesque. Their beauty, however, has the pathos of exile, and they are the most religious creatures in Tolkien's Middle-earth, with the high elves praying often to Elbereth, the star-kindling member of the Ainur. Arabesque elf and grotesque dwarf then transcend their origins in their friendship and in the growth towards understanding of each other's aesthetic. Gimli learns to love the wildness of Fangorn Forest, in which the elves have awakened the trees, while Legolas pledges to travel with his friend to view the underground glories of dwarf building and mining. For the viewing of the scaffolding of divine creation that I have attributed to the grotesque is evident also at the level of the creatures' own creative endeavours: Middle-earth is a worked-on series of habitats that bear the marks of elven, human, entish and dwarf manufacture.

Chesterton's God, in the introduction he wrote to the biblical book of Job, is primarily an artist who shows his work, and especially an exponent of the grotesque: 'To startle man, God becomes for an instant a blasphemer; one might almost say God becomes for an instant an atheist. He unrolls before Job a long panorama of created things, the horse, the eagle, the raven, the wild ass, the peacock, the ostrich, the crocodile. He so describes each of them that it sounds like a monster walking in the sun ... The maker of all things is astonished at the things he has made'.[29]

In the Browning monograph Chesterton uses the Behemoth in Job as another example of divine grotesque humour and wonder, as God asks Job if he could play with it as a kind of household pet.[30]

The God of the book of Job is a figure who uses the monsters and creatures of the wild to stress his distance from Job, and the futility of the latter's attempt to understand him. The stress on monstrosity is an educational tool. Indeed, Montaigne, in a celebrated passage about a monstrously deformed child, believes that the divine creation is, in its essence, not grotesque at all: 'What we call monsters are not so to God, who sees in the immensity of his work the infinity of forms that he has comprised in it; and it is for us to believe that this figure that astonishes us is related and linked to some other figure of the same kind unknown to man. From his infinite wisdom there proceeds nothing but that [which] is good and ordinary and regular; but we do not see its arrangement and relationship'.[31]

Tolkien too, in the Treebeard chapter, moves on to add relationship and arrangement by providing a whole spectrum of treelike/human existence, ranging from trees that move their roots to those awoken to speech by the elves to Huorns, who are ents become treeish, and ents who, like the prophet Amos, are 'shepherds of the trees' and contrast in their mastery of stone with the stony trolls. (They have power over stone because of the vigour of their rootish legs, which like those of trees can burrow through all sorts of terrain. Trolls, by contrast, can only turn things and people into stone.) By the time the reader has accustomed him or herself to this range of being, enthood has been rendered somewhat less grotesque and more 'natural'. Like Chesterton's God, Tolkien has made the reader astonished in order to make him or her wonder, but then provided the links that allow a less partial vision.

There are, however, a great many 'grotesques' in Tolkien's writing that are not assimilated in the way that the ents are, and who remain monsters in the medieval sense of a wonder, from the Latin 'monstrare', meaning 'to show' or point out. Like the God of Job's monstrosities they are either pedagogical tools which stress the distance between human perception and the divine, or, like illuminated capitals in medieval manuscripts, they exhort the reader to pay attention: look, understand and learn – by ruminating, just as the monster gnaws at the text.[32] As illustrated in medieval bestiaries or sculpted on cathedrals they express the power and infinite mystery of the divine creation. For the monsters of Tolkien's art are facts of Middle-earth life that the reader does not fully comprehend; and in so acting, they dramatize the unknowability of its universe. They accord with Ruskin's third class of grotesque effects in *Modern Painters*, which derive 'from the confusion of the imagination by the presence of truths which it cannot wholly grasp'.[33] It is the gaps between the symbols shown that provide their grotesque character. The nobleness that Ruskin accords this third mode is in accord with the theology of Thomas Aquinas who follows Dionysus the Pseudo-Areopagite in arguing that it is more appropriate for God to be presented by metaphors of a lower and bodily order than higher ones, 'for what He is not is clearer to us than what He is', and so 'similitudes drawn from things farthest away from God form within us a truer estimate that God is above whatsoever we may say or think of Him'.[34] Hence the monstrosity of the grotesque witnesses to the impossibility in comprehending the divine, and its monstrous quality precludes any misunderstanding or false literalism.

This aspect of the grotesque, as a mode of limited perception, is explored at length by Chesterton in *The Man Who Was Thursday* (1908). As the hero Gabriel Syme arrives at the breakfast party of anarchist conspirators on the balcony in Leicester Square, each of the men assembled is described in grotesque terms, as a contradiction. Monday is motionless as a waxwork, yet has a 'spasm of smile', Tuesday has the eyes of a Skye terrier coming out from the head of a revolutionary, Wednesday has square-cut clothes that have qualities of softness and infinitude that contradict their cut, Friday is an articulated skeleton, and Saturday the coarse matter-of-factness of a medical practitioner offset by sinister dark glasses.[35] Each of these men is un-grotesqued and normalized by revealing their grotesquerie as a form of disguise: they are all, in fact, detectives, but the figure of their leader, Sunday, remains wholly monstrous. He, it is revealed, is truly a contradiction, because he is both the detective in the dark room at Scotland Yard who sent them out on their adventure, and also the chief of the anarchists whom they sought to defeat. And as soon as he has admitted this fact, he jumps off the balcony like an india-rubber ball and races off by balloon and elephant, leaving behind a series of riddles that have no meaning at all: 'Fly at once. The truth about your trouser-stretchers is known' and 'The word, I fancy, should be "pink" '.[36]

Each of the group sees Sunday differently and in grotesque terms: to Bull he is 'a bouncing baby', to the Secretary he was 'loathsome and living jelly', to Ratcliffe he is 'an absent-minded tiger', to Gogol he is the sun, and to the Professor an eye and a nose that do not make a face.[37] Syme, however, finds a common theme running through these disparate impressions:

> 'Have you noticed an odd thing,' he said, 'about all your descriptions? Each man of you finds Sunday quite different, yet each man of you can only find one thing to compare him to – the universe itself. Bull finds him like the earth in Spring, Gogol like the sun at noonday. The Secretary is minded of the shapeless protoplasm, and the Inspector of the carelessness of virgin forests. The Professor says he is like a changing landscape. This is queer, but it is queerer still that I also have had my odd notion about the president, and I also find that I think of Sunday as I think of the whole world.' [38]

Syme goes on to argue that they see Sunday as a monster because they are only seeing the back of the world, and it looks brutal because they cannot see the front. Chesterton was fascinated by the idea of seeing things from behind. His primal memory of the toy theatre embraced the concept of seeing 'the very back-scene of the theatre of things', and he marvelled at the painter Watts's portrayal of backs of the human body in paintings such as *Love and Death* as examples of the mysterious unknowableness of the material, since we can never quite see our own back directly.[39] *The Napoleon of Notting Hill* (1904) opens with a clerk, Auberon Quin, following the backs of two of his co-workers along the street, but seeing the coat-tails of one of them as 'two black dragons . . . looking at him with evil eyes'.[40] This sense of the monstrosity of doubleness at the back of things is only resolved at the very end of the novel when Quin and the local revolutionary discuss the fictional basis of the devolutionary government created by the former and realize their mutual dependence.

In *The Man Who Was Thursday* the characters never do get round to the front of Sunday, as it were, since that is impossible. The only clue left to them as Sunday grows to fill the sky and all goes black is a 'distant voice' saying, 'Can ye drink of the cup that I drink of?'[41] The words are those of Christ in Matthew 20.22 to James and John, referring to his approaching suffering. In this way the text leaves a Job-like distance between the problem of the nature of reality and of God, while hinting at Christ as an answer to the problem of suffering, which had been openly discussed by the detectives and by 'The Accuser', Lucian Gregory, a figure in imitation of the Satanic accuser of Job in the Old Testament. Chesterton suggests that our monstrous conception of existence as a struggle to the death between competing groups is a partial and misleading one. He presents his figure of Sunday, not as God exactly, but as the mystery of existence. His monstrosity is, to some extent, our own construction, just as the quasi-medieval revillaging of London is Quin's fictional creation in *The Napoleon of Notting Hill*. To admit, however, that nature is cruel and meaningless is already to presuppose that there is a category of meaning by which it might be so judged: there has to be something that renders monstrosity monstrous, as it were. Hence for Chesterton the grotesque is always a hopeful mode and one that educates our perceptions. And the outcome of *The Man Who Was*

Thursday is to reveal, in classic orthodox fashion, that evil can only be a lack, and never a Manichean pitting of equal forces against each other.

Ruskin needed this understanding of the grotesque as a limited view of the divine as a prophylactic against false conceptions of God (especially in his younger evangelical days) in order to prevent himself from falling into image worship or amoral aestheticism. It can be seen in his practice of drawing only part of a building or cutting up illuminated manuscripts in order to distribute them to the various educational establishments of which he was patron. Art in this mode does not subsume divine power to itself but dramatizes its own limited nature. Yet paradoxically this allows for a more powerful art, as is illustrated in Ruskin's paired drawings of griffins reproduced in *Modern Painters*. A Lombardy Gothic griffin from Verona's cathedral is contrasted to a classical example from a Roman temple frieze. Although the Roman example is delicately executed, it is ornamental and inert, in contrast to the Lombardy griffin which more truly reproduces the leonine and aquiline nature of his hybrid identity in having the heaviness of a lion to strike, the eagle's grip in the back claw and bird-like wrinkled skin for further binding power. The former is a perfectly finished artistic invention and fails; the latter an imperfect, naturalistic piece of sculpture, and succeeds. After several pages of devastating analysis, Ruskin then moves to illustrate how the Lombardy griffin is actually a profound emblem of the divine power, evoking Ezekiel's vision of the creatures in the fiery chariot, and restraining evil with negligent ease in his grip on a winged dragon: 'The dragon tries to bite him, but can only bring his head round far enough to get hold of his own wing, which he bites in agony instead; flapping the griffin's dewlap with it, and wriggling his tail up against the griffin's throat; the griffin being, as to these minor proceedings, entirely indifferent, sure that the dragon's body cannot drag itself one hair's breadth off those ghastly claws, and that its head can do no harm but to itself.'[42]

I quote this passage at length because it seems so apposite to Tolkien's use of the grotesque. For Ruskin goes on to compare the griffin's hold on the dragon to that of the 'faithful and true imagination', which allows the head of the serpent free for a while

THE GROTESQUE

'that it may inflict in its fury profounder destruction upon itself'. In the same way many of the grotesque figures of Tolkien's fiction who are not so much examples of the playful grotesque but evil and truly monstrous are spared by the forces of good, so that they may go on to cause their own downfall. Both in their original fearful monstrosity and power, as well as in the way that power draws upon itself its own destruction, they witness to the Good. This is not only famously true of Gollum, who is spared on separate occasions by Bilbo, Gandalf, Frodo, Faramir and even by Sam, but also the case with Gríma Wormtongue, a human dragon in his guile and malice as well as his desire for Théoden's hoard, who is given every opportunity to redeem himself by joining his master in battle but chooses instead to return to Saruman. This last, similarly, is spared by Gandalf after the fall of Isengard, and later also mistakenly allowed to go free by the ents and offered a last chance at redemption by Gandalf and Galadriel. Even after his destruction of the Shire, Frodo offers mercy to both Saruman and Wormtongue, which they refuse, and the latter slits Saruman's throat only to be finished off before Frodo can speak by hobbit arrows. This mercy, in both Ruskin and Tolkien, is partly a reverential attitude to being and existence itself as a good thing. It is good to move and have one's being, but not to destroy others. The morally upright characters in Tolkien's novel are always unwilling to take life or assert power over it.

It is because Tolkien has an Augustinian attitude to evil as a privation – and not a positive force in itself – and a Thomist understanding of evil is a deficiency in being, which he shares with Chesterton, that he presents his evil human characters as physically warped and grotesque in the manner of medieval devils, who were represented in ugly and hybrid forms with bestial characteristics. Since human embodiment is a positive thing in itself, evil must be a warping of that nature. In the case of originally good people or wizards who have gone wrong, the duality of heavenly and bestial elements is present relatively chastely, so that Gríma becomes a serpent, 'wormtongue' with a 'wizened figure' at odds with his 'pale wise face' and 'heavy-lidded eyes', reminiscent of Dante's monster of fraud Geryon in *Inferno* 17, who had similarly the face of a just man and the body of a serpent, and a sting in his tail. As Gandalf breaks Wormtongue's spell over Théoden, Gríma becomes ever more monstrous; he hisses, sprawls and is thrust down on his belly like the judgement of the serpent in the Genesis myth of the Fall. Saruman is not initially presented in grotesque terms until after his defeat, when he literally becomes a voice, separate from his actual appearance, just as he had indeed become the vocal instrument for his master, Sauron. By the end of the novel he too has a bestial name, 'Sharkey', that is linked to 'old man' in Orkish but to 'shark' in English, as well as to a colloquial term for a fraudster. In exactly the same fashion as Ruskin's self-biting dragon, Saruman is killed by a part of himself, his 'tongue', Gríma, through whom his voice was conveyed in limp parody of Sauron's 'Mouth', the Lieutenant of the Tower of Barad-dûr (p. 872), who appears to parley with Aragorn and who has the face and slavering mouth of a wild beast. The grotesque presentation is a way of marking a fall from humanity, but achieves its evil aspects only by a bestiality that would be good in a wild beast or snake but is inappropriate in a man.

Gollum is the most obvious example of a person rendered grotesque by his loss of virtue and fall into unbeing, although his earlier existence as a water hobbit is the stuff of legend. Only his old name, Sméagol, sometimes recurs in his memory meaning burrower, and Bilbo encounters him deep underground in the Misty Mountains, where he now has the appearance of 'a small slimy creature' with great yellow eyes like telescopes (p. 67). His new name, Gollum, refers to the gobbling noises he makes in his throat, and he arouses disgust in Bilbo, and later in Sam and Frodo. The disgust comes from his departure from all the categories that make hobbithood: dislike of water, enjoyment of sociability and family closeness (for Gollum killed his relation and friend Déagol) and liking for cooked food (since Gollum eats raw fish and flesh). He is no longer physically recognizable as a hobbit, save for one moment near Cirith Ungol when he might have seemed to a watcher like an old weary hobbit (p. 699), but rather appears like a frog, grasshopper, insect or creeping thing. His hand is soft and clammy where it should be hard, and his eyes yellow or bright green. He offers all the difficulties of categorization that Harpham discerns in the true grotesque, all

THE GROTESQUE

the more complexly because his insect-like body speaks like a young child, using the third person to address himself – 'No food, no rest, nothing for Sméagol' (p. 700) – or addresses the absent 'Precious' as if it were his imaginary friend.

There will be more to say about Gollum in the next chapter but, for the moment, it is important to note his monstrous hybridity and the fact that he will, like Ruskin's dragon, defeat his own ends by falling into the fires of Mount Doom in his attempt to take the Ring from Frodo by biting through his finger. The fact that it is Frodo's finger, not actually Gollum's, that is detached only serves to make clearer how closely the two have become entwined, in a similar way to Isildur and Sauron, when the former sliced the latter's finger off and took the Ring which became his 'bane' and led to his own death by drowning.

The most grotesque figure of the whole *Lord of the Rings* is, however, the huge spider, Shelob, a descendant of Ungoliant who, as Melkor wounded the two Trees of Valinor, swallowed the light they held. She 'set her black beak to their wounds, till they were drained; and the poison of Death that was in her went into their tissues and withered them, root, branch, and leaf; and they died'.[43] Ungoliant is a somewhat mythical figure, in the sense that she is like a creature who makes or destroys the whole world, as in a number of traditional creation myths, and Melkor accuses her of this: 'Dost thou desire the world for thy belly?'[44] Shelob resembles her in combining physicality of the most disgusting nature with mental or metaphysical ambitions. She smells of excrement, emits bubbling sounds, gloats with her 'monstrous and abominable eyes' (p. 704), which seem to leap of their own accord, and she drinks human and elvish blood. To Sam she is the embodiment of horror:

> A little way ahead and to his left he saw suddenly, issuing from a black hole of shadow under the cliff, the most loathly shape that he had ever beheld, horrible beyond the horror of an evil dream. Most like a spider she was, but huger than the great hunting beasts, and more terrible than they because of the evil purpose in her remorseless eyes. Those same eyes that he had thought daunted and defeated, there they were lit with a fell light again, clustering in her out-thrust head. Great horns she had, and behind her short stalk-like neck was

> her huge swollen body, a vast bloated bag, swaying and sagging between her legs; its great bulk was black, blotched with livid marks, but the belly underneath was pale and luminous and gave forth a stench. Her legs were bent, with great knobbed joints high above her back, and hairs that stuck out like steel spines, and at each leg's end there was a claw. (p. 709)

Not only is Shelob classically monstrous but she represents the mixture and juxtaposition of opposed categories of the truly grotesque: soft and hard, small and huge, natural and man-made. Her size alone goes against our experience of spiders as smaller than ourselves; her horns and claw suggest quite different animals, and the whole description is both vivid and yet oddly difficult to 'see', since the body parts remain as parts rather than uniting in a single whole and her intentionality and obvious personhood are at odds with our understanding of spiderliness.

Shelob is threatening in another manner peculiar to the grotesque, namely through her assault on the integrity of the victim's body. Her own is porous, with webs woven out of it to entrap the hobbits, and poison ejected to stun and quieten her prey. She bleeds green ooze from her wounded eye after Sam's sword thrust; her threat is that of the disgusting, which seems to pollute and render unstable the bodily identity of the self. This is the model of the grotesque that Mikhail Bakhtin has written about in positive terms, as he sees it at work in the monstrous bodies of Rabelais's Pantagruel. For Bakhtin, the open-ended body offers a reconnection with the material cosmos and with life as becoming, a cycle of death and life.[45] He links it to medieval carnival, when the communal life of the people was expressed in opposition to the rules and dualisms of secular and sacred authority. Yet Tolkien's grotesque is the reverse of Bakhtin's porosity here. Like Chesterton, who wrote in his autobiography of his love of edges, 'and the boundary-line that brings one thing sharply against another',[46] Tolkien obviously liked clear and definite forms, as can be seen in his drawing style, with its inked outlines and love of pattern repeat. Again like Chesterton, Tolkien's grotesque monsters are viewed in relation to this privileging of form itself as a positive thing. For the point about the grotesque is that it

THE GROTESQUE

is clearly *seen* yet mysterious in its ontology. (Even faeces, which are so central an element in Rabelais's grotesque art have form; the disgust comes from their being placed in the wrong setting, or their being too close to something that culture wishes to keep separate and 'clean'.) The privileging of form in Tolkien is shown in his pencil drawing of a monstrous three-headed man, which shows the individual heads quite distinctly and clearly.[47] His most negative drawing, *Wickedness*, shows a pillared doorway that is utterly grotesque in having twisted columns with claws for feet and rapacious beaks for capitals, with a circumference of eyes and a five-fingered hand emerging but which is quite clear in outline.[48]

So the disgusting, engulfing Shelob has no positive valency in Tolkien's imaginative universe. Here we obviously have a grotesque that is quite other than the Ruskinian noble grotesque that reveals divine power, or Browning's ugliness of potentiality and the energy of creation. Like Bram Stoker's female serpent in *The Lair of the White Worm* (1911), the disgustingness and putridity of Shelob represent an ancient malice that seeks to undo form and development, like a maternal womb in reverse, with her webs a negative form of umbilical cord that seeks to withdraw the child back into nonbeing. It is interesting that Sam defeats her by means of a sword named 'Sting' by Bilbo, after it had so performed on a troop of malignant spiders in Mirkwood. To the spiders Bilbo appeared a creature like them but with a sideways sting, and Sam too is reduced to the status of an insect by Shelob's giant web and enormous size.

Shelob, however, raises a problem for the model of the grotesque that I have outlined so far. Not only can she in no way reveal the qualities of the divine, but her very life is murder. She seems to question the Thomist basis of Tolkien's metaphysics that I have been asserting, since how can a being, for whom existence itself is a good, be utterly evil? This is a problem that has been noted by Tom Shippey and by early readers of *The Lord of the Rings* in relation to the Orcs. If Eru created only good, how can there be orcs who seem to have no possibility of redemption?[49] Tolkien was obviously worried by this criticism, since he wrote an (unposted) but lengthy draft of a possible response. He begins by stressing the difference in his sub-created universe in relation to creation. Eru, his God, gave subcreative powers to his own Valar, guaranteeing 'that what they devised and made should be given the reality of Creation' even if they fell and produced evil beings as a mockery of 'the Children of God'.[50] Orcs are corrupted and remodelled pre-existing real beings, and part of the world, which is good. 'That God would "tolerate" that, seems no worse theology than the toleration of the calculated dehumanizing of Men by tyrants that goes on today. There might be other "makings" all the same which were more like puppets filled (if only at a distance) with their maker's mind and will, or ant-like operating under direction of a queen-centre'.[51]

Tolkien seems here to be wrestling with a world made before he had worked out all the ontological implications of his choices, but his intentions are clear: he aims to hold in orthodox Christian fashion, following Augustine and Aquinas, to a belief in the Creation as wholly good, and to existence itself as a good, which is not lost, even if one becomes Satan. As Aquinas says, 'Indeed, evil cannot exist by itself, since it has no essence ... Therefore, evil must be in some subject. Now every subject, because it is some sort of substance, is good of some kind ... So, every evil is in a good thing'.[52] Hence, despite their allegiance to Sauron, the orcs of the Tower of Cirith Ungol have a zany, quite comic discourse, showing the energy of being rather in the way in which Dante in *Inferno* 21 and 22 has his pantomime demons play tricks on the barrators and be deceived by them into falling into the pitch themselves, and makes them talk in a jokey exchange of insults. In both cases being has a kind of energy, even when it is put to unpleasant uses such as the farting of Dante's devil or the mutual destruction of Shagrat and Gorbag, which ends with the former orc licking the knife with which he has just polished off his colleague. Dante gives his devils deliberately bestial names, which Dorothy Sayers anglicizes as Libbicock, Dragonel, Guttlehog and Grabbersnitch, using a similar mix of animal and phallic imagery in grotesque hybrids.[53] Shagrat and Gorbag are much more grotesquely presented than the orcs who capture Merry and Pippin at Amon Hen, as if the forces of evil become not just more powerful but also more strikingly visible as evil, the nearer they are to their source and stronghold.

Yet if orcs are assimilable, albeit through the playful grotesque, to a metaphysic of the non-being of evil, Shelob is more difficult. For like her ancestress, she is a form of life that is nihilist in character and one which seems almost positive in its use of darkness as a medium of assault. Unlike the orcs, Shelob's origin is obscure: even the Eldar do not know who made Ungoliant, and with whom she mated to produce offspring. Ungoliant produces not darkness so much as 'Unlight' that 'seemed not a light but a thing with being of its own'.[54] Her descendant Shelob, although baulked at first by the phial of light from the Silmaril, Elendil's star which Galadriel had given Frodo, still manages to poison and entrap him. The light, indeed, seems to wax and wane in efficacy according to the faith and belief of the holder of the phial. But the power of Shelob and her desire for nothing but death seems to suggest a Manichean universe of competing and equal forces of light and darkness. Augustine speaks of evil as a wounding of good, or as an infection, whose status is only accidental, 'for the wound or disease is not a substance, but a defect in the fleshly substance'.[55] He is using 'substance' here in its philosophical sense of substantial being. But Ungoliant and Shelob seem to wound and infect their victims in a manner that is more metaphysically substantive: it is a sort of positive negativity. Sméagol has been Shelob's worshipper for this very reason, bowing down to her because her omnivorous darkness, which 'walked through all the ways of his weariness beside him, cutting him off from light and from regret' (p. 707). The ugliness of orcs may remind one of the loss of beauty, but the way in which Shelob negates difference itself stops Gollum from the pain of awareness of his lost self.

Shelob is only grotesque if light is shone upon her; otherwise she lives in a world without light, where there can be no individuation, no being and no contrast to make possible the juxtaposition and clash of the grotesque mode. In the same way Bakhtin's carnivalesque, porously grotesque body can only work as grotesque if the structure of Church feast, fast and creed is in place to render it other. Shelob's threat is everywhere in *The Lord of the Rings*: in Wormtongue's hold over Théoden's will, rendering him hopeless and lifeless, and in Éowyn's melancholia and distaste for life. Denethor is, of course, actually suicidal and seeks to take Faramir's life with him. Even the Rohirrim have a near-suicidal fatalism in their reckless battle hunger. Of course Shelob herself is not directly responsible for all this nihilism, but she represents it and embodies it as if she were an arachnic black hole.

And it is as embodiment of negativity without grotesque contrast that Shelob is important as the gate to Mordor for Frodo and Sam, as well as Gollum. For each of the first two hobbits learns, with the help of good memories of Tom, Galadriel and even of Elbereth Gilthoniel, to face up to the nothingness that Shelob embodies. Again Dante, whom Tolkien himself called 'a supreme poet', provides an analogy.[56] Before Dante and Virgil can leave Hell they must pass Dis or Satan, who is stuck in the hole at the bottom of Hell and is completely monstrous and horrible. No glamourized Miltonic Satan, Dante's is a grotesque, with three heads of different colours that chew on the bodies of traitors, the hairy body of an animal, claws and three pairs of great leathery wings which keep Hell arctic. Blood from his victims and tears from his six eyes dribble down his chins. The effect on Dante is extreme: 'How chilled and faint I turned then, do not ask, reader, for I do not write it, since all words would fail. I did not die and I did not remain alive; think now for thyself, if thou hast any wit, what I became, denied both life and death'.[57] The nonbeing that Dis causes is like that of Shelob in that he is a literal blockage to thought and life. He may be a parody of the Trinity, but his bulk fills the horizon and subsumes being. Dis is like Shelob also in that he does not kill outright but eternally chews his prey, just as she slowly poisons and devours her victims: Frodo is left between life and death like Dante's narrator. The way out for Dante, advised by Virgil, and Frodo by Sam, is to engage with Satan and not to run away. It is for Dante necessary to grasp Dis's hairy flanks and climb down his body. Similarly that is how Sam deals with Shelob, by facing her and not turning tail, engaging her bodily. In touching the monstrosity of evil as a denial of life and existence, each character is brought into the disgust and fear of the grotesque experience, as Sam like Dante finds himself right underneath, with 'the great bag of her belly' above his head. Where Dante's Satan aids his victim's escape despite himself, locked in his own frozen self-punishment, Shelob too brings about Sam's release by driving down upon his body and impaling herself on the blade of Sting. The only positive aspect to her being – her movement and freedom of action – is what causes her downfall. This is a similar dynamic to that of the damned souls in Dante's *Inferno*. They still have some simulacrum of a body with movement and feeling, and it is this positive aspect of their post-mortem existence through which their punishment is achieved. The wounding of Shelob and the death of Gollum have this same dimension of *contrapasso*, meaning literally 'step against', and judgement more metaphorically. It involves a certain poetic justice by which the punishment fits the crime, and in some sense expresses it. So Shelob, who like her mother wishes to engulf light and life, is wounded in the eye, while Gollum dies with the 'Precious' he had always sought, and thanks to his possession of it. Tolkien does not fully deal with the implications of the positive negativity he has allowed in his fictional world. Shelob's negativity is a risk in an imaginary universe that allows such creative power to its inhabitants, but it *can* be resisted by means of the grotesque. In that sense *The Lord of the Rings* seeks to correct the negativity let off the leash in *The Silmarillion* by the mystery about Ungoliant's origin.

In Dante and Tolkien, bringing the self close to the overwhelmingness of negativity provokes the grotesque, as self and other are juxtaposed in a monstrous hybrid. And it is this clash that allows the evil to be seen, and in being viewed in the horror of intimacy rather than distant terror, to be seen as what it is: a monstrosity, and thus a witness to the goodness of being. As Augustine wrote:

> Nothing, then, can be evil except something which is good. And although this, when stated, seems to be a contradiction, yet the strictness of reasoning leaves us no escape from the conclusion . . . Now what is an evil man but an evil being? For a man is a being? Now if a man is a good thing because he is a being, what is an evil man but an evil good? Yet when we accurately distinguish these two things, we find it is not because he is a man that he is evil, or because he is wicked that he is good; but that he is good because he is a man, and evil because he is wicked.[58]

Although this passage does end by sorting out evil from good, it puts them close up against each other, in a grotesque contradiction, which is then shown to be correct in so far as a wicked man *is* an 'evil good'. This monstrous paradox is true in a fallen world, where a man might choose to be evil. And it can do no harm to the concept of goodness, on which the evil is parasitic. Indeed, as Aquinas makes clear, evil only serves to show up the goodness of being by contrast and vice versa.

Tolkien's world does, however, have its Manicheans, for that is what Morgoth and Sauron have become, not just because they wish to claim equal if not superior power for evil, but because they denigrate the material and physical world and 'save' their subjects from it. The Nazgûl, for example, have lost bodily form as a result of their subjection to the power of Sauron, while he himself is reduced to a single eye. And while the human world of *The Lord of the Rings* is deliberately lacking in religious practice, save for one instance of grace before meals and its various funeral rites, Tolkien does refer in one of his letters to 'the false religion', and to 'the cult of Morgoth' set up by Sauron in Númenor.[59]

This false religion is a form of fetishism, which means, following Charles de Brosse and E. B. Tylor, the importing to inanimate objects of spiritual powers, characteristic of West African religious practice and the belief, in some cases, that one can put one's own powers or soul into the object for safety or command. Fetishism is closely allied to what happens in the grotesque image, for frequently the effect is derived from the admixture of animate to inanimate form, or the galvanism of an inert object. Hoffmann's tale 'The Sandman' has a celebrated series of scenes in which the protagonist views what he takes to be a beautiful girl through a telescope, who is actually an automaton. At a ball where the imposture and mechanical nature of Olympia are obvious to all, Nathaniel continues to address her as human, dance with her and make love to her. Only as her 'body' is carted off without its glass eyes is he awakened to his grotesque mistake.[60]

The Ring of Power in *The Lord of the Rings* is grotesque in this sense, because, like the Hoffmanesque automaton, it is treated as if it had agency and intentionality. Gandalf talks of it 'trying to get back to its master' and somehow precipitating its adventures from Isildur to Frodo: 'It had slipped from Isildur's hand and betrayed him; then when a chance came it caught poor Déagol, and he was murdered;

and after that Gollum, and it had devoured him. It could make no further use of him: he was too small and mean; and as long as it stayed with him he would never leave his deep pool again. So now, when its master was awake once more and sending out his dark thought from Mirkwood, it abandoned Gollum' (p. 54).

The Ring is grotesque because it is actually a fetish, in that it was forged by Sauron so as to have his own power within it, and to control others. In a sense he put his soul into it like the Congolese fetishist into his tree. So great is the power of the Ring that it causes everyone, even Gandalf, to treat it as an active agent; it is only Tom Bombadil who can withstand its power and be unaffected by its spell of invisibility. He plays with the Ring, throwing it up into the air like a mere trinket in a juggler's performance and puts it to his eye: 'for a second the hobbits had a vision, both comical and alarming, of his bright blue eye gleaming through a circle of gold' (p. 130). Making the Ring of Power into a bizarre monocle is grotesque – both 'comical and alarming' like the playful version of the mode, and it has a pedagogical aim: to unmask the glamour of the Ring.

Tom Bombadil can do this because he is unfallen in his relation to the world and its creatures. Moreover, as 'Eldest' he belongs to another Age, and is somewhat outside the present story, being included as a deliberate anachronism and anomaly. His relation to his own labour is completely unalienated in a Marxist sense: he makes all he needs without recourse to money or the market in a utopia worthy of John Ball's Eden, in which 'Adam delved and Eve span' and there was no 'gentleman' to turn the works of their hands into commodities.

Although I would not go so far as to attempt to claim the Cobbettish Tolkien for Marxism, his conception of the Ring as a form of critique has distinct analogies with Marx's own critique of commodity capitalism in section four of the first chapter of *Capital*, entitled 'The Fetishism of Commodities and the Secret Thereof'. Marx thought that nineteenth-century humanity had been deceived into believing that objects of exchange in the marketplace have a life of their own:

> It is clear as noon-day, that man, by his industry, changes the forms of the materials furnished by Nature, in such a way as to make them useful to him. The form of wood, for instance, is altered, by making a table out of it. Yet, for all that, the table continues to be that common, every-day thing, wood. But, so soon as it steps forth as a commodity, it is changed into something transcendent. It not only stands with its feet on the ground, but, in relation to all other commodities, it stands on its head, and evolves out of its wooden brain grotesque ideas, far more wonderful then 'table-turning' ever was.[61]

In the modern market economy we are disconnected from the things we produce; we lose relations between makers and consumers and are estranged even from the objects of our own labour. Relationships between things are substituted for those between people, and these commodities acquire an idolatrous character as fetishes: they are totally of our own creation but we fail to recognize them as such. In *The Lord of the Rings* one can contrast the way in which the palantírs, the seeing-stones made to enable communication between allies, have come to dominate their users to such an extent that the object drives the 'owner' and leads to Denethor's self-murder. Middle-earth is different from our modern world in that figures like Sauron really do have a certain creative power, but it is not to give real life exactly, but rather the ability to put one's will into an inanimate thing so as to galvanize it grotesquely into a parody of life. The three-headed monsters, for example, the Two Watchers of Cirith Ungol, are animated by malicious will from without into a horrendous parody of creatures that are like robot machines.

The Ring of Power is most like Marx's grotesque commodity, because it subsumes being and agency to itself and away from its users. Its primary relations are to the other Rings – 'One Ring to rule them all' – and the men who wear the 'nine for mortal men doomed to die' have lost all bodily form to it, becoming the shadowy 'Ringwraiths'. The effect of ring-bearing makes Bilbo feel 'like butter that has been stretched over too much bread' (p. 30), while Frodo becomes increasingly transparent. Sauron too has the shadowiest of forms, if form he has, having been reduced to scopophilia, being nothing but a great eye, an agent of unceasing surveillance fixated on its object. But this eye, as Frodo views it in Galadriel's mirror, is

THE GROTESQUE

'rimmed with fire, but was itself glazed, yellow as a cat's, watchful and intent, and the black slit of its pupil opened on a pit, a window into nothing' (p. 409). Sauron is as empty as his Ringwraiths, and his eye opens onto the void. Even his will-to-power is completely nihilistic: he seems to aim at the destruction of the very world he claims to wish to rule. Moreover, having put his will-to-power within the Ring, in fetishistic fashion, his authority collapses immediately the Ring is returned to its source. It loses its status as religious fetish, holding the soul of the worshipper at the same moment that it loses its status as commodity fetish in Marxian mode. In falling back into the fires of Mount Doom its origin is made plain, and its grotesqueness similarly becomes clear once its glamour is removed. Peter Jackson's film emphasizes the weaponry and size of the armed forces at Sauron's command as the source of terror. These facts are part of the truth of Sauron's power but not all: it is fear behind and above the actual physical effect of his army that disarms his opponents, exemplified by the flying dragons on which the Nazgûl ride. It is the same vertiginous negativity that Shelob represents. Once the Ring falls with Gollum into the fires, its trace remains only in the fact of the broken finger of Frodo's hand: there is literally nothing else left to show for it. In this way the finger becomes a sign of hope by means of its brokenness: it images both fall and redemption, just as Tolkien orchestrates both Ruskin's noble grotesque that dramatizes the gap between the human and divine, and the energies of Chesterton's grotesque of potentiality for a theology that is true both to the goodness of the creation and the fall into lack of being. But, as we shall see in the next chapter, the 'fall' of the Ring is the way back or, as Heraclitus put it, 'the way up and the way down are one and the same'.[62]

Notes

1. Chesterton, 'A Ballade on the Grotesque', in *The Coloured Lands*, p. 114.
2. Victor Hugo, *Cromwell*, ed. Annie Ubersfeld (Paris: Garnier-Flammarion, 1986), pp. 77–8.
3. On the Pre-Raphaelites' use of awkward gesture, see Tim Barringer, *Reading the Pre-Raphaelites* (London: Weidenfeld & Nicolson, 1998), pp. 34–5. On responses

to Millais's *Christ in the House of His Parents*, see Barringer, p. 40; and Timothy Hilton, *The Pre-Raphaelites* (London: Thames and Hudson, 1970), p. 41.

4. Charles Baudelaire, 'Une Charogne' (A Carcase), in *Flowers of Evil*, ed. Jonathan Culler, trans. James McGowan (Oxford: Oxford University Press, 1998), p. 149.

5. Quoted in Geoffrey Harpham, *On the Grotesque: Strategies of Contradiction in Art and Literature* (Princeton: Princeton University Press, 1987), p. 5.

6. Hugo, *Cromwell*, p. 78.

7. G. K. Chesterton, *Robert Browning*, English Men of Letters Series (London: Macmillan, 1903); G. K. Chesterton, *Charles Dickens* (London: Methuen, 1906).

8. Robert Browning, 'Soliloquy of the Spanish Cloister', in *The Poetical Works of Robert Browning*, ed. Ian Jack (London: Oxford University Press, 1970), pp. 374–6 (374).

9. Chesterton, *Browning*, p. 149.

10. Chesterton, *Browning*, p. 151.

11. G. K. Chesterton, *Criticisms and Appreciations of Charles Dickens* (London: Stratus, 2001), p. 62.

12. Harpham, *The Grotesque*, p. 8.

13. John Ruskin, *Complete Works of John Ruskin*, Library Edition, ed. E. T. Cook and Alexander Wedderburn, 37 vols (London: George Allen, 1905–12), 10, p. 240.

14. G. K. Chesterton, 'On Gargoyles' in *Alarms and Discursions* (London: Methuen, 1910), pp. 1–4 (2).

15. Chesterton, 'On Gargoyles', p. 4.

16. Chesterton, 'On Gargoyles', p. 2.

17. Wayne Hammond and Christina Scull, *J. R. R. Tolkien: Artist and Illustrator* (London: HarperCollins, 1995), p. 53.

18. Tolkien, 'Beowulf: The Monsters and the Critics', Sir Israel Gollancz Memorial Lecture, British Academy 1936, *Proceedings of the British Academy* 22 (London: Oxford University Press, 1958), p. 27.

19. William Dunbar, 'Surrexit Dominus de sepulchro' in *The Poetry of Scotland: Gaelic, Scots and English*, ed. Roderick Watson (Edinburgh: Edinburgh University Press, 1995), p. 80.

20. J. R. R. Tolkien, *Tree and Leaf*, p. 41.

21. Hammond and Scull, *Tolkien: Artist and Illustrator*, p. 51.

22. Ruskin, *Complete Works*, 5, p. 131.

23. See Wolfgang Kayser, *The Grotesque in Art and Literature*, trans. Ulrich Weisstein (New York: Columbia University Press, 1981), pp. 48–50.

24. Hammond and Scull, *Tolkien: Artist and Illustrator*, p. 53.

25. Tolkien, 'Mythopoeia' in *Tree and Leaf*, p. 87.

26. Harpham, *The Grotesque*, p. 5.
27. Tolkien, *The Silmarillion*, p. 45.
28. See Friedrich Schlegel, *Gespräch über die Poesie* (1800), discussed in Kayser, p. 86.
29. Quoted in Hugh Kenner, *Paradox in Chesterton*, intro. Herbert Marshall McLuhan (London: Sheed and Ward, 1948), p. 82.
30. Chesterton, *Browning*, p. 151.
31. Quoted in Harpham, *The Grotesque*, p. 78.
32. On the pedagogical function of monsters in illumination, see Asa Simon Mittman, *Maps and Monsters in Medieval England* (New York and London: Routledge, 2006).
33. Ruskin, *Complete Works*, 5, Part 4, chapter 8, p. 130.
34. Thomas Aquinas, *Summa Theologica*, Part 1, Q. 1, Art. 9, p. 16.
35. Chesterton, *The Man Who Was Thursday*, p. 53.
36. Chesterton, *The Man Who Was Thursday*, pp. 157 & 161.
37. Chesterton, *The Man Who Was Thursday*, pp. 165, 166, 167.
38. Chesterton, *The Man Who Was Thursday*, p. 168.
39. G. K. Chesterton, *Autobiography*, p. 15; *G. F. Watts* (London: Duckworth, 1904), pp. 62–4.
40. G. K. Chesterton, *The Napoleon of Notting Hill*, intro. Martin Gardner (New York: Dover, 1991), p. 10.
41. Chesterton, *The Man Who Was Thursday*, p. 183.
42. Ruskin, *Complete Works*, 5, p. 145.
43. Tolkien, *The Silmarillion*, p. 76.
44. Tolkien, *The Silmarillion*, p. 80. For creators and devourers, see *A Dictionary of Creation Myths*, ed. David Leeming and Margaret Leeming (Oxford: Oxford University Press, 1994).
45. Mikhail Bakhtin, *Rabelais and His World*, trans. Hélène Iswolsky (Bloomington: Indiana University Press, 1984), pp. 303–67.
46. Chesterton, *Autobiography*, p. 16.
47. Hammond and Scull, *Tolkien: Artist and Illustrator*, p. 83, fig. 77.
48. Hammond and Scull, *Tolkien: Artist and Illustrator*, p. 37, fig. 32.
49. Shippey, *The Road to Middle-earth*, pp. 174–5.
50. Tolkien, *The Silmarillion*, p. 195.
51. *Letters of Tolkien*, p. 195.
52. Thomas Aquinas, *Summa Contra Gentiles*, Book III, Providence, ch. 11, p. 61.
53. Dante Alighieri, *The Divine Comedy: 1 Hell*, trans. Dorothy Sayers (London: Penguin, 1949), p. 204.
54. Tolkien, *The Silmarillion*, p. 76.
55. Augustine of Hippo, *Enchiridion*, in *A Select Library of the Nicene and*

Post-Nicene Fathers of the Christian Church, gen. ed. Philip Schaff, 28 vols (Edinburgh and Grand Rapids MI: T & T Clark and Eerdmans, 1998), 3, p. 240.

56. *Letters of Tolkien*, p. 377.
57. Dante Alighieri, *Inferno*, trans. John Sinclair (Oxford: Oxford University Press, 1971), 34: 23–7, p. 421.
58. Augustine, *Enchiridion*, p. 241.
59. *Letters of Tolkien*, p. 194.
60. Kayser, *Grotesque*, pp. 72–8.
61. Karl Marx, *Capital: A Critique of Political Economy*, trans. Samuel Moore and Edward Aveling, ed. Frederick Engels, 3 vols (London: Lawrence and Wishart, 1954), p. 76.
62. Charles H. Kahn, *The Art and Thought of Heraclitus: An Edition of the Fragments with Translation and Commentary* (Cambridge: Cambridge University Press, 1979), pp. 74–5.

CHAPTER 3

PARADOX AND RIDDLES

> I only ask from Fate the gift
> Of one man well content.
>
> Him will I find: though when in vain
> I search the feast and mart,
> The fading flowers of liberty,
> The painted masks of art
>
> I only find him at the last,
> On one old hill where nod
> Golgotha's ghastly trinity –
> Three persons and one god.[1]

CHESTERTON IS FAMOUS for his inveterate use of paradox and, as in this short poem, for heaping paradox upon paradox with all the relentless efficiency of the stage conjurer, who pulls from his hat flags or rabbits with equal professional ease. An early reviewer opined that paradox should be 'used like onions to season the salad. Mr Chesterton's salad is all onions'.[2] The same reviewer accused Chesterton of not only standing truth on her head, but making her 'cut her throat to attract attention'. This last bizarre figure reveals something of the closeness of paradox to the grotesque, which is evident in the final couplet of 'The Happy Man' in which the three gibbets literalize the orthodox doctrine of the Athanasian Creed, with all the casual insouciance of the verb 'nod', which Chesterton goes on to rhyme, scandalously, with 'god'.

Like the grotesque, paradox puts contradictions together, but whereas in the former mode the monstrosity of the apposition baulks thought and reveals the unknowability and mystery of existence, paradox leads to a moment of recognition beyond the contradictions in which a truth becomes manifest. Paradox is therefore very close to the grotesque, and yet is in some sense its antonym, since it allows us to understand what we thought was straightforward – in the poem the nature of happiness – as complex or different from what we originally assumed, and yet illumined, whereas grotesque complexity leads to the cloud of unknowing.

As with defamiliarization and the grotesque so with paradox, Chesterton is developing in a more metaphysical and realist direction another of the favoured aesthetic modes of the 1890s: here the aphoristic method of Oscar Wilde, with whom Chesterton is often compared. In a 1909 article for the *Daily News*, Chesterton sought to distinguish two sorts of paradox in Wilde, 'the real epigram which he wrote to please his own wild intellect, and the sham epigram which he wrote to thrill the very tamest part of our tame civilisation'.[3] An example of the former is 'nothing survives being thought of', which Chesterton describes as 'death-dealing' rather than life-dealing but revealing an actual idea. For an example of the sham epigram, Chesterton cites the definition of an immoral woman as 'the kind of woman a man never tires of'. He continues, 'that vice never tires men, might be a tenable and entertaining lie, that the individual instrument of vice never tires them is not, even as a lie, tenable enough to be entertaining'.[4]

Chesterton views the first example as truly paradoxical, in that it suggests a truth revealed in and through the contradiction, whereas the second merely inverts a truism. Many of the epigrams of Wilde's plays – 'Divorces are made in heaven' or 'in marriage three is company and two is none' – have this 'death-dealing' character in that they confine behaviour within the dualities of the terms that the paradoxical method implies they wish to question.[5] Chesterton's own explanation for this was Wilde's desire to be all things to all men, to please the bourgeoisie, which meant that he could never commit himself to any one side of a polarity. Chesterton's own epigrammatic style can prove tiring, and his symbolic realism can leap too quickly to tie phenomena to one side or other of a cosmic conflict, but by and large he avoids Wilde's tendency to play to the dress-circle, even if he can, occasionally, play to the gallery – or the gods. This is because Chesterton actually believes in the solidity of phenomena (albeit also in their contingency) and can say, 'believe me there are real things'.[6] And this realism extends also to language itself, so that Father Brown stands for his author when he says of a revolutionary poet that 'a poem was an event for him'.[7] Like the symbolists, Chesterton sees language itself as material, and a poem as an object. The difference lies in the fact that he also sees language, like his revolutionary poet, as an event. That is, the words have life in themselves in a performative sense. For language for Chesterton does not have the transparency of nineteenth-century literary realism, nor the fetishistic opacity and separateness of the symbolist object, but the potency and explodability of a bomb. It is like the Torah as portrayed by the writer of the letter to the Hebrews: 'For the word of God is quick, and powerful, and sharper than any two-edged sword, piercing even to the dividing asunder of soul and spirit, and of the joints and marrow, and is a discerner of the thoughts and intents of the heart' (Hebrews 4.12, AV). The whole conceit of Chesterton's series of *Tales of the Long Bow* (1925) is driven by his anger at the trite conventionality of everyday linguistic laziness. This is not just the artist's dislike of cliché but of the philosopher's use of words merely as conventional signs and not events. In the first tale, Colonel Crane attracts social opprobrium by walking about his respectable neighbourhood and even to church wearing a cabbage on his head so that, eventually, he may enact the promise he made to 'eat his hat'.[8] He restores force and reality to his words by rendering them material and actual.

In his brilliant 1948 study of Chesterton's use of paradox, Hugh Kenner followed Chesterton's taxonomy of 'sham' and actual paradoxes in Wilde with a similar division in Chesterton himself, between what he called rhetorical and metaphysical forms. The second responded to the complexity of ultimate reality, but the first spoke of things that were in fact clear and simple, were our minds not clouded and dulled by conventional thinking, out of which Chesterton's epigrams seek to startle us into realization. The example Kenner gives of rhetorical paradox is Chesterton's definition of companionate marriage as 'so-called' because 'the people involved are not married and will very rapidly cease to be companions'. For Kenner this paradox relies solely on the substitution of terms, as Chesterton accused Wilde's epigrams of doing, because the contradiction is not in the things but the words. Yet I would argue that even here Chesterton is more metaphysical than Wilde, because his epigram depends upon the *realism* of an idea represented by the words 'companion' and 'marriage' in contrast to Wilde's flippancy. The epigrams, 'Bigamy is having one wife too many, monogamy is the same' or 'in marriage three is company, two is none' seek to destabilize marriage as a concept while relying on its stability as a social practice to make the joke.

Chesterton imitates this style in order to restore the links between signifier and its signified (the word 'marriage' with the concept), which have been divided and he does so by drawing attention to the separation between the two in order to show the importance of their reunion. In the same way, T. S. Eliot in *The Waste Land* would juxtapose the tragic response of the speaker of Goldsmith's poem 'When lovely woman stoops to folly' with '[she] puts a record on the gramophone', forcing the reader to acknowledge the dissociation of sensibility that this implies.[9] But while Eliot makes a kind of melancholy beauty out of these ironic juxtapositions, Chesterton's art goes much further towards the redemption and restoration of language, since the greater the disjunction between conventional speech and the thing or idea itself, the more extreme the paradox and, most crucially, the larger the opening for analogical relation.

Although analogy in the theological sense is associated with medieval thought, and especially with Aquinas, Chesterton seems to have come up with it on his own, so that as early as 1905 he is instructing his reader in its principles.

> [The reader] must realize the first and simplest of the paradoxes that sit by the springs of truth. He must surely see that the fact of two things being different implies that they are similar. The hare and the tortoise may differ in the quality of swiftness, but they must agree in the quality of motion. The swiftest hare cannot be swifter than an isosceles triangle or the idea of pinkness. When we say the hare

moves faster, we say that the tortoise moves. And when we say of a thing that it moves, we say, without need of other words, that there are things that do not move. And even in the act of saying that things change, we say that there is something unchangeable.[10]

The hare and the tortoise are alike in their potential for movement but unlike in the quality and speed of that movement. In this way analogy, likeness in difference, in proportionality, illustrates the way in which individual beings participate in being. In the case of God, analogy is important as ensuring an avoidance of too close and easy an understanding of his mystery. For just as the hare exists 'harily' and the tortoise 'tortoisely', they both have being in a manner according to their own nature. In tortoise terms, an individual member of that species may be swift or slow. Aquinas points out that 'we cannot speak of God at all except in the language we use of creatures' and also that 'there is a likeness, because in Genesis there is a resemblance between creatures and God: "Let us make man in our own image and likeness."'[11] Yet the goodness of God is not on a continuum with that of humans. As Hugh Kenner puts it: 'the answer of St Thomas and Chesterton is that goodness is possessed by man and by God, but not in the same way. The way in which men are good is proportionate to the being which men have; the way in which God is good is proportionate to the being which God has'.[12] The result of this analogical way of thinking is a world that offers a network of analogies consisting of unity with difference, and consequently an infinite opportunity for paradox. Indeed, the reader of a paradox is presented with the difference between two things, and seeks for that which unites them – their relation. This relation takes him or her back beyond the two contrasted things to their cause, which is God. In the sense in which humans share in divine qualities because of their cause being in God, Chesterton may, implicitly, be referring to the analogy of attribution as well as proportion. The analogy of attribution is a way of relating qualities shared by diverse beings through the one being the cause of the quality in the other.[13]

Because being itself is analogical, all systematic thinking has a paradoxical cast, and Kenner gives the example of belated identification, as when we realize that the winged mouse in our attic is a bat, and also the rationality of the *Summa*, in which Thomas's method is to 'resolve the paradox created by a previous imperfect solution'.[14] Indeed Thomas seems to delight in making the Fathers seem to contradict themselves, but then properly defines the terms so as to harmonize the thoughts and things. For both Chesterton and Aquinas, 'the world is a baffling place, incapable of being enmeshed in a phrase or a formula'.[15] This does not mean, however, that truth may not be found; it does mean that truth as we know it has a paradoxical cast.

Hence Chesterton's forays into detective fiction are not just essays in ratiocination but also enacted paradoxes of the complicated nature of existence. They tend to present facts in the form of a series of objects that appear utterly disconnected or even contradictory – thus imitating the method of the *Summa* – forcing the reader to search for the analogical principle that underlies them. In 'The Invisible Man', for example, the tale's title is its central paradox: four witnesses swear that no-one has entered Himalaya Mansions and Smythe's flat, yet his body has disappeared from it, to be found eventually in the canal; there is blood on the apartment's floor and footprints in the snow. A red herring is set up in the uncanny presence of Smythe's servant automata, and a horrid fancy strikes those entering the apartment 'that matter had rebelled and these machines had killed their master' or even eaten him.[16] The paradox of the invisible man is solved appropriately by a priest, whose role is to mediate between humanity and God. Father Brown can 'see' the invisible man to be a mediator like himself: a postman whose function as daily mediator of letters means that he is totally overlooked. Although this solution relies, like many others in the series, on a linguistic confusion, the paradox reveals something of the nature of being. For the invisible man can be seen to refer equally to the corpse, which ought to be in the flat but is not, and the headless 'butler' automatom as well as the murdering postman. Each is invisible in a different way, and it is by working out the analogical likenesses and differences in being that the case is solved.

Father Brown stories, however, are never neatly ended when the solution is reached. 'The Invisible Man' ends with a further mystery: 'Father Brown walked those snow-covered hills under the stars for many hours with a murderer, and what they said to each other will never be known'.[17] The little priest is a device whereby being is always conveyed over to the transcendent, to the baffling depths of the human soul, and the intrinsically paradoxical nature of humanity itself. For although Chesterton's detective tales are so concerned with objects, as we have seen in previous chapters, the grotesque features of their arrangement point back always to the strangeness of the human being who so placed them. So, for example, the story entitled 'The Man With Two Beards' focuses attention on the evidence of disguise and the improbably red false whiskers of the erstwhile thief, Michael Smith. When his body is found wearing a second red beard, it is this fact that exonerates him for Father Brown, and shows that he has been framed. ' "Hang it all," said Sir John Bales restlessly, "after all he was a convicted thief." "Yes," said Father Brown; "and only a convicted thief has ever in this world heard that assurance: 'This night shalt thou be with me in Paradise.' " '[18] The existence of a second beard was a form of honesty on the part of Michael Smith. He kept it as a salutary reminder of his criminal past, and it proves the reality of his character as a penitent thief, which is a paradoxical duality conceived of in the Christian scriptures themselves.

In Chesterton it is humanity itself that is the strangest paradox, as he expresses eloquently in the first chapter of *The Everlasting Man*, 'The Man in the Cave':

> The simplest truth about a man is that he is a very strange being; almost in the sense of being a stranger on the earth. In all sobriety, he has much more of the external appearance of one bringing alien habits from another land than of a mere growth of this one. He has an unfair advantage and an unfair disadvantage. He cannot sleep in his own skin; he cannot trust his own instincts. He is at once a creator moving miraculous hands and fingers and a kind of cripple. He is wrapped in artificial bandages called clothes; he is propped on artificial crutches called furniture. His mind has the same doubtful liberties and the same wild limitations. Alone among the animals, he is shaken with the beautiful madness called laughter; as if he had caught sight of some secret in the very shape of the universe hidden from the universe itself. Alone among the animals he feels the need

of averting his thought from the root realities of his own bodily being; of hiding them as in the presence of some higher possibility which creates the mystery of shame. Whether we praise these things as natural to man or abuse tham as artificial in nature, they remain in the same sense unique ... It is not natural to see man as a natural product ... It sins against the light; against that broad daylight of proportion which is the principle of all reality.[19]

This is a magnificent rhetorical *tour de force*, but it also recapitulates the elements of the Chestertonian poetics we have examined so far. It begins by defamiliarizing the ordinary to make us wonder at it. Secondly, it employs a grotesque focus to render mankind a sort of monster – 'a kind of cripple.' He becomes a walking paradox that is only resolvable by admitting, like Victor Hugo, his double origin as both bestial and divine. The procedure of turning the self into a grotesque has the same distantiating effect as of an object, and a self-alienation ensues. In *Orthodoxy* Chesterton sums it up as: 'whatever I am, I am not myself'.[20] Humanity is as much a mystery as God himself, and not only in its aspirations towards divinity but as an animal. The whole force of this long passage from *The Everlasting Man* is to show that we make no sense in animal terms, and that we cannot be explained in that way because we are simply not proportionate: the analogical differences are huge. 'Whatever I am, I am not myself' was written by Chesterton in the margin of Sir Oliver Lodge's catechism reconciling Darwinism and religion, and was in answer to the question, 'What, then, is meant by the Fall of man?' and therefore takes the self-alienation in some respect as an index of fallenness.[21]

The duality of humanity causes Chesterton to write fictions in which there are dialectically opposed pairings of characters, such as the artist Gabriel Gale and the madman James Hurrel in *The Poet and the Lunatics* (1929), or Father Brown and the ex-criminal Flambeau. Innocent Smith, the hero of *Manalive* (1912), turns self-estrangement into a joyful and even ecstatic alienation from the self. In works like *The Ball and the Cross* (1909), Chesterton appears to set up a quasi-Hegelian dialectic between opposed and irreconcilable virtues in the antithetical rationalist Turnbull and his opponent the Romantic Catholic McIan, who spend large parts of the novel seeking a safe place for a duel. But whereas according to Hegel's view the tragic heroine Antigone dies as a result of pushing a virtue to excess so that she suffers in an unideal world of limitation, Chesterton's dualities provoke the realization of a truth beyond themselves that does no violence to their integrity of vision.[22] Turnbull and McIan unite to take on the authoritarian tyranny of Professor Lucifer, and their contradiction is resolved not by synthesis but by a higher paradox, as their dropped swords accidentally fall into the shape of a cross.[23]

Moreover, duality of self is the key to Father Brown's success as a detective. He estranges his mind so as to 'play[ed] the part of the murderer' as his understudy, and imagines himself into the thought world of the particular crime so as to realize that he himself might have committed it under 'certain mental conditions'.[24] Father Brown uses the language of spiritual meditation to explain this exercise, but to his auditor, the American Grandison Chace, it appears a demonic practice and Brown a 'monster and murderer' with a 'vast void of dark behind', in which ghosts of criminals lurked ready to tear 'their master in pieces'.[25] It is Father Brown's acknowledgement of his own capacity for evil that renders him monstrous to Chace, but it is paradoxically this same capacity for imaginative duality that allows him both to solve crimes and save the criminals by bringing them to repentance and confession, as Flambeau himself is moved to act in this same story.

Tolkien from *The Hobbit* onwards follows Chesterton in presenting the human (or creaturely) person as a duality. His own approach to paradox relies greatly on Anglo-Saxon literature and its pleasure in using 'kennings', which are mini-riddles or condensed metaphors that render the known new and significant: for example, 'the swan's riding-place' for the sea, 'peace-weaver' for wife. On a larger scale Anglo-Saxon and other Northern literature was full of riddle poems or games, in which an object was described in a number of strange ways, or by reference to a variety of disparate and conflicting categories.[26] Like the paradox, the riddle sets up a series of contradictions that the reader or listener has to solve. The difference lies in the agonistic nature of the riddle. Where a paradox may be presented for purely readerly delight, the riddle intensifies the contradictions and the mystery and sets it as a deliberate problem, if not a contest, that emphasizes the metaphysical aspects of the trope. *The Hobbit*, for example, contains a highly agonistic riddle game played between Bilbo and Gollum in a cave beneath the Misty Mountains, in which Bilbo, like Oedipus before the Sphinx, riddles for his life. In the capital or 'neck' riddle, the word is indeed a sword, cleaving head from body if the player fails to join word to word. Gollum's first, simple riddle reveals the paradoxical quality of the form:

> What has roots as nobody sees,
> Is taller than trees
> Up, up it goes,
> And yet it never grows?[27]

The answer is a mountain, and its meaning is wrapped up in a sequence of antonyms: grows/does not grow, visible/invisible, tall/low, like trees/unlike trees. To guess the answer requires analogical thinking so as to discover something that develops in a way that is both like and unlike the growth of trees.

The riddles that follow in this contest all share this format of contradiction and analogy and are far from random. Gollum's riddle subjects are mountain, wind, dark, fish and time, and they embody his experience of physical isolation and despair and alienation from the company of living beings, caught as he is in a death-in-life form of longevity. For him the wind 'toothless bites', and 'mouthless mutters', the dark 'ends life, kills laughter', and even the fish riddle (which is repeated and extended in *The Lord of the Rings* to include the juicy sweetness of the flesh as Gollum chants it in the Forbidden Pool), is here quite alienating:

> Alive without breath,
> As cold as death;
> Never thirsty, ever drinking,
> All in mail never clinking.[28]

Bilbo's riddle subjects, in contrast, are all relational: teeth, sun on the daisies, an egg, a fish on a table eaten by a man and some given to a cat, and finally a ring. Teeth may refer to Bilbo's immediate fear of being eaten by Gollum but the sun and daisies are involved in mutual exchange, the egg is a treasure within a box and the last – 'no-legs lay on one-leg, two-legs sat near on three-legs, four-legs got some' – provides a picture of a whole domestic universe, in which a man shares his fish with his pet cat. It is an interesting variant on the Sphinx's riddle about what goes on four legs in the morning, two in the afternoon and three in the evening, to which the answer is: a man (crawling, walking, walking with a stick when old). Just as Tolkien wished to establish the participation in being of all things, so he here offers a 'realist' version of the riddle of man to include not just the stages of human life but also tables, fish and a cat. These riddle subjects situate Bilbo as a social and kindly individual in complete contrast to the 'fallen' Gollum, but his last riddle, 'What have I got in my pocket?' reveals a link with his opponent in the form of the Ring that will continue to the end of *The Lord of the Rings*. Winning the riddle contest and the Ring opens a fissure in Bilbo's subjectivity and inaugurates his assumption of the 'kenning' of 'bourgeois burglar' as Tom Shippey puts it, that will enable him to take an epic role in future events.[29] Indeed his ruse of invisibility to escape Gollum's eye and his clever idea of hiding the dwarves and himself in barrels to elude the elven-king are reminiscent of Odysseus's craftiness, both with the wooden horse at Troy and later in evading the Cyclops.

Another Anglo-Saxon mode of riddling used by Tolkien that is equally characteristic of ancient Greek literary practice is the presentation of identity in terms of epithets. Odysseus is routinely 'polymetis' in Homer, the diversely cunning or intelligent, but he is also a series of riddle epithets, such as 'Fatherpain' and 'no-one' (punning 'metis' or 'mê-tis') and he introduces himself back at Ithaca according to a whole series of riddling titles that refer to all he has undergone.[30] Similarly Bilbo announces himself to Smaug the dragon thus: 'I come from under the hill, and under the hills and over the hills my paths led. And through the air. I am he who walks unseen. I am the clue-finder, the web-cutter, the stinging fly. I was chosen for the lucky number. I am he that buries his friends alive and drowns them and draws them alive from the water. I came from the end of a bag, but no bag went over me'.[31] As dragons are verbal deceivers, so Bilbo mimics their misdirection with a series of epithets that are both riddles and paradoxes. There is a natural explanation for each of the seeming contradictions, and he, of course, is the answer to the riddle, but that selfhood is revealed to be no longer singular but multiple. As Gandalf exclaims after Bilbo's lyrical declamation over his neighbourhood at his coming home at the end of the novel: 'my dear Bilbo . . . Something is the matter with you! You are not the hobbit that you were'.[32] Although there is an element of the tragic in Bilbo's deepened identity, which is especially evident in his struggle to give up the Ring in the later novel, and gestured at in the Sackville-Bagginses' treatment of the returned Bilbo as an impostor, there is no doubt that his duality is to be seen as an advance. The title, 'elf-friend', which is used as a term of abuse by the other inhabitants of the Hill, reveals a paradoxical selfhood that seeks to exceed its own origins.

The Lord of the Rings follows *The Hobbit* in admitting a fissure in unitary subjectivity to all its major protagonists. Aragorn in particular is a riddle from his first appearance as a sinister, rough-spoken presence at the inn at Bree, under the epithet 'Strider'. He is associated with actual riddles: first, 'the sword that is broken' that Boromir and Faramir heard of in separate dreams, and secondly the riddle that Bilbo declaims at Rivendell:

> All that is gold does not glitter,
> Not all those who wander are lost;
> The old that is strong does not wither,
> Deep roots are not reached by the frost.
> From the ashes a fire shall be woken,
> A light from the shadows shall spring;
> Renewed shall be blade that was broken:
> The crownless again shall be king. (p. 241)

It is Aragorn who has not wandered but kept watch over the borders of the free world, unknown and unregarded by its inhabitants. His age is great because he is a descendant of the Númenóreans; as Isildur's heir he is heir also to the crown of Gondor. It is appropriate that this doubled figure seeks to marry another with double identity in Arwen, who is the daughter of Elrond and thus of dual human and elf ancestry. It will only be characters who achieve a sometimes grotesque duality of selfhood who will be able to turn the fortunes of Middle-earth, whereas someone with the unfallen unselfconscious unitary personhood of Tom Bombadil cannot. These fissured selves come to embody a sort of paradoxical truth, as illustrated early on by Frodo when he speaks up in the ferment of Elrond's council to take on the task of returning the Ring to its fire of original forging: ' "I will take the Ring", he said, "though I do not know the way" ' (p. 264). The narrator emphasizes the paradoxical nature of his offer by prefacing it with the words, 'as if some other will was using his small voice' (p. 263). Frodo is already two selves – wounded by the poison of the Black Rider's sword – and this psychic woundedness will grow ever stronger as he bears the Ring deeper into enemy territory.

The Ring has a double effect on Frodo, creating as it were two new selves to add to his hobbit identity. In one sense he becomes quite saintly in his patient endurance and physical translucency. This has caused a number of critics to accord him a Christological character, so that his encounter with Boromir on Amon Hen is read as a parallel temptation by Satan in the wilderness, and his journey to Mordor a journey towards his passion, in which Gollum plays the role of Judas and Sam that of Simon of Cyrene, who helps Jesus carry the cross in Luke 23.26.[33] Frodo under duress in Cirith Ungol is stripped and beaten like Christ, and Mount Doom becomes his Golgotha.

In another sense, however, Frodo is quite un-Christlike, since he is in sinful thrall to the Ring he bears. This causes him to view Sam, who had reluctantly taken the Ring when he thought his master dead, as a thief: 'Sam had changed before his very eyes into an orc again, leering and pawing at his treasure, a foul little creature with greedy eyes and a slobbering mouth' (p. 891). Frodo also later morphs from friend and kind master to Ring-slave on Mount Doom. When Gollum appears there Frodo has lost any pity for him but out of some 'stern, untouchable' authority, he addresses him as 'creeping thing' and prophesies that, if Gollum touch him again, 'you shall be cast yourself into the Fire of Doom' (p. 922). And when the cracks of Doom are reached, Frodo is of course unable to resist the Ring's will to power and claims it for his own, refusing to destroy it. The narrative therefore sets up a series of typological analogies with Christ, only to render them highly problematic. Where Hans Frei can argue that in the gospel passion narrative the intention-action identity of the biblical Christ becomes most evident – and Christ most himself – Frodo in his own 'passion' becomes instead a grotesque monster: half Christ and half Satan, and his 'transfiguration' in Christlike robes of white exquisitely ambiguous, with the 'wheel of fire' at his breast.[34]

This scene of Frodo as a tall white figure and Gollum as a cowering animal repeats an earlier encounter when Gollum vows to serve 'the master of the precious' (p. 604). On this first occasion, Frodo similarly treats Gollum with disdain, saying 'down, down' as to a recalcitrant pet dog. What Sam intuits on this first meeting is that 'they were in some way akin and not alien: they could reach each other's minds' (p. 604). Gollum/Sméagol is used most effectively by Tolkien to render Frodo himself grotesque. As the little trio of Frodo, Sam and Gollum cross the Dead Marshes and approach ever closer to Mordor, the relationship between Frodo and Gollum becomes ever closer, as the result of their shared knowledge of what it means to be a wearer of the Ring, and Sam feels both suspicious about Gollum's intentions and jealous of the secret understanding the other two seem to enjoy. To Frodo, Gollum is Sméagol, an attempt to reach out to the hobbit nature dormant within him; to Sam he is 'slinker' or 'stinker' (p. 698). Yet at the same time as this complication in relationships renders the narrative more readable and realist in its characterization, it renders all three hobbits monstrous in the sense that each seems to take on some elements of the other. On the slopes of Mount Doom this affinity makes Frodo and Gollum doubles of each other: neither wishes the Ring to be destroyed, and each seeks to take it for himself. So Frodo's self-divided character becomes evident at the same moment of his monstrously shared identity with Gollum. Even Chesterton could not have put the contradictions in any sharper a contiguity.

The scene on Mount Doom has claims to be the most grotesque

in the whole novel, not only in terms of the monstrous hybridity of Frodo's character but in its physical action by which, after a struggle of a body with an invisible assailant, Gollum bites off Frodo's hitherto invisible finger and dances with it on the brink of the fire. The reason why it is discussed here and not in the preceding chapter is because, paradoxically, Middle-earth is 'redeemed' in and through this grotesque moment, as Gollum's dance of victory causes him to slip and fall into the fire, finger, Ring and all. The tragic duality of personhood is therefore, with massive irony, the mode in which redemption is gained: redemption happens because evil causes its own destruction and the strength of the Ring is its own undoing. Tolkien appears to be reworking here the scene in George MacDonald's religious fantasy *Lilith* (1895), in which the repentant tyrant cannot die and escape the power of the Shadow until she unclasps her hand and sets free the water the childish Little Ones need to grow. Unable to pull her fingers apart, Lilith asks Adam to cut her hand off, after which she is able to sleep with the redeemed and her land is saved. For MacDonald this mutilation shows the limitation of the human will, and the need for divine grace. In Tolkien the failure of Middle-earth to save itself presents a world that makes the Incarnation a necessity. It is for this reason that the Ring's destruction occurs on 25 March (formerly in Britain the beginning of the year and the feast of the Annunciation of the news of Christ's birth to Mary) and not because this redemption has begun in Frodo's actions. For *The Lord of the Rings* illustrates the potential in the Northern pagan virtues to make Christianity 'good-to-think' in the same moment that it reveals the failure of Middle-earth to save itself.

It is for this reason, therefore, that the redemptive actions of the novel, of which there are many, are conceived in highly paradoxical terms. There is a creaturely contribution to the destruction of the Ring, not only in the whole project of the Fellowship but in the pity shown by a series of characters towards Gollum that allows him his moment of redemptive action. Pity itself, as Blake's poem reveals, has an equivocal value: 'Pity would be more,/ If we did not make somebody poor'.[35] It can be a virtue that depends upon a safe distance from the sufferer. Yet the pity Gandalf feels for Gollum is an awareness of his double selfhood – 'there was a little corner of his mind that was still his own' – and his fate as one that could have happened to anyone: 'I think it is a sad story . . . and might have happened to others, even to some hobbits that I have known' (p. 53). Gandalf enters imaginatively into Gollum's alienated selfhood in the manner of Father Brown understudying the criminals he tracks down. And Frodo's kindness to Gollum comes not so much out of pity as compassion, since as bearer of the Ring he shares an understanding of how it enslaved the former Sméagol. Most crucially, it is Sam who makes it possible for Gollum to get to the Ring on Mount Doom:

> Sam's hand wavered. His mind was hot with wrath and the memory of evil. It would be just to slay this treacherous, murderous creature, just and many times deserved; and also it seemed the only safe thing to do. But deep in his heart there was something that restrained him: he could not strike this thing lying in the dust, forlorn, ruinous, utterly wretched. He himself, if only for a little while, had borne the Ring, and now dimly he guessed the agony of Gollum's shrivelled mind and body, enslaved to that Ring, unable to find peace or relief ever in life again. (p. 923)

The duality in Sam allows compassion and solidarity with Gollum, while the distance from himself allows pity; the combination of the two allows Gollum to creep safely away. In the inability to act and strike Gollum with his sword lies Sam's contribution to the denouement.

Religious-minded critics are therefore not wrong to detect models of redemptive activity in *The Lord of the Rings*, but they err if they are unaware of the highly ambiguous and paradoxical nature of every example. This is particularly clear in the various battles in which Sauron's forces are engaged by the armies of Gondor and Rohan. The battle is a traditional figure for Christ's redemptive action, especially in Northern cultures, in which the hero Beowulf fighting Grendel can appear on a Christian stone cross, and in poems like Dunbar's 'On the Resurrection of Christ' and Langland's *Piers Plowman*, in which Christ jousts at Jerusalem like a knight at a tournament. 1 Corinthians 15.25–6 encourages this mode of interpretation: 'For he must reign, till he hath put all enemies under his feet. The last enemy that shall be destroyed is death' (AV). Tolkien is at his most Anglo-Saxon in the Battle of the Pelennor Fields, in which the Rohirrim 'sang as they slew, for the joy of battle was on them, and the sound of their singing that was fair and terrible came even to the City' (p. 820). The joy of the riders in battle is presented positively, echoing Chesterton's analysis of the paradox of courage as 'almost a contradiction in terms. It means a strong desire to live taking the form of a readiness to die'.[36] In contrast to Denethor's nihilism, this noble fatalism is the height of pagan virtue. Yet it is not Théoden who defeats the embodiment of death at this battle (although he mistakenly thinks he has), since Tolkien revises the heroic model to make the Nazgûl's defeat occur by means of the united but limited actions of the hobbit Merry and Éowyn, a woman, albeit a shield-maiden. Their engagement with the Black Rider is presented with the alliteration and exalted diction of an Anglo-Saxon poem, and the presentation of Éowyn is more heroic than that applied to any of the male characters who fight nobly to defeat Sauron:

> Still she did not blench: maiden of the Rohirrim, child of kings, slender but as a steel blade, fair yet terrible. A swift stroke she dealt, skilled and deadly. The outstretched neck she clove asunder, and the hewn head fell like a stone. Backward she sprang as the huge shape crashed to ruin, vast wings outspread, crumpled on the earth; and with its fall the shadow passed away. A light fell about her, and her hair shone in the sunrise. (pp. 823–4)

The emphasis on the womanly fighter eches Anselm's *Meditation of Human Redemption*, in which he wrote of the importance of Christ's own helplessness: 'But what strength can there be in such a weakness? . . . surely it is in weakness something hidden, because veiled in humiliation it is something concealed . . . O hidden might. A man appended to a cross suspends the eternal death impending on the human race'.[37]

Under Dernhelm's armour similarly there is something concealed: the body of a woman and therefore a threat to the Black Rider, who cannot be killed by a man. Yet although there are also parallels with the paradoxes of the Magnificat in this victory of the weak over the strong – 'he hath put down the mighty from their seat and hath exalted the humble and meek' – this agon is not an exact parallel with Christ's own battle. It takes two people, not one, to defeat this embodiment of death, and the need for two reveals a lack in Éowyn. Her courage is not in doubt, but it has a somewhat negative character. It comes not from love of life but a reckless desire for death. She too had been subject to the fatalistic rhetoric of Wormtongue, and her rejection by Aragorn and her belief that he rode to his certain death in the Paths of the Dead at Dunharrow leads her to despair. Paradoxically it is this despair that enables her to face the Lord of the Nazgúl, but she is also aided by Merry, whose name supplies the bubbling joy that she lacks. For the Black Captain threatens her not merely with death but 'the houses of lamentation' where her flesh will be devoured but her mind opened to Sauron: a death-in-life akin to his own, and a version of the torment of Dante's suicides who, separated from their bodies, are torn by harpies in *Inferno* 13. The narrative, moreover, separates out the elements of the death figure even further by having Théoden's horse become his 'bane' by falling on top of him, in ironic imitation of the winged steed of the Black Riders. Théoden dies believing (mistakenly) that he has killed the latter beast and in ignorance of the role of his niece, and Éowyn is left for dead by her brother who rides off in despair: 'Death! Ride to ruin and the world's ending' (p. 826). Finally, although the killing of the Black Captain is a great victory, not least because of his psychological effect in bringing fear to all on the battlefield, it is not decisive. Again, Tolkien invokes the model of Christ's atoning action, only to use it paradoxically, to show in what way the types fall short.

Aragorn enacts several aspects of Christ's atonement: the healing and harrowing, both of which involve rescue from death. The old Gondor riddle about the herb athelas is: 'Life to the dying/In the king's hand lying', and Aragorn uses it to bring healing to those like Éowyn who are suffering the death-sickness of the Nazgúl wound, as on a societal level he brings new life like a grail knight to the wasteland of Gondor, with its suicidal 'fisher king' and dying sacred tree. More central to the Passion narrative as recounted in the Apostles' Creed, like Christ Aragorn descends into hell to liberate the souls in Hades/Sheol, as traditionally Christ's spirit did on Holy Saturday and as the Orthodox Church portrays in its iconic representation of the Resurrection, which shows Christ reaching into Hell to bring Adam and Eve out. Aragorn takes the pathway of the dead through Dunharrow (which echoes the harrowing of Hell), and adds its shades to his army. Their participation then frees them from their captivity in an endless death-in-life, but they do not enter Paradise like the captives of Sheol, but die naturally. For Aragorn is no Christ but merely a figure like MacDonald's Adam in *Lilith*, who can release those enslaved in a half-life by the Shadow: 'whom he kills never knows she is dead, but lives to do his will, and thinks she is doing her own'.[38] Adam can give Lilith a bed in the House of Death and so can Aragorn give the King of the Dead and his company a natural end.

The most paradoxical of all the redemptive actions in *The Lord of the Rings* makes use of evil's capacity to defeat itself. As we have seen, the Ring ensures its own destruction, Sauron thoughtfully provides a nice broad highway up Mount Doom when Frodo is at his weakest, orcs fight among themselves so that Sam can rescue Frodo, and Sauron's army gives cover to the two hobbits, so that they march across the plain of Mordor in its livery. Again and again, evil fails because it is so strong, so extensive and so highly organized. This capacity of evil for self-destruction formed part of patristic theories of the atonement, which were based on the idea of a divine trick. It is evident in Venantius Fortunatus's hymn that is still regularly sung in Holy Week – 'Pange, lingua, gloriosi' ('Sing, my tongue, the glorious battle') – which includes the following stanza:

> Such the order God appointed
> When for sin he would atone
> To the serpent thus opposing
> Schemes yet deeper than his own,
> Thence the remedy procuring
> Whence the fatal wound had come.[39]

To the idea of Christ's death as a healing act, Venantius adds the concept of the 'pharmakos' or healing poison, but he also suggests that God tricks the devil. In patristic thought God's scheme revolves around Christ's dual nature as both divine and human. Gregory of Nyssa describes the human nature of Christ as a 'fish-hook' to catch the devil, 'hook, line and sinker'.[40] Augustine describes how this trick works:

> For we fell into the hands of the prince of this world, who seduced Adam and made him his servant, and began to possess us as his slaves. But the Redeemer came and the seducer was overcome. And what did our Redeemer do to him who held us captive? For our ransom he held out His cross as a trap; He placed in it as a bait His blood. He [Satan] indeed had power to shed that blood; he did not attain to drink it. And in that he shed the blood of Him who was not his debtor, he was commanded to render up the debtors.[41]

Augustine suggests that the cross was a sort of mousetrap with a human body as bait, following the tradition that death came into the world as a result of the Fall and that humanity 'owes' Satan (who is associated with death) a life. But Christ, being sinless, does not, and in taking Christ through death, Satan breaks the bargain and loses all of his other human debtors. In this way the beguiler, the Father of Lies, is himself beguiled. Anselm attacked the hook model of atonement in two ways: first, by denying that God could owe the devil anything, although he did not deny that humanity was in bondage to Satan – in this he is in agreement with Augustine, who did not accept that the devil's claim was just; and secondly, by arguing that God is truth and cannot be held to deceive anyone, even the devil.[42] However, it is possible for the devil to deceive himself: 'Someone deceives himself if he does not know the truth, if he does not believe it. He deceives himself if, seeing the truth, he hates it, despises it; thus Truth deceives no-one'.[43]

The fall of Sauron is in many ways due to his capacity for self-deception. For example, he assumes that Saruman has deceived him by hiding Pippin from him, believing Pippin carries the Ring. Similarly, Saruman is deceived by what he thinks he sees in the palantír: 'the biter bit, the hawk under the eagle's foot, the spider in a steel web', Gandalf says of him (p. 585). Saruman fails to comprehend also that anyone would choose to give up rather than use the

Ring. The opposing side succeeds against him partly through a greater capacity for imagination, and also through understanding how Saruman might reason. And Aragorn in particular makes use of this capacity for self-deception by acting as a bait. First, while still in the travel-worn guise of a ranger, he dons the sword of Elendil and reveals his status as heir of Isildur in the palantír. He aims to strike fear into Sauron by revealing his power and presence. Yet, as he later admits, showing himself in this way might have deflected Sauron's attention from the Ring-bearer. What Aragorn does may have a double function but is not in any sense a lie: it has the flavour of a knightly challenge about it, calling Sauron from his own land.

More akin to beguilement is Aragorn's strategy after the relief of Gondor. The war is not over, and Sauron has huge armies waiting within the walls of Mordor. In council with the other leaders of the free peoples, Aragorn proposes an audacious plan: to call again the eye of Sauron from his own land (and thus from Frodo) by confronting him at his very gates. Gandalf agrees and reveals the element of beguilement: 'We must make ourselves the bait, though his jaws should close on us. He will take that bait, in hope and in greed, for he will think that in such rashness he sees the pride of the new Ringlord, and he will say: "So! He pushes out his neck too soon and too far. Come on, and behold I will have him in a trap from which he cannot escape. There I will crush him, and what he has taken in his insolence shall be mine again for ever"'. (p. 862)

Thus will the beguiler be beguiled because he assumes that it is the power of the Ring that gives Aragorn the courage to confront him. In fact, of course, Aragorn has no Ring. He offers himself and those who choose to come with him sacrificially, to give the quest a chance. As Gandalf continues, 'it may be that we ourselves perish utterly in a blade battle far from the living lands, so that even if Barad-Dûr be thrown down, we shall not live to see a new age. But that, I deem, is our duty' (p. 862).

Sauron is, indeed, tricked by this strategy, but it is not an exact analogy to the Redemption of Christ. Since it is sinful mortals who are the bait there is no 'hook of divinity' here. In that sense there is no trick; they can and may die. But Sauron's own sense of supremacy will again be his undoing. Imrahil laughs as the troops set off: 'So might a child threaten a mail-clad knight with a bow and string of green willow! If the Dark Lord knows so much as you say, Mithrandir, will he not rather smile than fear, and with his little finger crush us like a fly that tries to sting him?' 'No, he will try to trap the fly and take the sting', says Gandalf (p. 864). Sauron wants to possess and spoil, not just kill the enemy. He provides his own beguilement in the form of the mithril-coat of Frodo, which suggests that he already holds him prisoner, and although this daunts the opposition more than he can realize, they hold firm. Sauron rather beguiles himself, because he is unable to conceive of motives and actions of unselfish love and humility. He had not even reckoned with the eagles, whose arrival causes the Nazgûl and their steeds to flee in terror. Yet although the bait at the Black Gates has some effect, it is not 'redemptive' in the manner of Christ's offering of himself, although in combination with the other redemptive actions it aids the overthrow of Sauron in that Age. The fact of the Shire's destruction under Saruman, which happens after the destruction of the Ring and the assaults on Lórien, shows the relativity of victory.

The ending of the novel is equally paradoxical and concerned with the duality of human subjectivity. It presents a mini-apocalypse in the 'Scouring of the Shire' by the returning hobbits, but sets up another series of biblical parallels only to deny them the finality of cosmic battle. Gondor's new tree that gives life to the city has something of the quality of the 'tree of life' in the new heaven and earth of Revelation 21–22; the title of the third volume, 'The Return of the King', has an apocalyptic force, and Aragorn's marriage to Arwen has echoes of the descent of the heavenly bride in Revelation 21. If the rituals of Aragorn's coronation are reminsiscent of Revelation, the scouring of the Shire has something of the quality of the realized eschatology of Jesus's first sermon, when he reads from the scroll in the synagagogue from Isaiah:

> The Spirit of the Lord is upon me,
> because he has anointed me
> to bring good news to the poor.
> He has sent me to proclaim release to the captives
> and recovery of sight to the blind,

to let the oppressed go free,
to proclaim the year of the Lord's favour. (Luke 4.18–19, NRSV)

In a comic mode, each of these actions is embodied in the hobbits' resistance: they free the prisoners, including the redoubtable Lobelia Sackville-Baggins and Fatty Bolger; they liberate the Shire from oppression and reveal the mendacity and double-speak of 'Sharkey' and his hobbit collaborators. 'The year of the Lord's favour' in Christ's speech refers to the Biblical concept of the Jubilee of Leviticus 25, a sabbath of sabbaths after 49 years, when a ram's horn was blown like Merry's horn, debts were to be cancelled and land brought back to God's ownership. There should be no work in Jubilee year but rather an endless harvest festival, which is what happens in the Shire in 1420, when there are miraculous harvests of corn, strawberries and golden-haired children.

The purpose of this implicit use of eschatological models is again to be thought of paradoxically. Although Aragorn's accession has strong echoes of Revelation, it is only historical and mortal, not immortal and divine. Indeed, Gondor has a certain hubristic quality in its aims to perfection and its attempt to reproduce Valinor in its centring itself around the tree, which derives its origin from the original two trees. Although the discovery of a new sapling introduces a note of hope for the future, the appendices continue Gondor's history into a time that falls away from the justice and peace of Aragorn's reign. The Shire does indeed continue in sleepy security after the expulsion of Saruman and death of Lotho and the miraculous fertility produced by Galadriel's gift of soil, but it has no place to offer Frodo, who is, like Christ after the sermon quoted above, dishonoured in his own country.

The ending of the novel is similarly ambiguous and something of a riddle. The majority of the major characters of the novel – Gandalf, Galadriel, Elrond, Bilbo and Frodo (and later also Legolas and Gimli) – sail for the Blessed Realm, while Sam, Merry and Pippin are left behind. Sam voices the reader's disquiet at this, when he realizes the goal of his mysterious journey with Frodo to be the Grey Havens: ' "And can't I come?" "No, Sam. Not yet anyway, not further than the Havens. Though you were a Ring-Bearer, if only for a little while. Your time may come. Do not be too sad, Sam. You cannot be always torn in two. You will have to be one and whole, for many years. You have so much to enjoy"' (p. 106).

The reader has, to some extent, been prepared for this separation. First, by the knowledge of the trajectory of the elves away from Middle-earth, and secondly by the distantiation of any characters except hobbits from the scouring of the Shire. Frodo was passive throughout that sequence of events, intervening only to advise against violent revenge. Elves and wizards have begun to retreat into the world of legend, like the monsters and ogres of the hymn: 'Though backward to storyland giants have fled/And the knights are no more, and the dragons are dead'.[44]

To make the separation keener, however, the reader is taken, through Frodo's consciousness, to the very border of the Blessed Realm, as he 'smelled a sweet fragrance on the air and heard the sound of singing that came over the water. And then it seemed to him that as in his dream in the house of Tom Bombadil, the grey rain-curtain turned all to silver glass and was rolled back, and he beheld white shores and beyond them a far green country under a swift sunrise' (p. 1007).

The entry to the divine land is rendered kinaesthetically, to bring the reader close to the experience, even to the extent of sharing the transition from natural (rain) to supernatural (glass that can 'roll back'). With the phrase, 'swift sunrise', however, the scene is whisked away from the reader's grasp as what had seemed a picture takes on agency and disappears. With Sam, the reader is left in view of only 'a shadow on the waters'. Sam returns and the novel ends with him also in the light: 'And he went on, and there was yellow light, and fire within, and the evening meal was ready, and he was expected. And Rose drew him in, and set him in his chair, and put little Elanor upon his lap.

He drew a deep breath. "Well, I'm back," he said' (p. 1008). Here too there is sight, sound and even smell in the propinquity of his supper. But although Sam's return to the family triad may be the instantiation of his being one and not two selves, as Frodo hopes, the reader is left with a double ending and a sense of dis-ease. The ending remains something of a riddle to be solved: indeed, Sam in his chair with the child resembles the answer to one of those puzzles like that which Bilbo set Gollum: 'No-legs lay on one-leg, two-legs sat near on three-legs, four-legs got some' (p. 72).

The main problem for the reader is how to separate in his or her mind two characters who have been a pair all through the novel, and who belong together. Despite his marriage, parenthood and obvious delight in Shire life, Sam is incomplete without Frodo, and Frodo an attenuated presence without Sam's earthiness. It is partly a problem of analogy, with Sam the 'answer' or common feature that unites Blessed Realm and Shire. It is in this context that the purpose of the eschatological parallels is made evident. Tolkien does not suggest both apocalyptic millennium in Aragorn's reign and realized eschatology in the Shire merely to show the limits of human attempts at inaugurating divine justice and human flourishing. They also prepare and precipitate the unease deliberately created by the double ending of the novel. The end of the world predicted by Christ and by the book of Revelation did not come, although it was inaugurated by Christ's resurrection. The problem of the believer in the time between was already an issue for St Paul in 1 Corinthians 15, where he laid out his belief in the resurrection of the dead. Tolkien, in his essay 'On Fairy-Stories' refers to this as the 'Great Eucatastrophe', when all our bodiliness shall share in some sense with our spirit – our Sam with our Frodo side. For Frodo hardly seems to have a body at all in the later parts of *The Lord of the Rings*, and even his pains back home in the Shire have a spiritual basis. Sam, on the contrary, is not just a reassuring physical presence but an active agent in the rebuilding of his community, and in forming human relationships. The true happy ending of the novel lies beyond the pages of the book, and yet is anticipated in moments such as Sam and Frodo's descent from Mount Doom, when Sam, a true Bunyanesque 'Hopeful', leads the lost and broken Frodo to safety, just as he had borne both Frodo and the Ring up to the summit, and found the burden surprisingly light. Sam is not to be reduced to an allegory of the body, for he is much more than that, but the separation of the two at the Grey Havens is emblematic of the sorrow of the separation of soul and body at death, while their solidarity gives a taste of the ecstatic reunion of soul and body at the Resurrection.

So the reader at the end of *The Lord of the Rings* 'solves' the riddle of their identity and separate *teloi* by an act of anagogical interpretation. In the four levels of scriptural interpretation outlined by Aquinas, and common to much patristic and medieval biblical interpretation – the literal, the allegorical (referring to Christ), the moral or tropological (applying the benefits to the soul) and the anagogical – the last meant reading the text in the light of the last things.[45] Tolkien's celebration of the 'sudden joyous turn' of a fairytale was not so much a realist trope of events turning out well as an anagogical anticipation of the Last Judgement. At the end of *The Lord of the Rings* it is up to the reader to hold the natural and supernatural ends of the characters together. And our own desire for a reunion of the characters beyond the separations of the last chapter is to provoke in us a longing for a happy ending that does not negate but fulfils the 'natural desire for the supernatural' that both Augustine and Aquinas taught, and which is most famously expressed by the former's *Confessions:* 'our hearts are restless until they rest in You'.[46] Tolkien goes even further than Augustine's autobiography that describes a soul yearning for the divine, by making his reader *perform* this desire for the transcendent, although in some cases – indeed many – the reader may not know what he or she longs for. In his *Feast of Creatures*, Craig Williamson describes riddling thus: 'the riddler invites us to witness a lyric epiphany as we see the world of our own shaping and realize that flesh is spirit embodied; spirit, symbolising flesh'.[47] To understand the answer to a riddle is to recreate the world anew, and thus to participate in the creation of meaning; and equally it is to allow the world of phenomena a subjectivity and otherness. Yet this recreation is also, in some sense, anagogical, in that the object is separated and the image 'dies', only to be resurrected in glory and in participation. Chesterton gives us a vision of the created order 'resurrected' in his dance at Sunday's house at the end of *The Man Who Was Thursday*, which is the resolution to the series of nonsensical riddles and answers left as he bounced before them by elephant and air-balloon. Yet the vison explodes as a 'nightmare', and it is up to the reader to work out how to hold together the natural and supernatural worlds. Tolkien too leaves us within the paradoxical, with the epiphany to work out for ourselves.

PARADOX AND RIDDLES

Both writers are sometimes accused of too easy a faith and too nostalgic a vision of the good. But in fact, they take their readers deep into the darkness and duality of the paradoxical, and the inability of the world to save itself.

Notes

1. Chesterton, 'The Happy Man', in *The Collected Poems*, p. 295.
2. Quoted in Kenner, *Paradox in Chesterton*, p. 15.
3. Kenner, *Paradox in Chesterton*, p. 41.
4. G. K. Chesterton, 'On Evil Euphemisms,' in *Come to Think of It* (London: Methuen, 1930), pp. 109–13 (109).
5. Oscar Wilde, *The Importance of Being Ernest*, Act 1, in *Complete Plays of Oscar Wilde*, intro. Tyrone Guthrie (London: Collins, 1965), pp. 21, 25.
6. G. K. Chesterton, 'A Ballade of Theatricals' (1912), accessed at *G. K. Chesterton's Works on the Web*, ed. Martin Ward at http://www.cse.dmu.ac.uk/~mward/gkc/books/titanicGKC.html (accessed 28 February 2007).
7. G. K. Chesterton, *The Secret of Father Brown* (Harmondsworth: Penguin, 1974), p. 171.
8. G. K. Chesterton, *Tales of the Long Bow* (London: Cassell, 1925).
9. T. S. Eliot, *The Complete Poems and Plays, 1909–1950* (London: Faber, 1980), p. 44.
10. G. K. Chesterton, *Heretics* (London: John Lane, 1905), p. 82.
11. Aquinas, *Summa Theologica*, 1a, q. 13, 5, p. 159.
12. Kenner, *Paradox in Chesterton*, p. 28.
13. Aquinas, *Summa Theologica*, 1a, q. 13, 5–7, pp. 158–68.
14. Kenner, *Paradox in Chesterton*, p. 20.
15. Kenner, *Paradox in Chesterton*, p. 21.
16. Chesterton, 'The Invisible Man', in *The Innocence of Father Brown*, p. 108.
17. Chesterton, *The Innocence of Father Brown*, p. 111.
18. Chesterton, *The Secret of Father Brown*, p. 50.
19. G. K. Chesterton, *The Everlasting Man* (San Francisco: Ignatius Press, 1993), p. 36.
20. G. K. Chesterton, *Orthodoxy*, p. 273.
21. The Chesterton Institute owns the copy of Lodge's *Substance of Faith Allied with Science: A Catechism For Parents and Teachers* (London: Methuen, 1905?), which is annotated by Chesterton. It was obviously important in his working out of the argument of the last chapter of *Orthodoxy*. He answers every one of the catechism questions, sometimes sarcastically – 'what is to be said of man's higher faculties?' 'as

little as possible' – but often seriously – 'What is meant by the Kingdom of Heaven?' 'The Republic of Earth among other things.' His own three questions have aspects of the argument of 'The Ethics of Elfland', for example, 'Q. Why can't pigs fly? A. I don't know that they can't. They don't. I don't know why'.

22. *The Hegel Reader*, ed. Stephen Houlgate (Oxford: Blackwell, 1998), p. 453.
23. Chesterton, *The Ball and the Cross*, p. 178.
24. Chesterton, *The Secret of Father Brown*, p. 170.
25. Chesterton, *The Secret of Father Brown*, pp. 171–2.
26. See Shippey, *The Road to Middle-earth*, Appendix A. for Tolkien's riddle sources, pp. 221–2. *The Exeter Book Riddles*, ed. Kevin Crossley-Holland (Harmondsworth: Penguin, 1978) is also a source for Bilbo's contest.
27. Tolkien, *The Hobbit*, p. 69.
28. Tolkien, *The Hobbit*, p. 71.
29. Shippey, *The Road to Middle-earth*, chapter 3, pp. 43–72 has this title.
30. Eleanor Cook, *Enigmas and Riddles in Literature* (Cambridge: Cambridge University Press, 2006), pp. 245–6. Cook cites Vernant and Detienne's study of 'metis' intelligence, *Cunning Intelligence in Greek Culture and Society* (Chicago: Chicago University Press, 1991) as associating Hermes-like trickster intelligence with riddling. It suggests a doubleness in both puzzle and puzzler.
31. Tolkien, *The Hobbit*, p. 190.
32. Tolkien, *The Hobbit*, p. 253.
33. Two of the more careful religious and Christological readings are Caldecott, *Secret Fire: The Spiritual Vision of J. R. R. Tolkien*, pp. 34–5; and Ralph C. Wood, *The Gospel According to Tolkien: Visions of the Kingdom in Middle-earth* (Louisville KY: Westminster John Knox Press, 2003).
34. Hans Frei, 'Theological Reflections on the Accounts of Jesus's Death and Resurrection', in *Theology and Narrative: Selected Essays*, ed. George Hunsinger and William C. Placher (Oxford: Oxford University Press, 1993), pp. 45–93.
35. William Blake, *Songs of Innocence and Experience*, ed. Geoffrey Keynes (Oxford and Paris: Oxford University Press and Trianon Press, 1975), p. 47.
36. Chesterton, *Orthodoxy*, p. 153.
37. Anselm, *Complete Philosophical and Theological Treatises*, trans. Jasper Hopkins and Herbert Richardson (Minneapolis: Arthur J. Banning Press, 2000), p. 419.
38. George MacDonald, *Phantastes and Lilith*, intro. C. S. Lewis (London: Gollancz, 1962), p. 386.
39. Venantius Fortunatus, 'Sing, my tongue, the glorious battle', in *The English Hymnal*, no. 95, pp. 78–9.
40. Gregory of Nyssa, 'The Great Catechism,' in *A Select Library of Nicene and Ante-Nicene Fathers of the Christian Church*, (Edinburgh: T & T Clark, 1994) vol. V,

p. 49: 'The deity was hidden under the veil of our nature, that so, as with ravenous fish, the hook of the Deity might be gulped along with the bait of flesh, and thus, life being introduced into the house of death, and light shining in darkness, that which is diametrically opposed to light and life might vanish'.

41. St Augustine, 'Sermon LXXX [cxxx]' in *A Select Library of Nicene and Post-Nicene Fathers of the Christian Church*, ed. Philip Schaff *et. al.* (Edinburgh: T & T Clark, 1996), p. 499.

42. See the discussion in Giles Gasper, *Anselm of Canterbury and His Theological Inheritance* (London: Ashgate, 2004), p. 165.

43. Anselm, *Cur Deus Homo* (London: Griffith, Farran, Okeden & Welsh, 1933), p. 11.

44. Jan Struther, 'When a knight won his spurs in the stories of old', *Songs of Praise* (Oxford: Oxford University Press, 1931), no. 354.

45. See Henri de Lubac, *Medieval Exegesis: The Four Senses of Scripture*, trans. Mark Sebanc, ed. Robert Louis Wilken (2 vols, Ressourcement: Retrieval and Renewal in Catholic Thought; Grand Rapids MI: Eerdmans, 1998).

46. Augustine, *Confessions*, trans. Henry Chadwick (Oxford: Oxford University Press, 1991), p. 3.

47. Craig Williamson, *A Feast of Creatures: Anglo-Saxon Riddle Songs* (Philadelphia: University of Pennsylvania Press, 1982), p. 36.

PART 2: PRAXIS

CHAPTER 4

FAIRY ECONOMICS: GIFT-EXCHANGE

Can I thank no one for the birthday present of birth?[1]

IN BIDDING FAREWELL to the fairies, Bishop Corbett's poem 'The Fairies' Farewell' that forms the epigraph to the Introduction to this book says goodbye also to their rewards – 'Yet who of late for cleanness,/Finds sixpence in her shoe?' For fairy presence almost invariably involves the bestowal of fairy gifts. I can state this with some confidence because the indefatigable analyst of the folk-tale structure, Vladimir Propp, includes the role of donor among the seven 'spheres of action' that drive the plots, while for A. J. Greimas exchange is one of the folk-tale's three possible narrative patterns.[2] Furthermore, these donors are frequently mysterious if they are not actually supernatural, as for example the wise women called to Sleeping Beauty's christening, or the aged crone who gives a cloak of invisibility to the suitor in the story of the twelve dancing princesses. Even seemingly commercial exchanges between fairy and human, such as Rumpelstiltskin's bargain with the miller's daughter or the magic beans exchanged by Jack for his mother's last cow have something incommensurable about them that reveals they do not really belong to the world of commerce and the 'free' market. Jack's beans are both ridiculous return for a substantially valuable commodity and then, after the beanstalk grows overnight, ridiculously 'other' in the sense that there is no way that the exchange is appropriate. In the case of Rumpelstiltskin's offer to spin straw into gold, the bargain begins in the language of giving – 'What will you give me if I spin it for you?' – appears to modulate to an economic contract with the handing over of a necklace and then a ring, but finally becomes a form of sacrifice as the firstborn son is pledged. These two tales describe the positive and negative poles of Propp's 'donor' function and reveal that to receive an object from a fairy source is to enter into a relation with the fairy-world that will involve some return. Even in fairyland there is no such thing as a free gift.

In our own world we too expect some return. For us gift-giving belongs to the private realm: we take off the price tag and wrap a commodity in tissue paper to remove it from the world of market-value and exchange; we turn it into a present, and thus restore it to the sacred: we enchant it, as it were. We strive to unite our taste with the character, desires and needs of the recipient so that a union may ensue between giver, gift and recipient. And as we give, so an expectation of receiving accompanies the gift, as the whole system of the exchanging of Christmas cards in our culture demonstrates. In 1925 Marcel Mauss, a French sociologist and nephew of the great Emile Durkheim, published a slender volume, *Essai sur le don* (*The Gift*), which argued that gift-giving in a number of pre-capitalist cultures in the past and the non-western present was not spontaneous archaic generosity but an alternative social and economic system. Mauss identified three parts to the system: giving, receiving and reciprocating, so that an obligation to give back was conferred on the receiver.

After Mauss, a flood of anthropological studies confirmed his findings. For as Christian belief and practice in the west declined, especially after the acceptance of Darwinian evolutionary theory, new universalizing explanations of human behaviour were needed. From the Enlightenment onwards sacrifice had been seen as central to all human cultures and religions, culminating in James Frazer's monumental study, *The Golden Bough*, in which the sacrifice of the priest/king to fertilize the soil was given in countless examples and seen as ubiquitous. (And, indeed, it would be easy to propound a Frazerian reading of *The Lord of the Rings*.) Mauss himself contributed to the sacrifice debate in 1898 in a work co-authored with Henri Hubert, arguing for a functionalist interpretation of sacrifice as the moving of the sacrifier from the profane to the sacred by means of the sacrificial object or person. Even there, in his model of *do ut des* (I give in order that you may give) an implicit reciprocity is being established.

What challenged the hegemony of sacrifice, in my view, was the experience of World War I, in which sacrificial theory became all too vividly realized in the carnage of youth. Mauss was a combatant and one of only a few of the Durkheimian school to survive the fighting. He saw his work on the gift as rendering some return to his friends' self-giving. As we know from John Garth's book *Tolkien and the Great War*, Tolkien too lost several members of his literary fellowship, and felt that he must be responsible for continuing their common project.[3] Indeed, one might develop this argument in relation to other members of the later Inklings group, especially Charles Williams, whose theology of reciprocal exchange was the result of supernatural visions of his fallen co-workers at the Oxford University Press.[4] Mauss, like Tolkien, was greatly influenced by Nordic culture and his gift essay draws on the collection of ancient Norse literature, the *Edda*, for its opening epigraph: 'a gift always looks for recompense'.[5] In the body of the work Mauss cites Germanic culture as an example of the preservation of gift-exchange 'to an extreme degree', through pledge, hostage, feast and other gifts.[6] And his highly influential (though now thought misleading) philological work deriving the double meaning of gift as both positive and negative from the Greek word for poison, also originated in his reading of the *Edda*.[7]

While anthropologists and ethnographers went quietly on their way attending to specific social instantiations of gift-exchange, cultural theorists pounced upon the idea for their own purposes. For Georges Bataille, gift theory restored life to the gifted object, and opposed the calculated nature of market relations in favour of an economics of excess.[8] He was drawn especially to Mauss's (again misleading, as later research has shown) description of the Native American potlatch in which excessive gift-giving and reciprocation led to the destruction of a tribe's whole possessions. For Jacques

Derrida, although a pure gift is impossible, it still points towards the idea of an excess that resists,[9] while for many unhappy with the alienated nature of modern capitalism gift-exchange offers a model of a more humane economic system that restores the links between producers and consumers, whereas capitalism turns objects into commodities, workers into 'hands' and instrumentalizes both. (A clear example of this in *The Lord of the Rings* is Saruman's dehumanizing treatment of his workers, who march under his 'hand' emblem.) Gift-exchange belongs to cultures in which the now 'dead' commodity is still alive, and the modern atomized individual a person is defined by webs of complex relations in which acts of exchange have sacred and peaceable value. So the attention of theorists from Pierre Bourdieu to Jean Baudrillard, despite their vaunted post-modernity, is at once nostalgic and utopian, even when they seek to emphasize the sometimes oppressive power relations that accompany gift-exchange.

We have come a long way from the fairy-tales with which I began this chapter, but this excursus into gift-exchange theory illuminates their function as told and then collected by the brothers Grimm and others on the cusp of the industrial and capitalist age. We can see how they embody and explore older economic relations and their dangers as well as their benefits. Rumpelstiltskin, for example, represents the ancient idea of pledge itself, which was usually embodied in the form of a divided document or coin. As he expresses his rage at the Queen's discovery of his name: 'in his fury he seized his left foot with both hands and tore himself in two right down the middle'. This act ends the tale and seems to deal in satisfactorily permanent fashion with the devilish goblin but it also establishes the permanence of the intertwining of human and fairy worlds in the story of a wealth built on supernatural gold. They are still within what Tolkien called 'the perilous realm' of faërie. As I come to discuss the use of fairy gifts in Chesterton and Tolkien we shall see that the former stresses the positive nature of the gift in his fiction and theological writing, while Tolkien gives us both poles of the gift, as reciprocity and as poison, probably because of his greater interest in Nordic mythology and, as will be argued below, its ethnography.

FAIRY ECONOMICS

As we have seen, 'The Ethics of Elfland' is a personal form of natural theology that seeks to show how Chesterton's experience of the world of phenomena itself drew him to belief in God. In that world the fairy-tale is his equivalent of the Old Testament, or rather his Virgilian prophecy because the Roman poet was read allegorically in the Middle Ages as writing a form of pagan scripture that could be used to point to the coming of Christ. If this seems bizarre, it is not unique, as modern proponents of Hasidic folk-tales also make the claim for reading them on the different levels by which scripture was interpreted in medieval times: the allegorical, the moral, the literal and the anagogical. What is unusual about Chesterton's project in *Orthodoxy* is that he seeks to establish a natural philosophical theology in the modern period. Ideas like that of the great 'Chain of Being' looked odd in the light of Darwinian theories of natural selection. Fairy-tales, however, are not natural but cultural productions and it is by means of these fictions that Chesterton comes to view the world itself as magical: utterly real and enchanted at one and the same time. As we have seen in the first part of this book, the fairy-tale first estranges us from the familiar, second engages us in that alienation with fear and the grotesque, third restores us to the real by enchantment but fourth, it allows us to receive the world back as a gift. 'The wonder', Chesterton writes, 'has a positive element of praise', and he goes on to elaborate: 'the goodness of a fairy tale was not affected by the fact that there might be more dragons than princesses; it was good to be in a fairy tale. The test of all happiness is gratitude, and I felt grateful, though I hardly knew to whom'.[10]

Life for Chesterton is to be received as a present precisely because it is not formless but a work of art; existence is a narrative like a fairy-story to be received as the literal birthday gift. 'Children are grateful when Santa Claus puts in their stockings gifts of toys or sweets. Could I not be grateful to Santa Claus when he put in my stockings the gift of two legs?' In invoking the fictional Father Christmas as an analogy for God, Chesterton seems to be on dangerous ground but it is typical of his audacity to use our cultural memory in order to arrive at belief in the divine, as we shall see in the next chapter. For why do we predicate a gift-giver? Why not just pass the gift from hand to hand? The reason, I believe, is that we need a third term in the act of exchange to render it meaningful and sacred. The whole system of gift-exchange whether in contemporary capitalist Britain or ancient Polynesia requires a transcendent that will be guarantor of the value of the gift. So it is no accident that our cultivation in our children of belief in Father Christmas goes on apace in a secularized world because without him our gift-giving would be revealed as the dreary manipulation of commodities that it so often really is. And it does not matter whether the spangled figure atop the Christmas tree is a fairy or an angel, because her role is in either case one of mediator and guarantor, whose role is to sanctify the presents stacked beneath the branches.

Chesterton's Elfland essay does not spell out his gift theology in any detail, but a reader of his various fantasies will encounter a number of works that seek to provoke this sense of the gifted and thus religious nature of existence. The pub sign in *The Flying Inn* (1914) becomes an image of sociality and pure reciprocity in a novel that describes an England turning towards puritanical prohibition and Islamicization. Beer is freely given under the inn sign from what appears to be a Cana-like never-emptied barrel as the sale of alcoholic drinks is forbidden. *Manalive* presents us with Innocent Smith, who burgles his own house, nearly kills a Cambridge college warden with a pistol and marries his own wife time and again so as to receive his own life back as a present. Again he follows the poetics I have outlined in this book: Innocent distances himself from his normal life, renders that distance grotesque through the extremity of his gestures, provides a riddle that is almost impossible to interpret but when the truth is revealed it demystifies the 'magic' of the medical and other experts who put him to a mock-trial. And once the paradox of his actions is explained the world is no less 'enchanted' but even more so.

Tolkien too seems to be reaching for a similar 'gifted' sense of enchantment in his discussion of the happy ending in his 'On Fairy-Stories' essay, in which he is anxious to prove that the 'happy ever after' of the form's conclusion is not a bland and easy tying up of narrative threads but a sudden turn, a surprise, to which he gives the name *eucatastrophe*:

FAIRY ECONOMICS

> This joy, which is one of the things which fairy-stories can produce supremely well, is not essentially 'escapist', nor 'fugitive'. In its fairy-tale – or otherworld – setting, it is a sudden and miraculous grace: never to be counted on to recur. It does not deny the existence of dyscatastrophe, of sorrow and failure: the possibility of these is necessary to the joy of deliverance; it denies, (in the face of much evidence, if you will) universal final defeat and in so far is *evangelium*, giving a fleeting instance of Joy, Joy beyond the walls of the world, poignant as grief.[11]

This emphasis on a happiness that breaks in from without like any catastrophe renders the ending an act of divine grace and therefore a gift rather than a wage fairly earned, even though it may have the poetic justice of the fairy reward. Tolkien stages these moments of eucatastrophe most effectively in the third volume of *The Lord of the Rings*: first, as Gollum's act of snatching the Ring achieves what Frodo could not; second, as Gandalf cries amid the carnage at the field of Cormallen: 'the Eagles are coming!' like the watchman of the city in Isaiah's prophecy; and third, as the effect of Sauron's fall reaches Faramir and Éowyn in the House of Healing:

> And so they stood on the walls of the City of Gondor, and a great wind rose and blew, and their hair, raven and golden, streamed out mingling in the air. And the Shadow departed, and the Sun was unveiled, and light leaped forth; and the waters of Anduin shone like silver, and in all the houses of the City men sang for the joy that welled up in their hearts from what source they could not tell. (pp. 941–2)

This last example is particularly apposite because it includes both the element of action from without as well as participation from below, so the lovers' hair moves in the wind, the sun leaps and the citizens sing despite their ignorance of why they are happy. For it is crucial to this conception of the religious nature of the happy ending that it is *both* God's gift but also a present that enables the real, the phenomenal world, to respond: to be itself. It is no accident that the date of these three events is 25 March, the feast of the Annunciation, the day when the Angel Gabriel announced the good news (the *evangelium*) of Christ's birth to Mary. She receives the gift of Christ conceived within her but her response is necessary also. In medieval churches one often sees images or paintings of Gabriel and Mary on opposite sides of the reredos or the east window, as if to emphasize the co-operation of angelic and human creations in inaugurating the Incarnation. Our eyes move from one figure to the other as we too join in this act of creative participation in God's gift of himself to us, as our act of vision draws together earth and heaven. The Orthodox prayer for vespers of Christmas Day embodies all that I have been saying:

> What shall we offer Thee, O Christ,
> Who for our sake was seen on earth as man?
> For every thing created by Thee offers Thee thanks.
> The angels offer Thee their hymn;
> The heavens, the star;
> The Magi, their gifts;
> The shepherds, their wonder;
> The earth, the cave;
> The wilderness, the manger;
> While we offer Thee a Virgin Mother,
> O pre-eternal God, have mercy upon us.[12]

This prayer stresses the co-operation of the whole cosmos, even the earth itself in the reception of the Christchild and is in accord with Tolkien's conception of the natural world as having its part to play in the redemption of Middle-earth from Sauron's and Saruman's possession. Chesterton too has a concept of reciprocity in the acceptance of the divine gift, as is shown most clearly in the astonishing last chapters of his fantastic novel *The Man Who Was Thursday*, written around the same time as *Orthodoxy*. Beginning as a social comedy, quickly the tale modulates into a spy thriller as the policeman protagonist gets himself elected to a secret anarchist council. Disguise after disguise is unmasked until what turn out to be six policemen/anarchists chase after the demonic revolutionary chief Sunday through the length and breadth of London and beyond until he eludes them by taking off in a balloon. Tracking him across country, the policemen suddenly find themselves in a fairy-tale world of waiting carriages, suites of luxurious rooms with costumes ready for their use, cold pheasant and a fancy-dress ball, and most bizarre of all: Sunday as himself the police chief who had sent them all off to fight the anarchists. The turn is one of the most sudden in all literature, with ragged and defeated protagonists all at once becoming princes – and actual days – of creation, like a child's fantasy of royal birth coming true. The extremity of the transition is necessary, however, to maintain the sense of the ending as coming from without and as a gift, even though the identity of the policemen as the six days of creation in Genesis 1 serves also to make them participants in the gift. The men believed themselves partial inventors of the reality of the anarchist league itself through their disguises and spying activities, but the ending renders them co-creators in a more important sense. As Syme, or Thursday, reawakens from what proves to be a dream, he does not leave it behind as a pleasant fantasy or horrid nightmare but 'felt he was in possession of some impossible good news'.[13] The good news is the *evangelium* of Tolkien's *eucatastrophe*, and the very excess of the story validates its status as divine gift.

Lewis Hyde made a study of the gift in relation to artistic production in which he argued that the artist manages to make his work more than a commodity by means of excess: he both accepts that his art is itself a gift from without, and he passes on his skill and 'the spirit of the gift' by the excessive, indeed sacrificial, nature of his artistic production.[14] The torrents of word-play and dizzying twists of plot and expectation are Chesterton's method of gift-exchange that calls the reader into a relation with him reminiscent of the *Crackerjack* television game of my own childhood, in which a young contestant's arms were loaded with prize after prize until he disappeared under the collapsing pile. Chesterton's writing has something of this almost overwhelming character, but it always requires the reader's participation: like Father Christmas, whom Chesterton resembled both spiritually and physically, he needs the co-creation of our imaginative response to solve his mysteries, and to hold together his paradoxes in the manner of the child's belief in Santa Claus despite the ubiquity and synchronicity of his presence in a variety of department stores, or his ability to enter chimneyless houses. Tolkien too perceived his own writing as a form of gift, as he wrote in a famous letter to Milton Waldman:

> Do not laugh! But once upon a time (my crest has long since fallen) I had in mind to make a body of more or less connected legend . . . which I could dedicate simply to England; to my country. . . . I would draw some of the great tales in fullness, and leave many only placed in the scheme, and sketched. The cycles should be linked to a majestic whole, and yet leave scope for other minds and hands, wielding paint and music and drama. Absurd.
> Of course, such an overweening purpose did not develop all at once. The mere stories were the thing. They arose in my mind as 'given' things, and as they came, separately, so too the links grew.[15]

This letter is celebrated as a manifesto of Tolkien's overall purpose in writing *The Lord of the Rings* and *The Silmarillion*, but less attention has been paid to the language he uses to express his desire: the words 'dedicate' and 'given' alert one to the nature of his work as a present, both as something with which he himself has been gifted, as the stories come from without, and as something not to be hoarded as a dead piece of tradition but as material to be reworked by other hands. The stories are like fairy gold, which is a blessing and even increases as it is freely passed along, but when hoarded turns to pitch.

Tolkien explores the gifted nature of artistic production in 'Leaf by Niggle', in which, as I rehearsed earlier, the unfortunate Niggle is constantly interrupted by the needs of his neighbours and fails to complete his painting of a tree. In the afterlife, he encounters the vision he had failed to accomplish:

> Before him stood the Tree, his Tree, finished. If you could say that of a Tree that was alive, its leaves opening, its branches growing and bending in the wind that Niggle had so often felt or guessed, and had so often failed to catch. He gazed at the Tree, and slowly he lifted his arms and opened them wide.
> 'It's a gift!' he said. He was referring to his art, and also to the result; but he was using the word quite literally.[16]

It is no accident that Niggle's subject is a tree because trees have been emblematic of the divine gift right back to the Garden of Eden and its Tree of Life, and Tolkien makes trees central to the origin of his own cosmos in the golden and silver lights of Laurelin and Telperion that lit the land of the Valar. The descendant of those trees is found by Gandalf blooming on the barren mountain outside Gondor at the end of *The Return of the King*. Its miraculous arrival as replacement for the dead tree in the palace courtyard was compared in the last chapter to the descent of the heavenly city with its tree of life in Revelation 21 and 22. There the New Jerusalem comes down like a bride in the wedding procession to inaugurate a new age of union between earth and heaven as a pure *gift* from God, and this tree similarly is a sign of divine presence in Aragorn's renewed Gondor. Making trees divine gifts ensures that we treat them with respect and not as possessions or dead objects to use as we wish.

There is more, however, to Tolkien's use of the gift than a theology of God the giver of all good things, and creation as a gift. Gift-exchange forms the basis of the novel's attempt to resist the power of the Ring, just as the Ring itself is the result of gift-exchange gone awry. For Tolkien's interest in gift is the means by which he approaches social ethics. While Tolkien's political views do not easily correspond to any political party of his day, as a devout Catholic with his own ethnological interests Tolkien in his fiction can be seen as seeking a more humane, less alienated form of sociality in the manner of Catholic social teaching of the early twentieth century, and its emphasis on a middle way between capitalism and communism. G. K. Chesterton and Hilaire Belloc developed these ideas as distributism, whereby land is redistributed and restored to all as smallholders, so that property lies in real material things for use and enjoyment, rather than in the form of abstract money. The basis for their movement was the encyclical, *Rerum Novarum*, and statements such as the following: 'the law, therefore, should favour ownership and its policy should be to induce as many people as possible to become owners . . . If workpeople can be encouraged to look forward to obtaining a share in the land, the result will be that the gulf between vast wealth and deep poverty will be bridged over, and the two orders brought closer together'.[17] Although distributism died as a political creed (partly through disputes about whether machinery should be allowed at all), its spirit lives on in localized responses to globalization such as the slow food movement, farmers markets and back-to-the-land developments. The Catholic project of a third way drives papal social teaching to this day and makes the theology of gift central to European Catholic thought. Distributism meant that everyone would have property, and therefore acts of exchange of real things were possible, which one might see as having something of a reciprocal nature, and as therefore much closer to gift-exchange than the capitalist economic system.

So it would not be surprising if Tolkien were drawn to explore alternative economic modes such as gift-exchange in his imaginative creations. The Shire in particular, while having employees, seems to allow its people some land for the odd cow or pig and the appearance of Hobbiton bears some resemblance to the interwoven village, field and homestead pattern that can still be seen today at Laxton in Nottinghamshire, where the old fieldstrip system that allowed country people to be partially independent of a cash economy still survives in a modified form.

And while it is unlikely that Tolkien read Mauss on the gift, he had direct and frequent recourse to Mauss's raw material in the sagas and myths that show gift-exchange in action both between humans and between gods and men. In the Anglo-Saxon poem *Beowulf*, for example, the question of the validity of gift-exchange is central to the poem, as recent scholars such as Robert Bjork have shown.[18] The centrality of the topic is evident even on a general reading, with Hrothgar, a kingly giver, rewarding Beowulf with golden arm-rings and other treasures for his destruction of the monster Grendel in Part I, and cementing with these gifts relations between their two societies. In Part II, the paucity of gift-giving scenes is evidence of a breakdown of ritual gift-exchange and thus a disintegration of Geat society itself, and the rites of the mead hall (the *meduseld*) are lost. An imitation of this breakdown is given by Tolkien in the scenes in the Edoras hall, also named Meduseld, in *The Lord of the Rings*. Language too is a gift-object in Anglo-Saxon culture, in which words are a form of deed, so that Wormtongue's perversion of speech prevents all forms of exchange and prevents the king from performing his role as gift-giver, illustrated by Théoden's failure to give Shadowfax to Gandalf, or keep his word to Gondor. Like Beowulf sacrificing himself to destroy Grendel's mother, Théoden has to restore the gift economy by becoming a gift himself in his heroic charge against the hosts of Mordor at the Battle of the Pelennor Fields, in which he gives his life.

There is, however, another possible source for Tolkien's knowledge of gift theory: *The Culture of the Teutons* (1909–12) by the Danish scholar Vilhelm Grönbech. Writing over ten years before Mauss, Grönbech identified and analysed the structure of gift-exchange, pledge and bargain in ancient Germanic and Nordic societies. Tolkien knew Danish, and was an admirer of the theologian Gruntvig, the Danish Grimm, so that he is likely to have come across *Culture of the Teutons* in his student years. It might also have been shown to him by his friend C. S. Lewis, a fellow admirer of Nordic culture and literature, with whom Tolkien met to declaim Anglo-Saxon verse and Icelandic sagas aloud.

For *The Lord of the Rings*, one of Grönbech's assertions is particularly germane: like the rewards of the fairies, gifts in Teutonic society were never free because they came with an obligation to receive and reciprocate. 'The receiver', he writes, 'is in the giver's power'.[19] Although this is something Mauss does assert and uses it to prove the competitive nature of gift-exchange, the ethically dangerous aspect of gift reception is stressed more strongly in Grönbech. Gifts are perilous to a person's soul or honour unless the recipient is ready to 'mingle . . . mind with the giver'.[20] To accept a gift is to join 'a mesh of obligations so strong that the whole state is moved if but one other point of the chain be properly grasped'.[21] This understanding of gift-exchange explains the significance of accepting a ring from Sauron. He named himself Annatar, 'Lord of Gifts', and used the rings he gave out to establish chains of domination and control.[22] Unlike the public nature of Hrothgar's gifts in *Beowulf* that unite two societies in peaceable and open connection, Sauron's gifts hide the actual assertion of complete control under a show of generosity. This is in harmony with Grönbech's insight that gift-giving can reveal or conceal the agonistic power in the social order. Its complexity and social interweaving, however, renders it unstable, which again makes sense of the way in which the Ring of Power is both utterly overwhelming in its effect on its recipient, but also revealing of Sauron's vulnerability. Once this tiny object falls into the Crack of Doom, Sauron's empire collapses.

The primary evidence for Tolkien's interest in gift-theory, as my example above indicates, is in his fictions themselves, from the opening chapter of *The Silmarillion*, in which the musical themes for the creation are the gift of Ilúvatar to the Ainur, to Niggle's delighted response to his completed tree-work in the tale 'Leaf by Niggle': 'It's a gift!'. These two examples involve an understanding of God as 'the giver of all good things', a biblical insight now being developed extensively in contemporary theology, but Tolkien develops also an anthropology that emphasizes the centrality of gift-exchange in human social and economic systems. And what attracts so many readers to Tolkien's *Lord of the Rings* is its development of societies marked by what Mauss calls 'total prestation': that is by relations of reciprocity that operate at all levels and in most complex chains of connection, all of which are both readable and yet never-ending.[23]

The narrative structures of *The Hobbit* and *The Lord of the Rings* are similar in taking their hobbit protagonists from a money culture that is, to some extent, modern in character (though, as I have argued, with distributist features) back to an encounter with more ancient societies who practise gift-exchange. This is enacted playfully and even satirically in *The Hobbit*, in which Bilbo begins as a suburban bourgeois with a contract for a percentage share of the profits of the dwarf treasure-recovery expedition. To the more archaic dwarves, Bilbo is a complete social outsider – the thief as his name of 'Bagg-ins' indicates – and is hired to do the actual stealing from the dragon. He is a kind of scapegoat who will bear prophylactically the transgressive nature of the enterprise: which means he will be the one to take all the blame and ward it away from the dwarfs. For, although dragons in Nordic culture represent the inverse of gift-exchange and distribution by their immobility and hoarding of treasures that should be shared, removing their hoard is often fateful, as in the case of Sigurd and Fáfnir in the saga of the Volsungs or Beowulf and Grendel's mother. Bilbo himself is lured by the dragon's gold and tempted to hoard, but he learns the value of gift-exchange through his (albeit dubious) bestowal of the arkenstone on the lakemen. He was attracted by its glitter and sought to hide his possession of it from the dwarves, but he freely gives it to the lakemen to use as a means of cementing peace between themselves and the dwarves: a *do ut des*, in effect. Bilbo ends the novel bonded to the dwarves by heirloom gifts of their making which, as we learn in *The Lord of the Rings*, exceed all the wealth of the Shire and thus resist any calculation of market value.

The Lord of the Rings is Tolkien's most sustained exploration of gift-exchange in action; but it is again explored through the hobbits and their 'halfling' character as half modern suburbanites, half pastoralists. From Bilbo's birthday-party arrangements we learn that the Shire has a cash economy, but it has a parallel private gift-exchange system of great importance and complexity. The Prologue informs us that hobbits 'delighted in parties, and in presents, which they gave away freely and eagerly accepted' (p. 2) revealing their kinship with Grönbech's Northmen, who were similarly attached both to getting treasures and to giving them. Since birthday presents are given as well as received, this involves the whole society in never-ending gift-exchange and causes the creation of an entire class of objects, 'mathom', that either form the contents of museums or end up being recycled as birthday gifts (p. 5). In imitation of gift cultures, present-giving creates close and labyrinthine relations among hobbits, paralleled by their equally labyrinthine webs of affinity by intermarriage, which is itself a form of gift giving, as Grönbech asserts, drawing attention to the Icelandic word for bride, *fridu-sibb*, and the Danish for marriage, *giftermal*.[24]

It is in this context of universal reciprocity that Gollum's act of possession of the Ring of Power appears so transgressive. Not only did he wrest the Ring from its finder Déagol, but he demanded it as a birthday present, despite the fact that he had already received a gift from his friend. Indeed, this story offers a sort of foundational myth behind the present-day hobbit birthday practice in the manner of Freud's derivation of the incest taboo from an original parricide by the primal horde of rivals for the patriarch's women and property. According to Freud in *Totem and Taboo*, this crime and its aftermath is the hidden origin of religion and human society, and memory of it survived only in exogamy (marriage outside the family or clan) and the ritual sacrifice of a father substitute.[25] Hobbit practice in the Shire might even be a response to the rumour of this traumatic murder by Sméagol, so that hobbits, like the Freudian horde, give up what was the original object of desire and rivalry.

In a letter to A. C. Dunn, written in 1958 or 1959, Tolkien himself plays the role of anthropologist in describing and elaborating upon gift-exchange in the Shire:

> Birthdays and the giving of gifts had a considerable social importance among Hobbits and were deeply rooted; it had a specific function and etiquette. The birthday-person was of old called a Ribadyan but later changed to Byrding. On his/her birthday the byrding both gave and received presents but the function and etiquette of receiving and giving gifts was different.
>
> With regard to receiving of gifts: The receiving of gifts was connected to kinship and it was a recognition of the byrding as a member of the whole family/clan and no present was given by the mother or father of the birthday-child but the reputed head of the family/clan (which normally was a male but could be female) was supposed to give a present. Those who were expected to give gifts (like to the Farewell-party) was limited to second cousins and to kin living within 12 miles, friends were not expected to give though they might if they wished. The person who received the gift would do this in private, it was very improper to open gifts in public.
>
> The giving of gifts was a personal matter and not limited to families. It was a sort of recognition of services and friendship for the past year.[26]

I quote this passage in full because it so clearly illustrates Tolkien's alertness to gift-exchange and his linkage of it to Anglo-Saxon and Nordic practices, especially to the establishment and maintenance of kinship relations. He even invents a term, 'byrding', for a practice that resembles Scandinavian bairn-fostering, and presents the birthday giving as enacting the 'incorporation' of a person into the family, or rather clan. Tolkien here sees the central social unit to be the wider group as Grönbech argues in *The Culture of the Teutons*, in which it is also called the clan. His older word for a birthday celebrant, 'ribadyan', includes 'rib', the Anglo-Saxon word for soul, suggesting the spiritual function of the exchanges as well as the social conception of soul among Teutonic peoples. If, however, as in its more common usage, it means a bodily rib, it stresses again the importance of gift-exchange in the establishment of the communal body.

As an aid to his own difficulty in giving up the Ring, Bilbo goes beyond normal hobbit custom and offers gifts on his birthday not only to friends and family but to everyone indiscriminately. And after what is, in effect, a sort of potlatch destruction of all his possessions, Bilbo goes off to offer himself to the elves at Rivendell as a *scop* (an Anglo-Saxon poet and story-teller) for the elves, whose own traditions he turns into songs.

Grönbech's chapter on the exchange of gifts also asserts that gifts have regenerating, active qualities and give rise to more giving, a quality also shared by the fairy-gifts of the folk-tale. This is illustrated in Frodo's own response to Bilbo's adoption of him as heir on his 'byrding', and the gift of the Ring. Frodo reciprocates by leaving his home and the Shire, and later offering himself at the Council of Elrond as restorer of the Ring to its place of origin. To prepare Frodo to make this gesture of ultimate reciprocity, the narrative of *The Fellowship of the Ring* charts a picaresque course in which the looseness of structure and seeming errancy of aim enacts a liminal stage in Frodo's development. Like an adolescent Masai warrior or young Zulu, Frodo prepares for initiation into adult responsibility and more ancient forms of sociality by being taken away from his tribe with his peers for ordeal and bonding. Tom Bombadil enacts the role of tribal elder in this rite, because his role and function in the novel is that of gift-giver (one very important also, as already mentioned, to fairy-tale structure, in which the protagonist is aided by a fairy godmother or old beggar with a magic cloak or ability). Bombadil is a manifestation of the giftedness of creation itself: he is delightful, surprising and (as adapters of the story indicate by omitting him) superfluous. This allies him to Gandalf, who has a similar ability to come to the hobbits' aid when least expected, and whose own characteristic gift of fireworks is a very pure form of gift – superfluous and self-oblatory in its cascades of sparks. Like Gandalf's, Bombadil's is a life lived in harmony with and mastery over nature but without domination. First encountered taking a love-offering of water lilies to Goldberry, he gives the hobbits all sorts of gifts: liberation, food, shelter and protection. Even his speech is a gift, because he offers more than is necessary for communication by speaking in verse. Like the artistic works described by Lewis Hyde in *The Gift*, his versifying avoids commodification by transcending the utilitarian and thereby becomes a gift to the reader. Tom Bombadil's words, indeed, have rhyme as well as metre, as in his first direct address to the hobbits:

> 'Whoa! whoa! steady there! . . . Now my little fellows,
> where be you a-going to, puffing like a bellows.'
> (p. 117 and my arrangement in lines of verse)

His speech also bursts into song at every opportunity, and also into nonsense: 'Hey dol! merry dol! ring a dong dillo', which introduces a further element of Bataillean excess to its already gifted character. Tom Bombadil can take, admire and even play with the Ring of Power because everything he touches he gives, including the treasure hoarded by the barrow-wight, which Tom exposes for redistribution to men and beasts alike. Tom takes one brooch but that is a gift for Goldberry and is to be worn in full memory and acknowledgement of the original wearer. Utterly fictive, Tom Bombadil with his localized mastery, his cottage and few acres is also distributism in action; utterly individual, he yet connects with the world of Middle-earth at all levels. (Indeed, he seems to be quite a Chestertonian figure with his love of comfort, pleasure in light verse, high uxoriousness and a certain rotundity.)

Focusing on gift-exchange reveals the importance of the later scenes of *The Fellowship of the Ring* at Rivendell, which have been criticized as static. Even in this, Tolkien is following Anglo-Saxon narrative modes, as a quotation from Grönbech makes plain:

> For us moderns, accustomed to seeing the poetry of a narration come to an end at the point where the hero has set his foot on the last of his foes, or the last of the demons, it is strange to see how in the old days . . . men could swoop down upon the sense of victory, create thereupon a counter-tension no weaker than the tension of the fight,

and write half the epic on the themes of triumph and feasting and games.[27]

This quotation is from the chapter on treasures, and what makes the counter-tension of these scenes is the delight in describing exchanges of gifts, both of gold but also of congratulations, jokes and songs, all of which are also seen as a form of exchange. As the 'Hamaval' urges: 'a man should be a friend to his friend and return gift for gift; men should receive mocking laughter with the same and a lie with a lie'.[28] So the Rivendell scenes describe gift-giving in the form of things but most of all exchanges of information. With often unfriendly groups to deal with, the Council of Elrond is an attempt to establish friendship through gifts of knowledge, but the capacity of words to be either gifts or weapons in Nordic societies makes the procedure dangerous. And it is the belief that words are actual objects of exchange but as such alive and active – 'the word must be alive, or simply must be the man himself' – that causes such consternation at the Council when Gandalf quotes aloud the orcish inscription upon the Ring: 'Ash nazg durbatulûk, ash nazg gimbatul, ash nazg thrakatulûk agh burzum-ishi krimpatul' (p. 247).[29] The gift of speech here that reveals Sauron's spell upon the Ring also acts as a weapon: the words are performative of that which they describe. And the Black Speech itself has been derived from elvish but in such a way that it too is a weapon, because it refuses that most common of vowels 'e' and with it the common good and the reciprocity of dialogic speech. Instead it enacts a gesture of aggression, 'menacing, powerful, harsh as stone', and forces the speaker's mouth into a retching shape as it forms and makes the vomiting gagging sounds of 'agh' and 'uk'.

The Fellowship of the Ring therefore emerges as a response to Sauron's threat by means of a group bonded by gift-exchange, who embark on a quest to complete the chain of reciprocity by restoring nature to itself. That the quest is ultimately successful is due partly to the interconnections between the different societies, but also due to the gifted nature of the objects at the Fellowship's disposal. For example, Merry is able to aid Éowyn to defeat the Ringwraith at the Battle of the Pelennor Fields because of his non-human, halfling status, but also because he has been given a sword forged long ago with runes to be effective against the sorcerer-king of Angmar, now declined to a Ringwraith. This sword was a gift from the barrow-wight's hoard given to Merry by Tom Bombadil, and with it came all the *dóm* ('its honour and power') of the sword's making and use, as well as the *frith* (kinship/bonding) of that powerful giver.[30] 'Frith' is an Old English word very rich in meaning, which Grönbech was one of the first to analyse. He interpreted it to mean the result of peaceable and friendly relations between individuals and groups in the Nordic world that link them in kinship. It was the consequence of successful gift-exchange and was linked to it directly. When Merry strikes the Ringwraith from below he acts in *frith*: first, with Éowyn herself who has borne him to the battle; secondly, with her uncle Théoden to whom he had sworn fealty; thirdly, with Tom Bombadil the giver of the sword; but fourthly, with those in the distant days of Westernesse who faced the same enemy and forged his weapon. Similarly it is the gift of Bilbo to Frodo of the mithril-coat that provides protection against the cave-troll in Moria. Again this is an object gifted at each stage of its history and passed in *frith* from the dwarves to Bilbo. As is usually the case in gift-exchange cultures, the object gathers value and virtue from each of its passings-on that become, as it were, part of its being.

Although only shadowy presences in Nordic mythology, Tolkien develops the race of elves as important fairy gift-givers and of these, as Galadriel states, Celeborn is 'giver of gifts beyond the power of kings' (p. 347). Lothlórien is a dangerous place precisely because it is a source of gift: if one can bond in *frith* with the purpose of the elves' gifts, such as glimpses into the mirror of Galadriel, they confer blessing and insight, but without that harmony of mind they are less beneficent. The elves offer elegies for Gandalf, boats and rope for the journey ahead, cloaks of their own weaving and food. Each present is 'enchanted' by its elvish origin, in the manner that Tolkien describes in his essay 'On Fairy-Stories' as the nature of magic. What is important for him is not the magic itself so much as the way in which ordinary everyday realities are made strange – enchanted – in order for the world to be restored to us in all its quiddity and beauty: as gift. So the elven lembas, for example, are completely useful and filling but have a sacrality as well as a deliciousness unknown to ordinary cram. This sacrality is not caused by the mysteriousness of the food's origin, but from the recognition of who made it. As the leader of the elves says, 'we put the thought of all that we love into all that we make' (p. 361).

The most important and personal gifts of the elves are those given – unexpectedly – by Galadriel when she appears in her swan ship offering the gift of song and then presents suited to the needs and character of each member of the Fellowship. Importantly, as in Norse and Anglo-Saxon practice, she accompanies her giving with the 'binding rite' of the cup, which she performs herself. The gifts themselves have this same binding quality both synchronically, in linking the recipients to the elves and to each other, and diachronically, in relating the recipients through gift with the historic past. This is particularly important for Aragorn: the sheath he is given is decorated with runes telling the lineage of the sword and thereby establishing his legitimacy as the rightful inheritor of Andúril. Sam is given the little box of earth that will literally unite the Shire to Lórien and allow the declining elven territory new life in the future; Legolas has a bow strung with an elven hair that expresses the brotherhood of Mirkwood and Lórien kingdoms; and Merry, Pippin and Boromir all have belts to emphasize the importance of union and loyalty. Gimli's request of a hair from Galadriel is not only a request for a pledge to engage in *frith* with the elven people, but it also marks his transcendence of the dwarven tendency to gold-lust and hoarding in favour of exchange, as Galadriel herself reveals as she says to Gimli, 'These words shall go with the gift . . . that your hands shall flow with gold, and yet over you gold shall have no dominion' (p. 367). Frodo's gift of the phial of light relates him not just to the elves but right back to the origin of the light in Eärendil's star and thus to the silmarils themselves, which owe their own light to the radiance of the two trees of Valinor. As Galadriel sang in her song of parting – 'Maybe thou shalt find Valimar' (p. 369) – so every one of her gifts not only looks back to the Edenic origin of Valinor but also forward in hope. In giving towards a future she may not share, Galadriel avoids the elvish temptation to embrace stasis and unchanging perfection.

CHESTERTON AND TOLKIEN AS THEOLOGIANS

The first volume of *The Lord of the Rings* then enacts the restoration of gift-exchange and the widening of *frith* as the way to undo the misuse of the gift relation by Sauron through the Ring of Power. At every stage of danger or need in the events that follow it is these and other gifts that allow success: the speed of Shadowfax, the leaf brooch that Pippin drops to mark his trail, the rope that allows Frodo to be rescued from the cliff-edge, the phial of light that overcomes the monstrous Shelob, the horn blown by Merry to raise the Shire. It is not by some totemic magic power that these objects become effectual but by their own powers accrued in their making and former use – by virtue of their relations and those they still act to effect. Indeed in the second and third volumes the hobbits themselves become gifts, not in ways that dehumanize but by creative use of their anomalous status. So Merry swears loving fealty to Théoden in a form of *frith*, while Pippin becomes a sort of ransom in payment for Boromir's life to Denethor, for *weregild* as compensation for an illicit death is also linked to the gift-exchange system in Anglo-Saxon culture. Similarly at Isengard and with the ents Merry and Pippin become ambassadors and a medium by which *frith* may be established between the various free peoples of Middle-earth.

In the central narrative of Frodo's quest, however, gift-exchange is shown to fail. On the slopes of Mount Doom Galadriel's phial seems useless and the Ring of Power itself becomes a protagonist, with a will of its own, proving the truth that Grönbech says Norsemen understood: 'It is not the giving that acts, they say, but the gift. None can, we learn, free himself from the influence of things about him, such as are in his own guardianship, and such as lie near enough to be entangled in his acts'.[31] Overcome by the Ring's will, Frodo shows its dominance precisely by his (illusory) assertion of his freedom to act: 'I do not choose now to do what I came to do' (p. 924). In the same way we are never more in the power of the fetishized commodity than when we rejoice in freedom of choice in the modern world of the 'free' market. It is, of course, only Gollum's intervention that causes the Ring to be taken down into the abyss, and that against his own will also. As Gandalf saw long before, Gollum had a role to play in the quest, although even he was unaware that this role would be that of a literal stumbling block, preventing Frodo from obtaining mastery. The scandal (linked etymologically to an offensive thing or stumbling stone in Greek as St Paul puns in 1 Corinthians 1.23) of Gollum's intervention is that it is the perverted and depraved river hobbit who saves Middle-earth, but he does so by re-establishing the circle of giving, reception and reciprocation inherent in the gift-exchange economy. As we saw in Chapter 3, in his identification and obsession with the Ring of Power Gollum had become objectified, losing all sense of himself as a person, split in two like Rumpelstiltskin. Frodo too suffers psychic disintegration and becomes dehumanized on the last part of his journey and it is his fellow-feeling with Gollum as ring-bearer that enables him to treat Gollum with kindness and sympathy. So although Frodo is unable actively to complete the cycle of giving, receiving and reciprocating by returning the Ring, he has already reciprocated by receiving Gollum as a gift not a burden and by setting him free after their bargain had been completed. In Gollum the Ring achieves its return and the circle is complete.

I have quoted frequently from Grönbech, which might suggest that although Tolkien does indeed employ gift-theory in his fiction, he owes his conception of the theology of gift to Chesterton and its ethnography to Grönbech, or to other expert sources, or even to his own familiarity with ancient northern materials, but has no contribution of his own to add. What, however, is singular and striking in Tolkien's portrayal is the means by which he discriminates between the good and the bad gift. This is a topic that Mauss only touches upon in his anxiety to prove the ubiquity and inescapability of the gift's reciprocation, while Grönbech emphasizes both the importance of knowing the one from whom one is receiving and the fateful nature of the gift, but does not proceed to identify the nature of that difference. By comparison, in the whole history of the Ring of Power from its secret forging to its later deceiving power, Tolkien shows clearly how gift-exchange can be perverted, and he offers criteria by which the good gift can be distinguished from the bad in terms of its clear and documented relation to origin, its circulation and the openness of its exchanges. In the figure of the Black Rider Tolkien reveals most effectively the alienating and oppressive effects of the bad gift.

A second way in which Tolkien has something to offer gift theory is the way in which he uses it to restore 'soul' to objects. Feminist theory has often criticized the way in which women are made into objects of exchange in marriage, but gift-exchange reveals the way in which items and people exchanged as gifts by no means lose their personhood. Indeed, it is by giving themselves that the hobbits grow and develop, both physically and morally and from 'flotsam and jetsam' (p. 546) to full personhood as Peregrin and Meriadoc. And objects thus exchanged become 'enchanted' by the act of giving into new value. Lastly, Tolkien develops in *The Lord of the Rings* an implicit theology that returns us to Chesterton's assertion in 'The Ethics of Elfland' that life in all its perilous beauty and fragility is itself a gift. So in the appendices that follow at the end of the novel we see Aragorn, gifted with life beyond the normal span, offering back his life in old age – not waiting for death to take him but completing the chain of reciprocation: 'I am the last of the Númenóreans and the latest King of the Elder days; and to me has been given not only a span thrice that of Men of Middle-earth, but also the grace to go at my will, and give back the gift. Now, therefore, I will sleep' (p. 1037). Only here does Tolkien's presentation of the gift move beyond his Anglo-Saxon and Nordic sources because, although death was defied and challenged by the bravery of the fearless Viking warrior, to present death as Ilúvatar's gift to mankind is to move into a completely new religious world: that of Christianity and the Incarnation, which lies ahead in the continuing history of Middle-earth.

Notes

1. Chesterton, *Orthodoxy*, p. 82.
2. Vladimir Propp, *The Morphology of the Folktale*, ed. Louis A Wagner, trans. Lawrence Scott (Austin: University of Texas Press, 1968), pp. 79–80; A. J. Greimas, *Du Sens: Essais Sémiotiques* (Paris: Éditions du Seuil, 1970), p. 245.
3. Garth, *Tolkien and the Great War*, p. 86.
4. Anne Ridler (ed.), *Charles Williams: The Image of the City and Other Essays* (London: Oxford University Press, 1958), p. 8.
5. Marcel Mauss, *The Gift: The Form and Reason for Exchange in Archaic Societies*, foreword Mary Douglas, trans. E. Halls (New York: Norton, 1990), p. i.

6. Mauss, *The Gift*, p. xiv.
7. Mauss, *The Gift*, p. 83.
8. Georges Bataille, *The Accursed Share*, 2 vols (New York: Urzone, 1988).
9. Jacques Derrida, *Given Time: Counterfeit Money*, trans. Peggy Kamuf (Chicago: Chicago University Press, 1992).
10. Chesterton, *Orthodoxy*, p. 82.
11. Tolkien, *Tree and Leaf*, p. 60.
12. Vespers for Christmas Day in *The Festal Menaian*, trans. Mother Mary and Archimandrite Kallistos Ware (London: Faber and Faber, 1969), p. 254.
13. Chesterton, *The Man Who Was Thursday*, p. 184.
14. Lewis Hyde, *The Gift: Imagination and the Erotic Life of Property* (New York: Vintage, 1983).
15. *Letters of Tolkien*, pp. 144–5.
16. Tolkien, *Tree and Leaf*, p. 85.
17. Leo XIII, *Rerum Novarum: On Capital and Labour*, 15 May 1891, paras. 46–47, online at www.vatican.va/holy_father/Leo_xiii/encyclicals (accessed 3 May 2007).
18. Robert Bjork, 'Speech as Gift in *Beowulf*', *Speculum* 69 (1994), pp. 993–1022.
19. Vilhelm Grönbech, *The Culture of the Teutons*, 2 vols (London: Oxford University Press, 1931), p. 6.
20. Grönbech, *Teutons*, p. 7.
21. Grönbech, *Teutons*, p. 10.
22. Tolkien, *The Silmarillion*, p. 287.
23. Mauss, *The Gift*, p. 1.
24. Grönbech, *Teutons*, pp. 6 and 54.
25. Sigmund Freud, *Totem and Taboo* in *Complete Psychological Works of Sigmund Freud*, ed. James Strachey, vol. 13 (London: Hogarth, 1962).
26. *Letters of Tolkien*, p. 291.
27. Grönbech, *Teutons*, pp. 12–13.
28. *Edda*, 'Words of Odin' stanza 42, quoted by Mauss, *The Gift*, p. xiv.
29. Grönbech, *Teutons*, p. 81.
30. Grönbech, *Teutons*, p. 27.
31. Grönbech, *Teutons*, p. 11.

CHAPTER 5

FAIRY POETICS: MAKE-BELIEVE

> Hark! Laughter like a lion wakes
> To roar to the resounding plain,
> And the whole heaven shouts and shakes,
> For God Himself is born again,
> And we are little children walking
> Through the snow and rain.[1]

IN THE PRECEDING CHAPTERS, we have seen how strongly realist is the philosophy that undergirds the fictional worlds of Chesterton and Tolkien, and how strongly participatory is their theology, which describes a universe of reciprocal exchanges, not only with other creatures, as in the gift relations of the previous chapter, but with God himself. Through the radiance of their forms, all the animate and inanimate creatures reveal their origin in the divine, as each 'deals out that being indoors each one dwells', as Gerard Manley Hopkins puts it, and 'selves – goes itself'.[2] One might therefore expect that the theory of imagination that undergirds this participatory vision would be a Romantic one in which, following Coleridge, the artist's imagination has a godlike capacity as 'a repetition in the finite mind of the eternal act of creation in the infinite I AM'.[3] While it is true that Tolkien does conceive the artistic imagination as a mode of secondary creation, following Maritain, who wrote that

the artist is 'an associate of God in the making of works of beauty
... and making use of created matter, he creates as it were in the
second degree', he would not agree with Coleridge's secondary
imagination as 'essentially *vital*, even as all objects (as objects) are
essentially fixed and dead'.[4] Similarly, despite the admiration both
Chesterton and Tolkien felt for the fantasy writing of George
MacDonald, I do not think they would concur with his (again
Coleridgean) remarks in an essay on the fantastic imagination:

> Man may, if he pleases, invent a little world of his own, with its own
> laws; for there is that in him which delights in calling up new forms –
> which is the nearest, perhaps, he can come to creation. When such
> forms are new embodiments of old truths, we call them products of
> Imagination; when they are mere inventions, however lovely, I should
> call them the work of Fancy: in either case Law has been diligently at
> work.[5]

The distinction between truth and its embodiment derives from
MacDonald's mode of Platonism and is quite foreign to Chesterton
and Tolkien's view of the work of art as a thing in itself, and a form
in the scholastic sense, in which its radiance is inseparable from its
formal qualities. MacDonald strives to the same end as they, but has
a less positive conception of the value of the material as against the
spiritual and disembodied. Indeed, one reason for Tolkien's anxiety
to avoid being read allegorically – despite his quite frequent use of
the mode in 'Leaf by Niggle' and his critical writings – is the avoidance of any interpretation of his writing that would remove a literal
interpretation from its meaning, and separate form and substance.

The difference from MacDonald lies in the wholly positive
valence both writers give to the invented and constructed nature of
the artwork. The more cheerfully fictive it appears, the more its
intelligibility and form become radiant and reveal its divine origin.
To use Tolkien's terminology in 'On Fairy-Stories', the artist 'assists
with the effoliation', and adds leaves to the tree of creation, as a
response to the skill and imagination with which he or she has been
gifted, whereas MacDonald's model is of the artist echoing at one
remove an original idea of the true, the good and the beautiful.[6]

Another important divergence from Romanticism in Chesterton

and Tolkien lies in their understanding of childhood. The absolute Romantic child of Wordsworth's 'Intimations of Immortality' has a privileged imaginative life as the innocent recipient of natural beauty beyond the reach of the adult. While Wordsworth's positive valuation of childhood experience and vision is a good thing and, as we shall see, is shared by the two later authors, it is accompanied, in 'Tintern Abbey' for example, by an immediacy that precludes reflection – 'wild ecstasy . . . dizzy raptures'.[7] The child receives only sensory impressions, so that it is rather the adult who has the active imagination that can 'half create' and half perceive, and add thought to sensation.[8] Like Rousseau and Blake, Wordsworth sets up a dualism between innocence and experience and nature and culture, one that has served to strand children across a hermeneutic chasm.

G. K. Chesterton, born into late-Victorian London rather than Wordsworth's rural Westmorland, had a quite different understanding of the relation of childhood and imagination. In Chapter 1, I gave an extended quotation from Chesterton's autobiography in which he describes his first memory, which is not of brooks and fields but 'the man with the golden key', who, it turns out, 'was about six inches high and proved on investigation to be made of cardboard' being a puppet in his father's toy theatre.[9] Where the boy Wordsworth saw the natural world 'apparell'd in celestial light' the young Chesterton saw manufactured cardboard and tinsel thus arrayed.[10] The adult Romantic poet mourns 'that there hath past away a glory from the earth' but Chesterton can renew his vision every time he puts his eye to a peep-show or watches a pantomime. His fiction and essays indeed offer endless defamiliarizations of the real world that allow the production of fantastic effects and the renewal of vision.

The 'golden key' sequence in the *Autobiography* tricks the unwary reader by its initial suggestion of realism before its revelation of artifice, but that is not how the child Gilbert experienced the scene, because he was consciously watching a performance. Chesterton indeed attributes this conscious quality to all children's play and attacks those who see in children's games only fantasy:

> The worst heresy of this school is that the child is concerned only with make-believe. For this is interpreted in the sense, at once

sentimental and sceptical, that there is not much difference between make-believe and belief. But the real child does not confuse fact and fiction. He simply likes fiction. He acts it because he cannot yet write it or even read it; but he never allows his moral sanity to be clouded by it. To him no two things could possibly be more contrary than playing at robbers and stealing sweets.[11]

What is implied here is that children's imaginative play is not, as Jean Piaget saw it, a retreat from reality into fantasy but an active act of creation akin to the work of an artist. It is the making of representations and thus mimetic in the way that art or drama are – it is closer to ritual. Therefore, rather than an indulgence in childish freedom from adult restraint before the 'shades of the prisonhouse' descend, play is a child's mode of engagement in an adult activity. Although, to make his point rhetorically effective, Chesterton inverts the Romantic position so completely that he seems to suggest that there is no element of the fantastic at work, his own examples of the power of the toy theatre and other childhood experiences show that the factual coexists with the fantastic.

Chesterton's understanding of children's play is in agreement with more recent studies by child psychologists such as Paul Harris's *The Work of the Imagination*. He concludes that the 'puzzling' emergence of pretend play in young children coincides with their developing language ability and helps them to understand causal principles by imagining alternative scenarios. Rather than blurring reality and fantasy in their play Harris provides evidence of experiments in which children deliberately explore a range of possible worlds and in which they are able empathically to take on roles of characters quite other than themselves.[12]

The magical and fantastical certainly have their place in children's imagination and Harris writes of experiments that prompt children to explain phenomena as 'magical,' such as E. V. Subbotsky's 1994 presentation of some so-called rejuvenating water which could work given some magic words.[13] Most children of four and five years old refused to try the experiment despite the promise of a reward, evidently afraid of the possibility that it might work. Even here, however, Harris sees a continuity with adult behaviour, comparing such responses to the nervous care to keep away from the kerb of a person walking home at night after watching a film about a car accident.[14] There is no objective reason why an accident would be more likely but the imagination infuses one's appraisal of a real situation. Similarly for children there is a 'semi-permeable boundary between the world of the imagination and the world of actual possibilities'.[15]

Harris even argues that children can be quite sophisticated literary critics, citing another study by Subbotsky in which preschool children were questioned about the possibility of time travel and penetration of a solid barrier. All children denied the possibility of the latter and nearly all of the former and yet they acknowledged that these transformations could happen in a fairy tale.[16] They are therefore as alert to literary conventions as any adult audience and the telling of fairy-tales to children by an older person is a collaborative enterprise in the activation of narrative tension and its resolution. This again is like Chesterton's man with the golden key who was made through the manipulation of a piece of balsa wood by a father who fashioned the theatre for the delight of his son, who himself collaborated to produce an imaginative creation.

Tolkien's 'perilous realm' of faërie represents this 'semi-permeable boundary' between the ordinary world and that of the imagination. It is not to be equated with the imagination but with the desire 'to survey the depths of space and time' and 'to hold communion with other living things'.[17] Tolkien is quite precise about its function, which is 'the realisation, independent of the conceiving mind, of imagined wonder'.[18] For this reason, stories of fairies that turn out to be a dream are unsatisfactory, because what is needed is real belief in what occurs, not only so that literary belief can be maintained through the reality effect of the fiction, but because *faërie* is a mode of exploring the real through the imagination. Chesterton and Tolkien do not actually say 'I believe in fairies', but they write about the possibility of such beings in a world, or plurality of worlds. Faërie is the fictive site (in the sense of the constructed work of art) where the intuition of other modes of material life apart from our own may be explored. Hence it is crucial that it is a mode of exploration not only for children but for adults, so that Tolkien spends considerable space at the beginning of his essay not only arguing that fairy-stories are as much if not more for grown-ups than for children, but promoting maturation as a good thing: 'the process of growing older is not necessarily allied to growing wickeder, though the two do often happen together. Children are meant to grow up, and not to become Peter Pans. Not to lose innocence and wonder, but to proceed on the appointed journey'.[19]

The model of imagination that Tolkien and Chesterton construct aims, therefore, to restore reason to fantasy, and ally childish intuitive rationality (the sense the child has that 'There *is* an Is') with wonder. The child is central because not only does he or she have this intuition of being but allies it with a sophisticated literary sense and capacity for make-believe in a deliberate act of artistic creation. In this way Tolkien and Chesterton invert the Romantic and Edwardian association of the child with credulity and with a totally separate consciousness from that of adults. And one way in which both writers celebrate the imaginative alliance of children and adults is through the figure of Father Christmas. Even now, although some modern parents agonize over the ethics of pretending that an old man in red parks his reindeer on their roof and shoots down the (possibly non-existent) chimney into their children's bedrooms, the custom persists, driven partly by childhood tradition as studied by the Opies' *Lore and Language of Schoolchildren*, as well as a natural pleasure in surprise presents.[20] For Chesterton, Father Christmas was an important figure of resistance to modern utilitarianism, who represented hospitality and community over self-sufficency, excess over capitalist calculation and generosity over commercial values. His Santa Claus is therefore a resource for adults as well as children. In one short story, 'The Shop of Ghosts', he appears as a sleepy and senile Battersea back-street shopkeeper to his adult admirers the writers Charles Dickens and Ben Jonson, who wrote about him, as well as to Richard Steele's fictional Christmas host, Sir Roger de Coverley and the legendary Robin Hood.[21] This shopkeeper refuses to take money for his box of toy soldiers on the grounds of his old-fashioned habits, and appears close to death. When Dickens ascertains that Father Christmas has always felt that he was dying, he declares 'I understand it now . . . you will never die'.[22]

What Chesterton is claiming here for this figure is the status of a cultural imaginary, a communal fantastic creation that children and adults alike have united to promote, in what he calls elsewhere an 'extra-belief', or product of 'creative credulity'.[23] This is the imaginative power that acknowledges *both* the cardboard of the man with the golden key and equally the gold of his crown. In another article Chesterton writes of the effect of water in the toy theatre produced by 'rank behind rank of escaloped blue walls as groundpieces, moved in opposite directions so that the crests seemed to toss and dance'.[24] The young Gilbert knew exactly how this effect was achieved but this awareness did not preclude imaginative engagement: he felt 'an ecstasy of apprehension . . . I knew it was not water, but I knew it was sea'.[25] Here the scalloped paper does not merely symbolize the sea; nor does it disappear in order to produce an illusion of water. Rather, it has a material iconicity precisely because of its fabricated nature. In other words, the scalloped waves can be seen to participate in that which they represent, as in Coleridge's theory of the creative imagination in chapter 13 of his *Biographia Literaria*, but without losing their cardboardiness and artificially activated movement.[26] In that sense the theatre is like an Orthodox icon, which is a most unrealistic and stylized representation of Christ, but by the very fact of that conventionality – the fact that any icon must follow standard outlines and forms of its subject – the icon mediates his presence and is itself holy. There is thus a mini-drama of presence and absence in its apprehension. Paul Ricoeur's study of metaphor indeed argues that this clash of iconic and non-iconic elements is what actually produces meaning and keeps metaphors 'alive'.[27]

Like the toy theatre, Father Christmas has obviously fictive qualities. Even in the Renaissance masques he was presented as an anachronism; in that sense he was always dying like the aged shopkeeper in Chesterton's story, in which even Robin Hood is surprised to see him still alive. Like the icon he has a series of clothes and attributes that render him instantly recognizable and easily imitated. Chesterton, writing of Dickens's characters, sees a certain similarity: 'they are creatures like Punch or Father Christmas. They live statically, in a perpetual summer of being themselves'.[28] This quality he calls mythical, not in the sense of something untrue, or a narrative that explains the origins of the world, but as a personage that is irreducible, the truth of which cannot be abstracted from its particularities but which can be shared in any number of versions.

Markers of Father Christmas's fantastic nature are to be found in the extraordinary sequence of letters that J. R. R. Tolkien wrote for his four children over a period of twenty years. As one might expect from the author of *The Lord of the Rings* these are highly elaborate productions, copiously illustrated, with a full cast of characters, including the childlike Polar Bear and his nephews, snowboys, and a mysterious 'Green Brother' for Father Christmas.[29] Also included is a complete goblin alphabet and beautifully designed imitation stamps. Despite attempts at realism such as the discovery of ancient cave paintings and bear claw marks to parallel the discoveries of Lascaux, and references to the Depression and World War II, all of which have some effect on life at the North Pole, there are several cheerfully fictive elements. There is a literal, oddly Aubrey Beardsley-like, curvy North Pole that occasionally has to be mended, a currency of polar kisses and a firework let off by mistake that 'shook all the stars out of place, broke the moon into four – and the Man in it fell into my back garden. He ate quite a lot of my Christmas chocolates before he said he felt better and climbed back to mend it and get the stars tidy'.[30]

The references to mending bring into prominence the fictive nature of the story as does the nursery-rhyme man in the moon. As Paul Harris points out, pre-school children already comprehend the physical causes and limits of motion and agency so that the man in the moon clambering back up would have been understood as a physical impossibility. That does not, however, mean that the children would have disbelieved the story either. As several experiments have demonstrated, the more children learn about the principles of physical causation, the more examples they are able to imagine of violations of those same principles. One 1991 study showed that despite a group of young children being quite sure that a box was empty and having proved it by seeing inside, a number of them still explored the box to see if the creature they had openly invented as part of the experiment was inside. The analysis of the resulting data suggested that they could entertain a suspension of the normal rules in the case of magic.[31]

In the case of Father Christmas, many children carry on believing or entertaining the possibility of his existence, even though they are also aware of the possibility that it is their parents who tiptoe in to fill the stockings. This was surely the case with some of the Tolkien children such as Priscilla, who was still getting letters in 1941 when she was eleven. She asked that year for the latest Alison Uttley story about Moldy-Warp, making it likely that she had *Little Grey Rabbit's Christmas* from the year before, in which it is Little Grey Rabbit herself who fills the stockings for Hare and Squirrel.[32] Again, Uttley leaves the possibility of Father Christmas's reality open since there is a suggestion that he cannot reach the cottage because of the snow. Priscilla's 1940 letter includes an impossibility in showing Polar Bear dancing with penguins, who belong to the southern hemisphere, although an explanation is included to the effect that they are 'evacuees' as well as reinforcements for the fight against the goblins.[33]

All the way through Tolkien's letters a double effect is engendered. On the one hand the 'reality effects' that allow congruence between the world of the North Pole and that of the children are numerous: different handwriting styles for the main characters, with a dialogic effect as Polar Bear scribbles cheeky and misspelt comments on Father Christmas's text, comic explanations for late delivery and even different signatures on the drawings. Conversely, the letters include such impossibilities as snowboys who write in snow ink, a tree at the Pole visible from Oxford, and a Santa Claus as old as the Christian era itself. Not only does this collision of realism and fantasy produce the life of the image as in Ricoeur's dynamic concept of the metaphor, but it parallels the effect of nursery rhymes such as 'Hey, Diddle, Diddle' and 'Goosey, Goosey, Gander' in which ordinary items are put together in unlikely conjunction or impossible action – 'The cow jumped over the moon'. These have their effect not because they are nonsense but rather mixtures of semantic sense and metaphoric nonsense, and the pleasure comes from an awareness of the collision.

The educational theorist Kieran Egan tries to make sense of

children's delight in nursery rhymes and fairy-stories by attending to the way in which children acquire cognitive tools. He argues that 'the generation of opposites and mediating between them seems to be basic to human thinking when shaped by language', and demonstrates how small children orient their perceptions of the world through antonyms such as cold/hot, dry/wet, small/large, etc. as these terms are applied to their own bodies.[34] Learning to mediate between these opposite terms is the stuff of understanding, and Egan goes on to place talking animals like Peter Rabbit between binaries such as nature/culture, while 'ghosts are to life and death as warm is to hot and cold'.[35]

Father Christmas is similarly a mediating figure between outside and inside, nature and culture, hot and cold. His mode of entry down the chimney marks his liminality and incarnates the 'semi-permeable boundary' that Harris used to describe the child's ontological framework, and which I have compared to Tolkien's realm of faërie. His mediatory significance goes much further than this, however, and to understand this we must return to the Tolkien family. For not only did the children receive annual letters from Father Christmas, they sent (unpublished) replies, to which 'he' responded – 'I feel quite well all the same, very nice of Michael to ask' – as did Polar Bear – 'p.s. I like letters and think Christofers are nice' – and answered questions. Priscilla sent her own drawings and messages from a host of her toys, one of whom, Bear Bingo, hung up his own stocking and received presents. These letters from the young Tolkiens are more elaborate versions of the lists of desired presents countless children still send up the chimney or to Father Christmas's 'official' Post Office address, while others respond by leaving carrots for the reindeer or sherry for Father Christmas himself.

This collaborative effort by the children is much more than a utilitarian means to acquire the toys they really want as presents. It allows them some response to the act of giving and it solidifies the mediation that Father Christmas represents. Whether the main gifts from the family are conveyed through Father Christmas or whether he fills stockings with little extra gifts extraneous to the main presents under the tree, he presides over the gift process and becomes its originator. The normal state of affairs is suspended in which everything children possess, from the food they eat to the clothes they wear, is given by their parents. This is not an ideological masking of a reality since the dependence of children on their parents and guardians is universally manifest. As Chesterton asserts, 'In dealing with childhood, we have a parental right to command it – because we should kill the childhood if we convinced it'.[36] Rather, that dependence is made even more visible but in an 'enchanted' form because the dependence of children is no longer a relation of lack in regard to the child, or one of possible resentment or drain on resources for the parent. It is now an infinite outpouring of generosity to which children can respond independently of their parents.

There is a weighty debate among cultural theorists about whether there can ever be a 'pure' gift that is free of any return and I do not intend to engage it here, since the Father Christmas ritual is by no means a project that seeks to remove the response-gift relation. Instead it seeks to express the sacredness of that relation. It is no coincidence in my view that Father Christmas's importance as a gift-giver to children increases and is emphasized in advanced capitalist economies in which market values have invaded the domestic world. For it is a custom that resists such values, as in Dickens's own Santa, the 'Ghost of Christmas Past' in *A Christmas Carol* and his criticism of Scrooge. Father Christmas represents modes of exchange quite inimical to those of the cash nexus and looks back to a pre-capitalist world, but he is not nostalgic in relation to children, because he also disallows the pre-modern absolute right of the father over the child that treats him or her as a form of property.

The figure of Father Christmas is then an actual mediation between the antonyms child/parent and one which establishes the relation between them as a sacred thing, neither a concession by the parent nor a right on either side. He represents something beyond them both which grounds and orients the relation between them. Secondly, Father Christmas establishes a crucial distance between parent and child, which is as important as their relation – indeed, it is only by opening up a space between them that the child can be given full presence. This distantiation makes explicit the sacredness of the child in the sense of the holy as that set apart, akin to the Jewish custom of offering (symbolically) the firstborn son to God, following Numbers 18.15–18. In both cases the rite acknowledges an origin for the child that is not equated with the parent.

Thirdly, the Father Christmas custom allows child and parent to collaborate in Chestertonian make-believe, as guardians of the liminal space opened up by this interplay of relation and distance. I have already described Santa Claus as a liminal figure because of his ambiguous relation to inside and outside: he is literally on the threshold or *limen*. Victor Turner and other anthropologists have also applied the term to rites of passage, and Father Christmas is a kind of literalization of this figure as well as a figure whose cult itself forms a rite of passage from childhood to adolescence, as the children move from utter credulity to 'make-believe'.[37] Tolkien enabled this sensitively by messages back to the older children from Father Christmas – 'I don't forget people even when they are past stocking age, not until they forget me' – while C. S. Lewis makes Father Christmas himself the helper who takes the initiates from childhood to mature adulthood in *The Lion, the Witch and the Wardrobe*, where he appears in snowbound Narnia as the first sign of the turn of winter towards spring, and gives the children adult presents: swords, a dagger, bow and arrows and a phial for healing.[38] Paradoxically, it is the children's continued capacity for imaginative belief as children that makes possible their intervention and actual later 'rule' of Narnia as its Kings and Queens.

Tolkien's *Lord of the Rings* has no actual Father Christmas, even one in pagan mode, but he has an equivalent figure in the person of Tom Bombadil. As we have seen, Middle-earth is intended to appear authentic, with a preface in mock-anthropological style about hobbit culture and a density of history, myth and language that makes even the world of Harry Potter seem comparatively thin. It is presented moreover, as Tom Shippey has demonstrated, in relation to our own world, as a possible *legendarium* of its pre-Christian past and its languages, set out to fill gaps and solve problems in Indo-European etymologies.[39] And yet, on the very edge of the Shire, the young hobbits encounter the bizarre figure of Tom Bombadil, who is so extraneous to the development of the main narrative that he was omitted not only from Peter Jackson's recent film trilogy, but even from the generally faithful BBC radio dramatization. Tom appears like a helper in a fairy-tale and sings to release Pippin and Merry from Old Man Willow while later, in response to Frodo's crying of his name, he rescues the hobbits from the barrow-wights. As was argued in the previous chapter, Tom is primarily a gift-giver, in which role he resembles Father Christmas. Like Father Christmas Tom is quite outside modern economic relations and on finding the treasure hoard in the barrow, immediately distributes some as gifts and leaves the rest for any who might come upon it. Also like Father Christmas he is very old, with the same rosy cheeks, a big (brown) beard and an age coterminous with the created order. He shares also the role of mediator, as he links the hobbit Shire and the world of men, the ancient past and the present, nature and culture in his communication with trees and other living things. His name, from a Dutch doll belonging to Michael Tolkien, and his stomping, singing and dancing persona, allow him also to negotiate the distance from childhood to adulthood. So also does his title, 'Eldest', which points at once to his great age but also his relation to younger people as one of a series. As an elder in a rite of passage, Tom also delivers the hobbits from childhood fears of the uncanny, which are represented by the animation of the inanimate in Old Man Willow and the ghostly barrow-wights, making them ready to engage the world of men at Bree and the life-in-death of the Black Riders.

Tolkien included Tom Bombadil as a deliberate enigma, as someone who did not fit the world of the novel.[40] His inclusion serves to draw attention to the fictive, made-up nature of the writing, and this is made pellucid in the way in which he talks always in regular metre and rhyme. Tom is an extreme example of the delicate fictiveness endemic in the novel as a whole, which is far from simple fantasy. That hobbit ethnography in the preface to which I alluded can itself be taken as a way of granting credibility and depth to the hobbit race, but equally as a way of marking the fictionality of those same hobbits, so that the anthropology becomes a sort of game, especially when it comes to the way hobbits diverge from sounding like small town or suburban *Little Britain* with their gardening and gossip, by having enormous and bare hairy feet. And at the most critical moments in the journey across Mordor to deliver the Ring, Sam Gamgee has recourse to self-conscious reflections on the literary nature of Frodo's quest: 'I wonder what sort of a tale we've fallen into?' (p. 696). The role of the reader of *The Lord of the Rings* is thus a double one, in which he or she 'receives' the novel as a reality in which to enter and believe but also as a self-consciously made-up fiction in which he or she can collaborate. Hence in his letters Tolkien referred, self-deprecatingly, to his desire to provide a 'mythology for England' that would be open to elaboration and development by others. As he argued in relation to the function of fairy-tale, his novel would provide both an escape from the limitations of the ordinary world but also a recovery of a clear understanding of those same diurnal realities. Imagining believes but it also makes; it is a form of *poiesis* but also *praxis*. It involves the creation of stories that will help us to shape our communal and individual lives.

In stressing the active and collaborative 'make-believe' involved in reading Tolkien's fiction or celebrating Father Christmas, I do not mean to imply that elves, hobbits and Santa Claus are untrue. Nor did Chesterton, who wrote thus about Father Christmas in his most serious work, *The Everlasting Man*: 'Father Christmas is not an allegory of snow and holly, he is not merely the stuff called snow afterwards artificially given a human form, like a snowman. He is something that gives a new meaning to the white world and the evergreens, so that the snow itself seems to be warm rather than cold. The test therefore is purely imaginative. But imaginative doesn't mean imaginary'.[41]

There is something real about Father Christmas; he is an invention in the literal sense of the word's Latin root in the verb *invenire*, meaning 'to meet with' or 'to come upon' something. Like Tom Bombadil he has a mythic quality because he is too big for the setting in which he finds himself: he is too large for his legendary chimney. He means more than can be expressed in an idea: for Chesterton he is personal as a result of his divine origin. Similarly Tolkien ended his lecture 'On Fairy-Stories' theologically by suggesting that 'all tales may come true' in the infinity of the divine life, and Sam Gamgee's sense of narrative self-reflexivity is the result of an understanding of human life itself as a narrative ontology.[42]

Whether or not one wishes to embrace divine transcendence, to give meaning to childhood and to relations within the family beyond the necessary and utilitarian, is already to introduce a 'religious' dimension. Historians of religion often date the beginnings of religion in the rites of burial, which give a significance to life that goes beyond the 'natural' and renders human relations sacred. To encourage children to hang up stockings on Christmas Eve is similarly to suggest a background to the child's life that is beyond rational calculation. Early humans gave gifts to the dead to witness that life itself is a gift, and in the same way Father Christmas gives to children, and adults through him, because *they themselves are the gift*. This is the universal response of adults to a newborn baby, which combines surprise at the newness and reality of life suddenly made apparent. The child Jesus in Matthew 2.11 was given gifts of gold, incense and myrrh not so much because he needed those things but because they expressed what he was: kingly gold, priestly frankincense and sacrificial myrrh. He himself was to be seen as the divine gift. As Chesterton puts it, 'The idea of embodying goodwill – that is, of putting it into a body – is the huge and primal idea of the Incarnation. A gift of God that can be seen and touched is the whole point of the epigram of the creed. Christ Himself was a Christmas present'.[43]

The gospels also present a scene in which the adult Jesus reveals that all children are to be seen as gifts. This is the version of the episode in the New Revised Standard translation of Mark 9.36–7: 'Then he took a little child and put it among them; and taking it in his arms, he said to them, "Whoever welcomes one such child in my name welcomes me, and whoever welcomes me welcomes not me but the one who sent me" '. This text acknowledges childhood to be something of value and importance in itself and relates that quality to the divine. The child is the gift of God himself. Mark 10.13–15 develops the concept further: 'People were bringing little children to him in order that he might touch them; and the disciples spoke sternly to them. But when Jesus saw this, he was indignant and said to them, "Let the little children come to me; do not stop them; for it is to such as these that the kingdom of God belongs. Truly I tell you, whoever does not receive the kingdom of God as a little child will never enter it" ' (NRSV).

The phrase 'truly I tell you' is a marker of the counter-cultural nature of Christ's claim in a society for whom children before their bar-mitzvah are not even under the law but answer to their parents as to God himself.[44] In Matthew (and Luke following him) children are shown to have a privileged attitude of openness or receptivity, and whereas in Mark they are the gift, in Matthew and Luke they receive the gift of the kingdom. In both cases there is no suggestion that children have a particular virtue of innocence or purity, but there is something about childhood that is paradigmatic and valuable and lies in the acts of giving and receiving. That children are ready to receive, according to John Pridmore's exhaustive study of this passage, is not by virtue of some subjective special quality they might possess, but because they are weak and dependent, relying on the adult world for their protection.[45]

Jesus's actions too are as important here as his words. In Mark he actually places a small child inside the circle of his initiates, taking him out of his familial role and relating him (or her) to the adults as one of themselves. In Matthew the same effect is made through the phrase 'to such as these' (των τοιούτων) which creates a new class of children and adults who receive the kingdom as a gift. It could rightly be said that the Christian Church has never quite embodied this vision, and has indeed traduced it very often, but these two scenes lie behind our modern understanding of the importance of childhood. Those who use this story to argue for the privileging of childhood innocence or some other quality fail to notice that both Mark and Matthew show Jesus moving children and adults closer together, although without denying the specificity of the child's status. The disciples are to realize their solidarity with the child or, as Roger Cox puts it, 'what is important . . . is the possibility of finding in childish things, and with luck in children themselves, a renewed humanity'.[46]

In this chapter I have tried to show that for Chesterton and Tolkien childhood imagination can be allied to adult modes of artistic expression, and adult admittance of ambiguity has its parallel in nursery rhyme and fantasy fiction. The cult of Father Christmas has been shown to be a site that allows relations between adults and children to be articulated and rendered 'magical' through an awareness of gift-exchange. I have referred to the Christian gospels not only for a model of childhood that can unite as well as separate the age-groups, but also because these stories show Jesus constructing adult discipleship in direct relation to childhood. Make-believe is an appropriate activity for children and adults, because we know that we shape and order the time of childhood for our young according to the possibilities we imagine for them; and making-believe together means that children too collaborate in the construction of their own imaginative horizon of meaning. As we have seen, children have the ability to hold in their mind myriad possibilities of being and modes of activity, but this is not totally dissimilar to the various world interpretations of quantum mechanics that posit an entanglement of infinite superpositionings of alternative realities. A custom such as hanging up Christmas stockings has its place as part of a larger project in which children collaborate in imagining a world not of fixed phenomena but of endless and surprising possibilities, and which means far more than it appears. For as G. K. Chesterton wrote: 'Some complain that parents will not tell their children whether Santa Claus exists or not. The parents do not tell them for the excellent reason that they do not know'.[47]

Chesterton's perceived 'childishness' has led to his cultural marginalization, while the fact that Tolkien wrote fictions that can be enjoyed by adults and children alike has been cited to his detriment as not tackling specifically 'adult' experiences. As against such assessments, this chapter has sought to show how important a realignment of adult and child imaginative collaboration is for our social wellbeing. Our culture puts enormous pressure on children, who have become guarantors of cultural value in the post-Enlightenment world. Parallel to the idealization of women in the nineteenth century, the worship of innocence in children has not precluded their abuse and mistreatment. Indeed, there is a symbiotic relation between fetishization and misappropriation, so that the sexual abuser of children necessarily destroys that which he most desires: namely, childhood 'otherness'. Somehow, our society needs to find a way in which to acknowledge both the differences between children and adults – the distinctiveness of the present time of childhood experience – and a narrative that offers a passage between infancy and maturity. Chesterton and Tolkien follow the gospels in positing a collaborative childlikeness for both adults and children, but their work is not simply a commendation of childhood. Tolkien specifically chides those who divide the human race into the pretty 'Eloi' children and the dark 'Morlock' adults tending their machines of H. G. Wells's *The Time Machine*.[48] Both Chesterton and Tolkien reject the 'separate haven' idealization of infant innocence of writers such as R. L. Stevenson by decrying equally the 'separate haven' of adult experience. In 'A Defence of Baby-Worship', Chesterton begins by asserting that we all instinctively treat babies as marvels, and their infantile limitations with 'dark affection and dazed respect', but then proceeds to argue that we should treat adult blunders in the same way.[49] For, as Chris Jenks has pointed out, 'the concept of "childhood" serves to articulate not just the experience and status of the young within modern society but also the projections, aspirations, longings and altruism contained within the adult experience'.[50] We adults look to children to understand ourselves: both the past from which we have come and the future beyond our own lifespan.

Notes

1. G. K. Chesterton, 'The Wise Men', *The Daily News*, 25 December 1905.
2. Gerard Manley Hopkins, in *Poems and Prose*, ed. W. H. Gardner (Harmondsworth: Penguin, 1972), 'As kingfishers catch fire', p. 51.
3. S. T. Coleridge, *Biographia Literaria*, ed. George Watson (London: J. M. Dent, 1975), p. 173. I am not dealing here with the later Coleridge and *The Statesman's Manual*, but solely with certain Platonic aspects that continue into MacDonald.
4. Jacques Maritain, 'The Purity of Art', in *Art and Scholasticism*, p. 49; Coleridge, *Biographia Literaria*, p. 173.
5. George MacDonald, 'The Fantastic Imagination', in *A Dish of Orts: Chiefly Papers on the Imagination* (London: Marston, 1893), p. 2.
6. Tolkien, 'On Fairy-Stories', in *Tree and Leaf*, p. 63.
7. William Wordsworth, 'Lines composed a few miles above Tintern Abbey,

in *Lyrical Ballads*, New Riverside Edition, ed. William Richey and Daniel Robinson (Boston: Houghton Mifflin, 2002), p. 113.
8. Wordsworth, 'Tintern Abbey', pp. 112–13.
9. Chesterton, *Autobiography*, p. 15.
10. Wordsworth, 'Tintern Abbey', p. 113.
11. Chesterton, *Autobiography*, p. 63.
12. Paul L. Harris, *The Work of the Imagination* (Oxford: Blackwell, 2000), p. 54.
13. Harris, *Imagination*, p. 182–3.
14. Harris, *Imagination*, p. 173–4.
15. Harris, *Imagination*, p. 173.
16. Harris, *Imagination*, p. 180–1.
17. Tolkien, *Tree and Leaf*, p. 18.
18. Tolkien, *Tree and Leaf*, p. 19.
19. Tolkien, *Tree and Leaf*, p. 42.
20. Iona and Peter Opie, *The Lore and Language of Schoolchildren* (Oxford: Oxford University Press, 1959).
21. G. K. Chesterton, 'The Shop of Ghosts', in *The Spirit of Christmas: Stories, Poems, Essays*, ed. Marie Smith (London: Xanadu), 1984, pp. 27–31.
22. Chesterton, *The Spirit of Christmas*, p. 31.
23. G. K. Chesterton, 'Some Fallacies and Santa Claus', in *The Spirit of Christmas*, p. 54.
24. G. K. Chesterton, 'The Pantomime', in *The Common Man* (London: Sheed and Ward, 1950), p. 266.
25. Chesterton, 'The Pantomime', p. 266.
26. Coleridge, *Biographia Literaria*, pp. 153–60.
27. Paul Ricoeur, *The Rule of Metaphor: Multidisciplinary Studies in the Creation of Meaning in Language* (London: Routledge & Kegan Paul, 1978).
28. Chesterton, *Charles Dickens*, p. 62.
29. J. R. R. Tolkien, *Letters From Father Christmas*, ed. Baillie Tolkien (Boston: Houghton Mifflin, 1999).
30. Tolkien, *Father Christmas*, p. 26.
31. Cited in Harris, *Imagination*, pp. 175–6.
32. Alison Uttley, *Little Grey Rabbit's Christmas* (London: Collins, 1940), pp. 41–2. Miss Tolkien confirmed to me that she did indeed possess this title in the series.
33. Tolkien, *Father Christmas*, pp. 140–1.
34. Kieran Egan, 'The Cognitive Tools of Children's Imagination', EECERA Conference Paper, 2001, at Kieran Egan's faculty webpage at http://www.educ.sfu.ca/kegan (accessed 23 March 2006). See also his study, *The Educated Mind: How Cognitive Tools Shape Our Understanding* (Chicago: Chicago University Press, 1997).

35. Egan, p. 7.
36. Chesterton, 'More Thoughts on Christmas', in *The Spirit of Christmas*, p. 43.
37. Victor Turner, *The Ritual Process: Structure and Antistructure* (London: Routledge, 1969).
38. Tolkien, *Father Christmas*, p. 66; Lewis, *The Lion, the Witch and the Wardrobe*, pp. 98–101.
39. Shippey, *The Road to Middle-earth*, pp. 28–54.
40. *Letters of Tolkien*, p. 192.
41. Chesterton, *The Everlasting Man*, p. 104.
42. Tolkien, *Tree and Leaf*, p. 63.
43. Chesterton, 'The Theology of Christmas Presents', in *The Spirit of Christmas*, p. 49.
44. See John Pridmore, 'The New Testament Theology of Childhood', MA thesis, University of Nottingham, 1967, pp. 69–73. It was publised under the same title by R. Buckland in Hobart, Australia in 1977.
45. Pridmore, New Testament, pp. 146–57.
46. Roger Cox, *Shaping Childhood: Themes of Uncertainty in the History of Adult-Child Relations* (London: Routledge, 1996), p. 207.
47. Chesterton, *The Spirit of Christmas*, p. 55.
48. Tolkien, *Tree and Leaf*, pp. 42–3.
49. G. K. Chesterton, 'A Defence of Baby-Worship', in *The Defendant* (London: Dent, 1901), pp. 147–53 (151–2).
50. Chris Jenks, *Childhood* (London: Routledge, 1996), p. 136.

CONCLUSION
A, a, a, DOMINE DEUS

I said, Ah! What shall I write?
I enquired up and down.
                      (He's tricked me before
with his manifold lurking-places.)
I have looked for His symbol at the door.
I have looked for a long while
                      at the textures and contours.
I have run a hand over the trivial intersections.
I have journeyed among the dead forms
causation projects from pillar to pylon.
I have tired the eyes of the mind
                      regarding the colours and lights.
I have felt for His Wounds
                      in nozzles and containers.
I have wondered for the automatic devices.
I have tested the inane patterns
                      without prejudice.
I have been on my guard
                      not to condemn the unfamiliar.
For it is easy to miss Him
                      at the turn of a civilisation.

I have watched the wheels go round in case I might see the living creatures like the appearance of lamps, in case I might see the Living God projected from the Machine. I have said to the perfected steel,

CONCLUSION

be my sister and for the glassy towers I thought I felt some beginnings of His creature, but *A, a, a, Domine Deus*, my hands found the glazed work unrefined and the terrible crystal a stage-paste . . . *Eia, Domine Deus.*[1]

I BEGAN THIS BOOK with Bishop Corbett's lament for the fairies, which mourned the loss of the enchantment of their dancing and also their exercise of poetic justice shown in rewarding the dutiful housemaid and in pinching the tell-tale. The fairies mediated a providential universe that Corbett's poem equated with Catholicism, and which operated a natural justice lost since the coming of the Puritan changelings. The poem by David Jones which prefaces my conclusion is also a lament: for the disenchantment of the modern world, in which the mediation that would render the steel truly one's sister in the manner of St Francis's Canticle of the Sun is lacking.

This book has been based upon the contention that the writing of Chesterton and Tolkien has been no escape from, but rather a facing up to, the loss of sign-making capacity 'at the turn of a civilisation', and a response to the draining of shared meaning from cultural discourse in the twentieth century. I have sought to demonstrate that the literary tropes used by both writers have been the means of witnessing to this desolation, but at the same time the beginning of a response. The same is true of 'A, a, a, DOMINE DEUS', in which the enjambed lines balance and stabilize the poem in the very same action by which their arrangement seems to break its flow and disjoint experience. Moreover, the title of the poem is taken from the Vulgate translation of Jeremiah 1.6, in which the prophet responds to news of God's election with 'Ah, Lord God! Truly I do not know how to speak, for I am only a boy' (NRSV). The triple 'a' in the Latin translation preserves a sense of childish inarticulacy. Jeremiah's inability to respond is solved by God putting his hand on the boy's mouth, thereby placing within it the words that Jeremiah lacks. The point of human expressive failure becomes the opportunity for the divine speech: the point of dereliction is where God can act. It is, in accord with the argument of my last chapter, by taking the stance of a child that one can begin the task of relating earthly and heavenly realities. And it is at the point of loss, when Christ is hidden or Santa Claus is dying or the fairies departing, that the need for their mediation becomes most apparent.

There are two kinds of difficulty expressed in 'A, a, a, DOMINE DEUS': the problem of how to relate modern technological production to the divine, and the problem of inarticulacy. We have seen how Chesterton and Tolkien answer the first by rendering *all* experience fantastic, either by the former's recourse to defamiliarization, or the latter's invented universe. In this way distantiation or even alienation can be refigured as wonder. The second problem is expressed and overcome by means of the employment of paradox and the grotesque which, like Jones's poem, dramatize the difficulties of articulation in such a way as to gesture towards the reality that they cannot comprehend.

Jones's lines, which were published in a number of different fragments from 1938 onwards, may have been prompted by his reading of Maritain. In 'The Purity of Art' Maritain wrote:

> Confronted with the work of beauty, as has already been said, the mind rejoices without discoursing. If art then manifests or expresses *in matter* a certain radiation of being, a certain form, a certain soul, a certain truth – 'Oh! You'll make *a clean breast of it* in the end,' said Carrière to a sitter – it does not express it in the soul conceptually and discursively. It suggests without conveying absolute knowledge, and expresses what our ideas are impotent to signify. *A, a, a,* exclaims Jeremias, *Domine Deus, ecce nescio loqui.* But song begins where speech breaks off, *exsultatio mentis prorumpens in vocem.*[2]

Maritain's footnote makes it clear that because this knowledge comes through the material object – the statue or poem – it is therefore capable of 'obscure experimental perception' of that 'direct intellectual knowledge of the particular which is the privilege of the angelic mind', and not the human.[3] Art therefore can take us beyond what we are capable of understanding intellectually and give us a form of direct access to particulars, just as the form of Jones's poem, which imitates the ancient Welsh poet Taliesin's 'The Battle of Goddeu' holds together the comprehension of the modern and technological that he himself cannot achieve.

CONCLUSION

Tolkien performs a similar exercise to Jones in his late tale *Smith of Wootton Major*, which is set in a society that has similarly lost all connection with the sacred.[4] Its Great Hall, which in the notes Tolkien equates with the parish church, has lost not only its Catholic decoration and beauty but also its function. All that survives is the Feast of Good Children, held every 24 years. The huge cake baked as part of the ceremony is itself debased and secularized, with a diminutive prettified fairy on top. Yet despite this fall into sentimentality, the cake becomes the medium of relation when the fairy king, the baker's apprentice, hides the passport to faërie inside, and it is eaten by the young Smith. The 'paste' itself enables signification, in the same manner in which David Jones argued that a birthday cake could be a mode of art and sacramental in its showing-forth of the anniversary.[5]

In the case of cake and poem alike, the reason why signification is still possible is because they are both things, just as the pylon and nozzles are things: they participate in being. As confections, bearing the marks of their manufacture, they also witness to creativity. To Tolkien's narrator the fairy on the cake may have been a parody but she was part of a thing – the cake – and also a thing in herself, even with a degree of radiance: 'in her hand was a minute wand of ice sparkling with light'.[6] The story itself is also a thing – a confection – which mediates an experience of the fairy world in the adventures of Smith, and his encounters with the Fairy Queen. Tolkien had been asked to write an introduction to George MacDonald's fairy-tale *The Golden Key*, but found himself unable to do so and provided his own story instead. He claimed that this was because he found somewhat too much allegory in MacDonald's fable but then set about, contradictorily, providing allegorical interpretations of his own tale, such as the references to the Great Hall as the village church mentioned above. As I have already argued, Tolkien's dislike of allegory was not a rejection of figural interpretation but was rather a protest against the subsuming of the literal level of meaning: the *mythos* by the *logos*. As the quotation by Maritain given here attests, art communicates by its form, which is grasped intuitively. Hence the best way to respond to *The Golden Key* is to write another story or make some other thing. MacDonald himself was re-writing the

CONCLUSION

tale entitled *The Golden Key* that concluded the collection of tales by the brothers Grimm. *Smith of Wootton Major* is another 'turn' of the story about a key and concerns a silver star that enables entry into faërie, just as the stories themselves by Grimm and MacDonald do, and also Chesterton's man with the golden key in the toy theatre. But what is important here is that all of these works of art *perform* their subject: their subject is entrance to the sacred and the enchanted, and they take the reader into the borders of that experience – or at least they point towards it. The Grimms' 'The Golden Key' ends with the opening of the box, but we do not know what lies inside; MacDonald's key opens a mountain that leads its protagonists *beyond* this world into 'the country whence the shadows fall'.[7] Tolkien takes his protagonist deep into faërie *within* this life to encounter beauty and terror that mean more than can be expressed.

If Chesterton and Tolkien are theologians, as the title of this book claims, it is because they offer a theology of art as practice. Practical Theology as it is taught in seminaries and theological colleges is very often the taking of theological ideas and realizing them in practical activity, or reflecting upon experience with theological tools. In contrast, Chesterton and Tolkien show how making – *poiesis* – opens the way to God and the way to encounters with the world. Their theurgic theology is practical in taking the reader into an intuition of being through the enchanted experience of art. It is a theology therefore that is inseparable from its instantiation and in which writing becomes mediation just as it reveals mediation. As a gift it likewise cements social relations and draws attention to the exchanges between people, and with the sacred. It is thus a true golden key which will never disappear like MacDonald's, for as Tolkien writes in 'Mythopoeia':

In Paradise perchance the eye may stray
from gazing upon everlasting Day
to see the day-illumined, and renew
from mirrored truth the likeness of the True.
Then looking on the Blessed Land 'twill see
that all is as it is, and yet made free:

CONCLUSION

> Salvation changes not, nor yet destroys,
> garden nor gardener, children nor their toys.
> Evil it will not see, for evil lies
> not in God's picture but in crooked eyes,
> not in the source but in malicious choice,
> and not in sound but in the tuneless voice.
> In Paradise they look no more awry;
> and though they make anew, they make no lie.
> Be sure they still will make, not being dead,
> and poets shall have flames upon their head,
> and harps whereon their faultless fingers fall:
> there each shall choose for ever from the All.[8]

Although in Aristotle and the scholastic tradition distinction is made between the ethic of making (*poiesis*) and that of doing (*praxis*), the former under the aegis of art and the latter of prudence, choice and the virtues rule each equally if in different ways. And in the narrative ontology that we have seen as forming experience in Chesterton and Tolkien the shaping of a life as a work of art is as much to do with art and beauty as it is with prudence and choice. In the conclusion to 'Mythopoeia' we see how choice becomes a faultless act of the restored will, as in Augustine's essay *On Free Choice of the Will*, where the diversity of goods that individuals seek does not mean that wisdom is not common to everyone: for 'each shall choose for ever from the All'.[9] In heaven, however, the freedom of the will to choose diverse goods is expressed through art: prudence is now free to dance like Dante's cardinal virtues in the terrestrial paradise, since there is no longer any possibility of a wrong action. She can join wisdom, 'playing before [God] at all times'.[10]

I have claimed that Chesterton and Tolkien use the fairy world as a means of engendering a theology of positive mediation. 'Mythopoeia' is an excellent confirmation of this proposition, in that Tolkien envisages mediation even in paradise, where the artist's eye is allowed to stray 'from gazing upon everlasting Day/to see the day-illumined, and renew/from mirrored truth the likeness of the True'. This centrality of mediation is where the Christological aspect of art is located. Maritain states in *Art and Scholasticism* that if 'art requires

CONCLUSION

that nothing shall attain the work but *through itself as intermediatory*' then this is a trace of its Trinitarian character. 'It is through His Word and His art that God attains, controls and realises, everything he does. And in the same way it is *through his art* that the human artist ought to attain, control and realise, all his work'.[11] In Tolkien's essay 'On Fairy-Stories' it is finally the life of Christ that unites primary and secondary art and collapses the distinction between history and fiction, real and imagined, human and faërie, and thereby provides the eucatastrophe that lies behind and justifies every fictional happy ending. Through a belief in the Incarnation, however, every mediation can have this Christological character. Fairies are not God, nor Christ, but nevertheless, 'God is the Lord, of angels, and of men – and of elves'.[12] In the Christian dispensation, anything can mediate the divine, and anything can image mediation itself. Faërie is the site of this mediation in Tolkien and Chesterton, and a way of rendering it visible.

Yet perhaps the main trajectory of faërie mediation is towards this world, and towards its redemption from our greedy appropriation. I have stressed throughout this book the importance of theological realism in our cultivation of respect towards the world beyond the self. Chesterton and Tolkien offer us different ways to achieve this joyous apprehension of otherness. The earlier writer always takes us back to the diurnal world to see it with new eyes, and this will be the beginning of our reconciliation with nature, if we are to live peaceably and without further harm to the earth and its atmosphere. Tolkien, as we have seen, always takes us further along towards the transcendent. Like David Jones, Tolkien's vision can be seen as more consoling – an escape from modern technology that confirms we are stuck with it in the here and now. In a world that is so lacking in any kind of vision at the moment – social, political or religious – there is a desperate need for imaginings of otherness that can act as critique and prompt us to action. And Tolkien's 'other' world is always in relation to our own, and his fantastic opens a space in which we can imagine and entertain the seemingly impossible in such a way that we can both literally and metaphorically 'assist in the effoliation and multiple enrichment of creation'.[13] For it is only through the re-enchantment of the world

CONCLUSION

by our creative vision that we will find the courage and resources to prevent its rape and destruction.

Notes

1. David Jones, 'A, a, a, DOMINE DEUS', in *The Sleeping Lord and Other Fragments* (London: Faber, 1974), p. 9.
2. Maritain, *Art and Scholasticism*, p. 47. The second piece of Latin is from Aquinas's Prologue to the Psalms, translated as 'the exultation of the mind, bursting forth in the voice'.
3. Maritain, *Art and Scholasticism*, p. 150.
4. J. R. R. Tolkien, *Smith of Wootton Major*, extended edition, ed. Verlyn Flieger (London: HarperCollins, 2005).
5. David Jones, 'Art and Sacrament', in *Epoch and Artist: Selected Writings*, ed. Harman Grisewood (London: Faber, 1959), p. 164.
6. Tolkien, *Smith*, p. 14.
7. Jacob and Wilhelm Grimm, *Selected Tales*, ed. Joyce Crick (Oxford: Oxford University Press, 2005), p. 276; George MacDonald, *The Golden Key*, illus. Maurice Sendack and afterword by W. H. Auden (London: Bodley Head, 1972), p. 78.
8. Tolkien, *Tree and Leaf*, p. 90.
9. Augustine, *On Free Choice of the Will*, trans. Thomas Williams (Indianapolis: Hackett, 1993), p. 49: 'Surely it does not follow from that assumption that wisdom itself is not one and common to all, simply because the goods that human beings discern and choose in it are many and various. That would be like thinking that there must be more than one sun, simply because we perceive many and various things by its light'.
10. Proverbs 8.31 as quoted by Maritain, *Art and Scholasticism*, p. 28.
11. Maritain, *Art and Scholasticism*, p. 102.
12. Tolkien, *Tree and Leaf*, p. 73.
13. Tolkien, *Tree and Leaf*, p. 73.

BIBLIOGRAPHY

Works by Chesterton and Tolkien

Chesterton

Alarms and Discursions (London: Methuen, 1910).
Autobiography (Thirsk: House of Stratus, 2001).
The Ball and the Cross, Martin Gardner (ed.) (New York: Dover, 1995).
'The Ballad of the White Horse', in *The Collected Poems*, pp. 225–336.
The Catholic Church and Conversion (London: Burns and Oates, 1960).
Charles Dickens (London: Methuen, 1906).
The Club of Queer Trades (London: Harper Bros, 1905).
The Collected Poems of G. K. Chesterton (London: Cecil Palmer, 1927).
The Coloured Lands, ed. M. Ward (London: Sheed and Ward, 1938).
Come to Think of It (London: Methuen, 1930).
The Common Man (London: Sheed and Ward, 1950).
Criticisms and Appreciations of Charles Dickens (London: Stratus, 2001).
The Defendant (London: Dent, 1901).
The Everlasting Man (San Francisco: Ignatius Press, 1993).
The Flying Inn (London: Methuen, 1915).
G. K. Chesterton's Works on the Web, Martin Ward (ed.) at http://www.cse.dmu.ac.uk/~mward/gkc/books/titanicGKC.html
Greybeards at Play: Literature and Art for Old Gentlemen (London: Brimley Johnson, 1900).
Heretics (London: John Lane, 1905).
The Incredulity of Father Brown (Harmondsworth: Penguin, 1974).
The Innocence of Father Brown (London: Penguin, 1950).
Magic: A Fantastic Comedy (London: Martin Secker, 1926).
Manalive (Mineola, NY: Dover, 2000, rpt.).

BIBLIOGRAPHY

The Man Who Was Thursday: A Nightmare, K. Amis (intro.) (Harmondsworth: Penguin, 1986).
The Napoleon of Notting Hill, M. Gardner (ed.) (New York: Dover, 1991).
The Secret of Father Brown (Harmondsworth: Penguin, 1974).
Orthodoxy (London: Bodley Head, 1908).
Robert Browning (London: Macmillan, 1903)
The Spirit of Christmas: Stories, Poems, Essays, M. Smith (ed.) (London: Xanadu, 1984).
Tales of the Long Bow (London: Cassell, 1925).
Thomas Aquinas and St Francis of Assisi, R. McInerny and J. Pearce (eds) (San Francisco: Ignatius Press, 2002).
G. F. Watts (London: Duckworth, 1904).
The Wisdom of Father Brown (Harmondsworth: Penguin, 1970).
'The Wise Men,' *The Daily News*, 25 December 1905.

Tolkien

'Beowulf: the Monsters and the Critics,' *Proceedings of the British Academy* 22 (London: Oxford University Press, 1937), pp. 245–95.
Farmer Giles of Ham (London: HarperCollins, 2000).
The Hobbit: Or There and Back Again (London: HarperCollins, 2001).
'Leaf by Niggle', in *Tree and Leaf*, pp. 93–118.
The Letters of J. R. R. Tolkien, H. Carpenter and C. Tolkien (eds) (London: George Allen and Unwin, 1981).
Letters from Father Christmas, B. Tolkien (ed.) (Boston: Houghton Mifflin, 1999).
'On Fairy-Stories', in *Tree and Leaf*, pp. 1–81.
The Lord of the Rings (3 vols; London: HarperCollins, 1997).
The Silmarillion, C. Tolkien (ed.) (London: HarperCollins, rev. edn, 1999).
Smith of Wootton Major, V. Flieger (ed.) (London: HarperCollins, extended edn, 2005).
Tree and Leaf Including the Poem Mythopoeia, The Homecoming of Beorhtnoth Beorhthelm's Son (London: HarperCollins, 2001).

Secondary Texts and Other Works Cited

Anderson, B., *Imagined Communities: Reflections on the Origin and Spread of Nationalism* (London: Verso, 1983).
Anselm, *Complete Philosophical and Theological Treatises*, J. Hopkins and H. Richardson (trans.) (Minneapolis: Arthur J. Banning Press, 2000).

BIBLIOGRAPHY

—— *Cur Deus Homo* (London: Griffith, Farran, Okeden & Welsh, 1933).
Auden, W. H., *Collected Poems*, E. Mendelson (ed.) (New York: Vintage, 1991).
Augustine of Hippo, *Enchiridion*, and 'Sermon LXXX [cxxx]', in *A Select Library of the Nicene and Post-Nicene Fathers of the Christian Church*, P. Schaff (ed.); (28 vols; 3; Edinburgh and Grand Rapids MI: T & T Clark and Eerdmans, 1998).
—— *Confessions*, H. Chadwick (trans.) (Oxford: Oxford University Press, 1991).
—— *On Free Choice of the Will*, T. Williams (trans.) (Indianapolis: Hackett, 1993).
Bakhtin, M., *Rabelais and His World*, H. Iswolsky (trans.) (Bloomington: Indiana University Press, 1984).
Bann, S. and J. Bowlt (eds), *Russian Formalism: A Collection of Articles and Texts in Translation* (Edinburgh: Scottish Academic Press, 1973).
Barringer, T., *Reading the Pre-Raphaelites* (London: Weidenfeld & Nicolson, 1988).
Bassham, G., and E. Bronson (eds), *The Lord of the Rings and Philosophy* (Chicago: Open Court, 2003).
Bataille, G., *The Accursed Share* (2 vols; New York: Urzone, 1988).
Baudelaire, C., *The Flowers of Evil*, J. Culler (ed.), J. McGowan (trans.) (Oxford: Oxford University Press, 1998).
Baudrillard, Jean, *Symbolic Exchange and Death* (Nottingham: Nottingham Trent University Press, 1993).
Beerbohm, M., 'Diminuendo', in Mermin and Tucker (eds), *Victorian Literature 1830–1900*, pp. 1097–1100.
Belloc, H., *An Essay on the Restoration of Property* (Norfolk VA: HIS Press, 2002).
Beowulf: An Edition, B. Mitchell (ed.) (Oxford: Blackwell, 1998).
Bjork, R., 'Speech as Gift in *Beowulf*', *Speculum* 69 (1994), pp. 993–1022.
Blake, W., *Songs of Innocence and Experience*, G. Keynes (ed.) (Oxford and Paris: Oxford University Press and Trianon Press, 1975).
Borges, J., 'On Oscar Wilde', in *Borges: Selected Non-Fictions*, W. Weinberger (ed.), E. Allen, J. Levine and E. Weinberger (trans.) (New York: Viking, 1999).
Bourdieu, P., *Outline of a Theory of Practice* (Cambridge: Cambridge University Press, 1977).
Bown, N., *Fairies in Nineteenth-Century Art and Literature* (Cambridge: Cambridge University Press, 2001).
Caldecott, S., *Secret Fire: The Spiritual Vision of J. R. R. Tolkien* (London: Darton, Longman and Todd, 2003).
—— D. Rance and G. Solari, *Tolkien, Faërie et Christianisme* (Geneva: Ad Solem, 2002).
Carpenter, H., *J. R. R. Tolkien: A Biography* (London: George Allen and Unwin, 1977).

BIBLIOGRAPHY

Cessario, R., *A Short History of Thomism* (Washington DC: Catholic University of America, 2005).

Chance, J., *Tolkien the Medievalist* (Routledge Studies in Medieval Culture and Religion, London: Routledge, 2002).

Coleridge, S. T., *Biographia Literaria*, G. Watson (ed.) (London: J. M. Dent, 1975).

Cook, E., *Enigmas and Riddles in Literature* (Cambridge: Cambridge University Press, 2006).

Cox, R., *Shaping Childhood: Themes of Uncertainty in the History of Adult-Child Relations* (London: Routledge, 1996).

Crossley-Holland, K., (trans.), *The Exeter Book Riddles* (Harmondsworth: Penguin, 1978).

Curry, P., *Defending Middle-Earth: Tolkien, Myth and Modernity* (London: HarperCollins, 1998).

Dante Alighieri, *The Divine Comedy: 1 Hell*, D. Sayers (trans.) (London: Penguin, 1949).

—— *Inferno*, J. Sinclair (trans.) (Oxford: Oxford University Press, 1971).

—— *Paradiso*, C. Singleton (ed.) (Bollingen series; New Haven: Yale University Press, 1973).

—— *Purgatorio*, C. Singleton (ed.) (Bollingen series; New Haven: Yale University Press, 1973).

Derrida, J., *Given Time: Counterfeit Money*, P. Kamuf (trans.) (Chicago: Chicago University Press, 1992).

Dowling, L., *Language and Decadence in the Victorian Fin de Siècle* (Princeton: Princeton University Press, 1986).

Dulac, E., *Picture Book for the French Red Cross* (London: Hodder and Stoughton, 1915).

Edda, in *The Poetic Edda*, Carolyne Larrington (trans.) (Oxford: Oxford University Press, 1996).

Egan, K., *The Educated Mind: How Cognitive Tools Shape Our Understanding* (Chicago: Chicago University Press, 1997).

—— 'The Cognitive Tools of Children's Imagination,' EECERA Conference Paper, 2001, Kieran Egan's faculty webpage at http://www.educ.sfu.ca/kegan

Eliot, T. S., *The Complete Poems and Plays, 1909–1950* (London: Faber, 1980).

The English Hymnal, P. Dearmer, R. Vaughan-Williams, *et al.* (eds) (Oxford: Oxford University Press, 1906).

Filmer-Roberts, K., 'Presence and Absence: God in Fantasy Literature', *Christianity and Literature* 47 (1) (1997), pp. 59–76.

Flieger, V., *Splintered Light: Logos and Language in Tolkien's World* (Kent OH: Kent State University Press, rev. edn 2002).

BIBLIOGRAPHY

—— *Interrupted Music: The Making of Tolkien's Mythology* (Kent OH and London: Kent State University Press, 2005).
Forster, E. M., *Collected Short Stories* (Harmondsworth: Penguin, 1972).
Frazer, J., *The Golden Bough: A Study in Magic and Religion* (15 vols.; London: Macmillan, 1915).
Frei, H., 'Theological Reflections on the Accounts of Jesus's Death and Resurrection', in G. Hunsinger and W. Placher (eds), *Theology and Narrative: Selected Essays* (New York: Oxford University Press, 1993).
Freud, S., *Totem and Taboo* in J. Strachey (ed.), *Complete Psychological Works of Sigmund Freud* (Standard Edition; vol. 13. London: Hogarth, 1962).
Garth, J., *Tolkien and the Great War: The Threshold of Middle-earth* (London: HarperCollins, 2003).
Gasper, G., *Anselm of Canterbury and His Theological Inheritance* (London: Ashgate, 2004).
Gill, E., *Art and Prudence* (Ditchling: Golden Cockerel Press, 1928).
Gosse, E. (ed.), *The Allies' Fairy Book* (London: Heinemann, 1916).
Gregory of Nyssa, 'The Great Catechism,' in A. Roberts and J. Donaldson (eds), *A Select Library of Nicene and Ante-Nicene Fathers of the Christian Church* (Second Series; Edinburgh: T & T Clark, 1994).
Greimas, A., *Du Sens: Essais Sémiotiques* (Paris: Éditions du Seuil, 1970).
Grimm, J. and W. Grimm, *Selected Tales*, J. Crick (ed.) (Oxford: Oxford University Press, 2005).
Grönbech, V., *The Culture of the Teutons* (2 vols.; London: Oxford University Press, 1931).
Hammond, W. (ed.), *J. R. R. Tolkien Centenary Conference* (Milton Keynes: Tolkien Society, 1992).
—— and C. Scull, *J. R. R. Tolkien: Artist and Illustrator* (London: HarperCollins, 1995).
Harpham, G., *On the Grotesque: Strategies of Contradiction in Art and Literature* (Princeton: Princeton University Press, 1987).
Harris, P., *The Work of the Imagination* (Oxford: Blackwell, 2000).
Hilton, T., *The Pre-Raphaelites* (London: Thames and Hudson, 1970).
Hopkins, G. M., *Poems and Prose*, W. H. Gardner (ed.) (Harmondsworth: Penguin, 1972).
Houlgate, S. (ed.), *The Hegel Reader* (Oxford: Blackwell, 1998).
Hugo, V., *Cromwell*, A. Ubersfeld (ed.) (Paris: Garnier-Flammarion, 1986).
Hyde, L., *The Gift: Imagination and the Erotic Life of Property* (New York: Vintage, 1983).
Jack, I. (ed.), *The Poetical Works of Robert Browning* (London: Oxford University Press, 1970).

BIBLIOGRAPHY

Jenks, C., *Childhood* (London: Routledge, 1996).
Jones, D., *The Anathémata: Fragments of an Attempted Writing* (London: Faber, 1952).
—— *Epoch and Artist: Selected Writings*, H. Grisewood (ed.) (London: Faber, 1959).
—— *In Parenthesis* (London: Faber, 1937).
—— *The Sleeping Lord and Other Fragments* (London: Faber, 1974).
Kahn, C., *The Art and Thought of Heraclitus: An Edition of the Fragments with Translation and Commentary* (Cambridge: Cambridge University Press, 1979).
Kayser, W., *The Grotesque in Art and Literature*, U. Weisstein (trans.) (New York: Columbia University Press, 1981).
Kenner, H., *Paradox in Chesterton*, H. McLuhan (intro.) (London: Sheed and Ward, 1948).
Kipling, R., *Limits and Renewals* (London: Macmillan, 1932).
Kraus, J., 'Tolkien, Modernism, and the Importance of Tradition', in Bassham and Bronson (eds), *The Lord of the Rings and Philosophy*, pp. 137–49.
Kumar, K., *The Making of English National Identity* (Cambridge: Cambridge University Press, 2003).
Lansman, P. and I. Velody (eds), *Max Weber* (London: Unwin, Hyman, 1989).
Leeming, D. and M. Leeming (eds), *A Dictionary of Creation Myths* (Oxford: Oxford University Press, 1994).
Leo XIII, *Actes de Leo XIII* (2 vols; Paris: Maison de la Bonne Presse, 1903).
—— *Rerum Novarum: On Capital and Labour*, 15 May 1891, online at www.vatican.va/holy_father/leo_xiii/encyclicals
Levenson, M., *The Genealogy of Modernism: A Study of English Literary Doctrine, 1908–1922* (Cambridge: Cambridge University Press, 1984).
Lewis, C. S., *The Lion, the Witch and the Wardrobe* (London: Collins, 1988).
—— *Surprised by Joy: The Shape of My Early Life* (London: Geoffrey Bles, 1955).
de Lubac, H., *Medieval Exegesis: The Four Senses of Scripture*, R. L. Wilken (ed.), M. Sebanc (trans.) (2 vols.; Ressourcement: Retrieval and Renewal in Catholic Thought, Grand Rapids MI: Eerdmans, 1998).
Maas, J., P. Trimpe and C. Gere *et al.*, *Victorian Fairy Painting*, J. Martineau (ed.) (London: Royal Academy of Arts, 1998).
MacDonald, G., *A Dish of Orts: Chiefly Papers on the Imagination* (London: Marston, 1893).
—— *The Golden Key*, W. H. Auden (afterw.), M. Sendack (illust.) (London: Bodley Head, 1972).
—— *Phantastes: A Fairy Romance*, C. Lewis (intro.) (Grand Rapids MI:: Eerdmans, 2000).
—— *Phantastes and Lilith*, C. Lewis (intro.) (London: Gollancz, 1962).

BIBLIOGRAPHY

Maritain, J., *Art and Scholasticism*, J. Scanlan (trans.) (London: Sheed and Ward, 1930).
—— *Theonas: Conversations of a Sage*, F. Sheed (trans.) (London: Sheed and Ward, 1923).
Mary, Mother and K. Ware (trans.), *The Festal Menaian* (London: Faber and Faber, 1969).
Marx, K., *Capital: A Critique of Political Economy*, F. Engels (ed.), S. Moore and E. Aveling (trans.) (London: Lawrence and Wishart, 1954).
Mauss, M., *The Gift: The Form and Reason for Exchange in Archaic Societies*, E. Halls (trans.), M. Douglas (forew.) (New York: Norton, 1990).
Mermin, D., and H. Tucker, *Victorian Literature 1830–1900* (Fort Worth: Harcourt Brace, 2002).
Mittman, A., *Maps and Monsters in Medieval England* (New York and London: Routledge, 2006).
Mortimer, P., 'Tolkien and Modernism', *Tolkien Studies* 2(1) (2005), pp. 113–29.
Oddie, W., 'Mass Communication and the Culture of Death', http://www.chesterton.lt/index.php?id=316
Opie, I. and P. Opie, *The Lore and Language of Schoolchildren* (Oxford: Oxford University Press, 1959).
Packer, A., S. Beddie and L. Jarrett, *Fairies in Legend and the Arts* (London: Cameron and Tayleur, 1980).
Percy, T., *Reliques of Ancient English Poetry* (3 vols.; London: L. J. Dodsley, 1765).
John Pridmore, 'The New Testament Theology of Childhood', MA thesis, University of Nottingham, 1967.
Propp, V., *The Morphology of the Folktale*, L. Wagner (ed.), L. Scott (trans.) (Austin: University of Texas Press, 1968).
Purkiss, D., *Troublesome Things: A History of Fairies and Fairy-Stories* (Harmondsworth: Penguin, 2001).
Ricoeur, P., *The Rule of Metaphor: Multidisciplinary Studies in the Creation of Meaning in Language* (London: Routledge & Kegan Paul, 1978).
Ridler, A. (ed.), *Charles Williams: The Image of the City and Other Essays* (London: Oxford University Press, 1958).
Ruskin, J., *Complete Works of John Ruskin*, Library Edition, E. Cook and A. Wedderburn (eds) (37 vols.; London: George Allen, 1905–12).
Shippey, T. A., *The Road to Middle-earth* (London: George Allen and Unwin, 1982).
—— *J. R. R. Tolkien: Author of the Century* (London: HarperCollins, 2000).
Songs of Praise, P. Dearmer (ed.) (Oxford: Oxford University Press, 1931).
Shklovsky, V., 'Art as Technique', in *Russian Formalist Criticism: Four Essays*,

BIBLIOGRAPHY

L. Lemon and M. Reis (trans.) (Lincoln: University of Nebraska Press, 1965), pp. 3–24.

—— 'The Resurrection of the Word (1914)', in Bann and Boult (eds), *Russian Formalism: A Collection of Articles and Texts in Translation*, pp. 41–47.

Stein, G., *Writings and Lectures 1911–1945*, P. Meyerowitz (ed.), E. Sprigge (intro.) (London: Peter Owen, 1967).

Strathern, M., *The Gender of the Gift: Problems with Women and Problems with Society in Melanesia* (Berkeley: University of California Press, 1988).

Thomas Aquinas, *Summa Contra Gentiles*, V. Bourke and A. Pegis (trans.) (5 vols.; Notre Dame IN: University of Notre Dame Press, 1975).

—— *Summa Theologica*, Fathers of the English Dominican Province (trans.) (22 vols; London: Burns, Oates and Washbourne, 1920).

Thomas, E., *Poems of Edward Thomas*, W. de la Mare (ed.) (Oxford: Oxford University Press, 1975).

Todorov, T., *The Fantastic: A Structural Approach to a Literary Genre*, R. Scholes (forew.), R. Howard (trans.) (Ithaca NY: Cornell University Press, 1975).

Turner, V., *The Ritual Process: Structure and Antistructure* (London: Routledge, 1969).

Uttley, A., *Little Grey Rabbit's Christmas* (London: Collins, 1940).

Vernon, M. (ed.), *Tolkien Influenced and Influencing: 17th Tolkien Society Seminar* (Cambridge: Tolkien Society, 2005).

Ward, M., *Gilbert Keith Chesterton* (London: Sheed and Ward, 1944).

Watson, R. (ed.), *The Poetry of Scotland: Gaelic, Scots and English* (Edinburgh: Edinburgh University Press, 1995).

Weisheipl, J., 'The Revival of Thomism: An Historical Survey', http://www.op.org/Domcentral/study/revival.htm

—— *The Picture of Dorian Gray*, R. Mighall (ed.) (Harmondsworth: Penguin, 2000).

Wilde, O., *Complete Plays of Oscar Wilde*, T. Guthrie (intro.) (London: Collins, 1965).

Williams, R., *Grace and Necessity: Reflections on Art and Love* (London and Harrisburg PA: Continuum/Morehouse, 2005).

Williamson, C., *A Feast of Creatures: Anglo-Saxon Riddle Songs* (Philadelphia: University of Pennsylvania Press, 1982).

Wood, R., *The Gospel According to Tolkien: Visions of the Kingdom in Middle-earth* (Louisville KY: Westminster John Knox Press, 2003).

Wordsworth, W. and S. T. Coleridge, *Lyrical Ballads*, W. Richey and D. Robinson (eds) (New Riverside Edition; Boston: Houghton Mifflin, 2002).

Zipes, J., *Victorian Fairy Tales: The Revolt of the Fairies and the Elves* (London: Methuen, 1987).

INDEX

Aiken, Joan 42
Anselm, St 103, 106
Aquinas, St Thomas 13, 15, 19, 25, 37–9, 67, 71, 75–6, 80, 90–2. 112
Aragorn, xi 98–9, 104–9, 111, 137, 140
Aristotle 12, 20, 167
Arwen 99, 108
Augustine, St 71, 76–7, 79, 106, 167

Bakhtin, Mikhail 74–5, 77
Ball, John 81
Bate, Robert Shelton 3
Bataille, Georges 119, 134
Battle of Maldon xi
Baudelaire, Charles 57
Baudrillard, Jean 120
Beardsley, Aubrey 57, 149
Beerbohm, Max 30
Belloc, Hilaire 13, 127
Beowulf ix, xi, 60–2, 128–30
Bible
    Genesis 72, 125
    Leviticus 109
    Numbers 153

Isaiah 108–9, 111
Jeremiah 163
Ezekiel 70
Amos 66
Job 66–7, 69
Matthew 69, 156–7
Mark 50–1, 156–7
Luke 49–51, 99, 109, 157
John 49–50
Acts 50
1 Corinthians 102–3, 111, 139
Revelation 108, 111
Bilbo (Baggins) 43–4, 71–2, 75, 82, 96–8, 109, 111, 130–3
Bjork, Robert 128
Blake, William 101
Bombadil, Tom 7, 81, 110, 133–6, 153–5
Borges, Jorge Luis 29
Boromir 98, 137
Bourdieu, Pierre 120
Brosse, Charles de 80
Brown, Father x, 15, 34, 89
Browning, Robert 58–9, 75

Caldecott, Stratford 13
Carlyle, Thomas 32

INDEX

Carpenter, Humphrey xi
Celeborn 22, 136
Chance, Jane viii
Chateaubriand, François René de 56
Chaucer, Geoffrey 8
Chesterton, Gilbert Keith
  Autobiography 35, 144–5
  Ballad of the White Horse x-xi
  The Ball and the Cross 33, 94
  The Catholic Church and Conversion 15
  The Club of Queer Trades 31
  The Coloured Lands xii–xiii, 53
  'A Defence of Baby Worship' 159
  'The Donkey' 34
  'The Ethics of Elfland' *see Orthodoxy*
  The Flying Inn 122
  The Everlasting Man x, 93–4, 155
  G. K.'s Weekly 16
  'O God of Earth and Altar' 15
  'The Happy Man' 87
  'The Head of Caesar' from *The Wisdom of Father Brown* 47–8
  'Introduction to the Book of Job' 66
  'The Invisible Man' from *The Innocence of Father Brown* 35, 92–3
  Magic: A Fantastic Comedy 48
  Manalive 31, 94, 122
  The Man Who Was Thursday 31, 38, 49, 67–70, 112, 124
  'The Man with Two Beards' from *The Secret of Father Brown* 93
  The Napoleon of Notting Hill 69
  'On Gargoyles' 59–60
  'The Oracle of the Dog' from *The Incredulity of Father Brown* 47
  Orthodoxy x, 8, 19, 38, 94, 121, 124
  'The Ethics of Elfland' 2, 11, 121, 140
  The Poet and the Lunatics 94
  'The Queer Feet' from *The Innocence of Father Brown* 35
  'The Resurrection of Father Brown' from *The Incredulity of Father Brown* 47, 50
  'The Secret of Flambeau' from *The Secret of Father Brown* 95
  'The Secret People' 6
  'The Shop of Ghosts' 147–8
  Tales of the Long Bow 89
  Thomas Aquinas 17
  'The Wise Men' 142
Christmas, Father 121–2, 125–6, 147–58
Christie, Agatha 3
Claudel, Paul ix
Coleridge, Samuel Taylor 15, 30, 142, 148
Corbett, Richard 1–2, 117, 163
Coverley, Sir Roger de 147

Cox, Roger 157

Dante Alighieri 4, 23, 45, 56, 71, 76, 78–9, 104, 167
Dark Rider (see Ringwraith)
Dawkins, Richard 9
Dearmer, Percy 14
Denethor 77, 82, 103, 138
Derrida, Jacques 119–20
Dickens, Charles xii–xiii, 32–3, 58–9, 147–8, 152
Dionysus, the Pseudo-Areopagite 67
Distributism 13–14, 16, 127–8, 130, 134
Dowling, Linda 29–30
Dulac, Edmund 4
Dunbar, William 61, 102
Dunn, A.C. 132
Dürer, Albrecht 62
Durkheim, Emile 118–9

Edda, Poetic 60, 119
Egan, Kieran 150–1
Elanor 110
Eliot, Thomas Stearns ix, 31, 90
Elrond 99, 109, 133
English Hymnal 15
Éomer 41, 77
Éowyn 77, 103–4, 123, 135
Ewing, Julia 3

Faramir 71, 98, 123
Fëanor 22
Flieger, Verlyn viii, 53
Forster, Edward Morgan 5
Fortunatus, Venantius 105–6

Frazer, Sir James ix, 118
Frei, Hans 100
Freud, Sigmund 45, 131–2
Frodo 24, 72–3, 77–8, 80, 82–3, 99–102, 105, 107, 109–11, 123, 133, 137–9

Gabriel 123–4
Galadriel xii, 22–3, 65, 71, 77–8, 82, 109, 136–7
Gandalf 43–51, 71, 80–1, 98, 101–2, 106, 108–9, 123, 127, 133
Garth, John viii, 3, 119
Gilbert and Sullivan 29
Gill, Eric 16, 20–1
Gilson, Etienne 16
Gimli 49, 65, 109, 129, 137
Goldberry 134
Graves, Robert 3
Gregory of Nyssa 106
Greimas, Algirdas Julien 117
Grimm Brothers 4, 120, 166
Grönbeck, Vilhelm 129–35
Grundtvig, Nikolai Frederik Severin 129

Harpham, Geoffrey 63, 72
Harris, Paul 145–6, 149–51
Headlam, Stewart 14
Hegel, Georg Wilhelm Friedrich 95
Heraclitus 83
Hoffman, Ernst Theodor Wilhelm 80
Holbein, Hans 62
Homer 97

INDEX

Hopkins, Gerard Manley 142
Hubert, Henri 119
Hugo, Victor 56–8, 60, 94
Hume, David 9
Hyde, Lewis 125, 134

Ilúvatar (see Eru)
Isildur 98, 107

Jackson, Peter 64, 83, 154
Jenks, Christopher 159
Jones, David ix–x, 8–9, 165, 168
   In Parenthesis ix–x, 3–4,
   Anathémata x, 30–1
   'A, a, a, DOMINE DEUS'
   162–4
Jonson, Ben 147
Joyce, James ix-x 18

Kant, Immanuel 37
Kenner, Hugh 59, 89–91
Kipling, Rudyard 4, 7
Kumar, Krishan 4

Lang, Andrew xii, 3
Langland, William 102
Legolas 50, 65, 109, 137
Le Guin, Ursula 22
Leonardo da Vinci 62
Lewis, Clive Staples x, xiii, 47, 129, 153
Leo XIII, Pope 12–13
Locke, John 36
Lodge, Sir Oliver 94

MacDonald, George xv, 143
   Phantastes 47

The Golden Key 165–6
Lilith 101, 105
The Princess and the Goblin 3
Maeterlinck, Maurice xii
Mare, Walter de la 3
Maritain, Jacques x, 16–25, 37–8, 51–2, 142–3, 164–8
Marx, Karl 81–2
Mary, Blessed Virgin 123–4
Maurice, Frederick Dennison 15
Mauss, Marcel 118–19, 128–30, 139
Melkor 19, 73
Merry (Meriadoc Brandybuck) 76, 103–4, 109, 135–6, 137–8, 140, 154
Millais, John 57
Milton, John 56
Montaigne, Michel 66
Murray, Fr Robert xii
Müller, Max 29

Noel, Conrad 14
Noyes, Alfred 3

O'Connor, Mgr John 15–16
Oddie, William 14
Opie, Iona and Peter 147

Pascal, Blaise 58
Paul, Jean 62
Peter Pan 3
Percy, Thomas 4
Piaget, Jean 145
Pippin (Peregrine Took) 76, 106, 109, 137–8, 140, 154
Pius XI, Pope 13

INDEX

Potter, Harry 24, 42, 153
Pound, Ezra 31
Pridmore, John 157
Propp, Vladimir 117–18
Pullman, Philip 42
Poe, Edgar Allan 57
Power, Revd Norman 49

Rabelais, François 74–5
Rackham, Arthur 4
Raphael Sanzio 62
Rerum Novarum 127
Ricoeur, Paul 148–50
Ring of Power 24, 80–3, 97–8, 100–2, 127, 131–2, 134, 138–9
Ringwraiths (Nazgûl, Dark Riders) 83, 103–4, 108, 136, 139
Rossetti, Dante Gabriel 57
Ruskin, John 59–62, 65, 67, 70–3, 83
Robin Hood 147–8
Rose (Gamgee) 110

Sam (Samwise Gamgee) 71–5, 78, 99–102, 105, 109–11, 137, 155–6
Saruman 49–50, 71, 106–9, 120, 124
Sauron 24, 73, 76, 81–2, 102, 104, 124, 129, 138
Sayers, Dorothy 76
Schlegel, Karl Wilhelm Friedrich 56, 62, 65
Shakespeare, William 56
Shelley, Mary 62–3
Shelob 73–80

Shippey, Tom viii, ix, 75, 97, 153
Shklovsky, Vladimir 31–40, 44
Smaug 61, 97
Stein, Gertrude 37
Stevenson, Robert Louis 159
Stoker, Bram 75

Taliesin 164
Tennyson, Alfred 2
Théoden 71–2, 77, 103–4, 129, 138
Thomas, Edward 5–7
Todorov, Tzvetan 44–50
Tolkien, John Ronald Reuel
  'Beowulf: The Monsters and the Critics' xi, 61
  The Father Christmas Letters 149–51
  Farmer Giles of Ham 61–2
  'Goblin Feet' 2
  'The Homecoming of Beorhtnoth, Beorhthelm's Son' xi
  Leaf by Niggle xiv, 21, 23, 126–7, 130, 143
  'Mythopoeia' 25, 49, 166–7
  'On Fairy-Stories' xii–xiii, 18, 24, 39–40, 61, 122–3, 143, 168
  Smith of Wootton Major 165–6
  Wickedness 75
Tolkien, Michael 154
Tolkien, Priscilla xiii, 150
Tolstoy, Leo 33–6
Treebeard 41, 63–4, 66
Turner, Victor 153
Tylor, Edward Burnett 80

Ungoliant 73, 77, 79

INDEX

Uttley, Alison 150

Virgil 31
Volsung Saga 61, 130
Vasari, Giorgio 62

Waldman, Milton 126
Ward, Maisie xi, xiii, 16

Watts, Frederick 69
Weber, Max 8
Wells, Herbert George 159
Wilde, Oscar 29–31, 57, 88–90
Williams, Charles xiii, 119
Williamson, Craig 112
Wordsworth, William 144

CPSIA information can be obtained at www.ICGtesting.com
Printed in the USA
LVOW12s1924170813

348399LV00020B/581/P